D1237013

THE FUTURE OF
CHRISTOLOGY

THE FUTURE OF
CHRISTOLOGY

Roger Haight, S.J.

continuum

NEW YORK • LONDON

2005

The Continuum International Publishing Group Inc
15 East 26 Street, New York, NY 10010

The Continuum International Publishing Group Ltd
The Tower Building, 11 York Road, London SE1 7NX

www.continuumbooks.com

Copyright © 2005 by Roger Haight

All rights reserved. No part of this book may be reproduced, stored in a retrieval system, or transmitted, in any form or by any means, electronic, mechanical, photocopying, recording, or otherwise, without the written permission of the publishers.

Printed in the United States of America

Library of Congress Cataloging-in-Publication Data

Haight, Roger.
   The future of Christology / Roger Haight.
      p. cm.
   Includes bibliographical references and index.
   ISBN 0-8264-1764-7 (hardcover : alk. paper)
   1. Jesus Christ – Person and offices. 2. Christianity and other religions.
   3. Catholic Church – Doctrines. I. Title.
   BT203.H35 2005
   232 – dc22

                      2005019629

CONTENTS

PREFACE

❦

THIS BOOK APPEARS six years after *Jesus Symbol of God*.[1] An explanation of how it relates to that work will provide a good introduction to a brief overview its contents.

The first book is an extensive monograph proposing a systematic christology. It is meant as a proposal to practitioners of the discipline who themselves represent the churches. It is fairly technical in character and comprehensive in its scope. That comprehensiveness, however, also entailed a necessity to abbreviate a good number of discussions en route to mapping out various positions.

This current work is not a monograph but a collection of articles, not a comprehensive work but a series of occasional essays that respond to particular questions and address particular audiences. Its systematic character consists only in the set of presuppositions and the approach that remain consistent with the earlier book. All but two of the chapters, on Jesus research and missions, were written after *Jesus Symbol of God*.

I have been asked whether it would be possible to re-present *Jesus Symbol of God* in a shorter and more accessible format. In some respects this volume serves that function. The selected essays are arranged so that their order roughly corresponds to the unfolding of *Jesus Symbol of God*. The language of exposition is simpler because the essays were either written for oral delivery or envision an audience that did not necessarily include professional Christian theologians. Although these essays were slightly revised for publication in this volume, they have not been substantially rewritten. They thus contain a good deal of repetition of some fundamental themes that continually have to be brought forward as the premises of the discussion. While they do not advance the fundamental argument contained in *Jesus Symbol of God*, they push forward certain

---

1. Roger Haight, *Jesus Symbol of God* (Maryknoll, N.Y.: Orbis Books, 1999).

aspects or highlight certain themes that are elicited by the topics under consideration.

The first essay, "Jesus Research and Faith in Jesus Christ," draws out the significance of Jesus research for the overall project of understanding Jesus Christ and his place in Christian faith. It is placed first in order to underline the fact that historical and exegetical research is having a major impact on dogmatic theology and to suggest one place where that influence is felt. The essay develops a distinction between a historicist and a dogmatic imagination. It then suggests that one of the ways in which postmodern culture affects Christian faith is through Jesus research; this material reschools the Christian imagination by its focus on Jesus of Nazareth. In this scenario, doctrinal conceptions are relocated in the structure of faith as interpretations of Jesus of Nazareth.

Chapter 2, entitled "The Logic of Christology from Below," builds on the first by describing a method in christology; it offers a concise recapitulation of the method employed in *Jesus Symbol of God*. The dense, schematic form of the essay represents an effort to cut through some of the complexity of the larger work. It depicts an approach to understanding Jesus Christ that is elicited by and corresponds with New Testament research reflected in the first chapter. Much of the negative criticism of and the positive response to *Jesus Symbol of God* is connected to an appreciation of the method that drives it.[2] A holistic understanding of the presuppositions and premises that make up a fundamental theology and some appreciation of the logic of an approach to christology "from below" are crucial for following the essays of this book.

Chapters 3 and 4 revolve around the theme of salvation, the deepest and most central question that Christianity as a religion addresses. No other theme receives more attention in *Jesus Symbol of God* than the notion of salvation. I go back to it here. The first of these two essays was written in the context of an interdisciplinary symposium on human freedom. This context and the broad, secular audience addressed necessitated an appeal to common human experience and led to highlighting the framework provided by the doctrine of creation in order to make sense of salvation relative to the value and exercise of freedom in this world.

---

2. A fuller account of that method is contained in Roger Haight, *Dynamics of Theology* (Maryknoll, N.Y.: Orbis Books, 2001).

One can, of course, explain salvation by focusing on sin and deploying one's constructive argument by using the framework provided by the distinction between a natural order of creation and a supernatural order of grace and redemption. But I believe that, while this distinction served well to reinforce an appreciation of the gratuitous character of God's grace and salvation, it has become dysfunctional in so many ways that it should be abandoned in the interest of communication with a broader world. Insider language must be translated into a more common idiom to become intelligible to both a secular and a religiously pluralistic world.

The essay on the theology of the cross, chapter 4, is of a piece with the experience of salvation as it examines objective redemption theory and the question of what Jesus did for our salvation. It offers a response to several issues: the forceful, dramatic question raised by the film of Mel Gibson, "The Passion of the Christ," released in 2004 and seen throughout the Christian world, the more explicit queries addressed to *Jesus Symbol of God* asking for more attention to the suffering of Jesus Christ, and, more generally, the meaning of Jesus' suffering and death for Christian self-understanding. In the traditional Christian language directed toward what Jesus did for human salvation, the cross holds an important and almost central place, so much so that its meaning is often taken for granted. The essay tries to break through the reflex use of formulas learned by rote with critical questions about the meaning and the value of physical suffering that in the end might help to sort out just what is going on in this ingrained Christian speech. The essay seeks to answer such questions as these: What are we actually saying about Jesus' suffering? What are outsiders hearing? Should we be revising this language or using it more carefully? These questions will certainly not be answered satisfactorily for all Christians, but the conversation is worthwhile.

The next three essays, chapters 5, 6, and 7, revolve around the issues raised by a new consciousness of the world's religious pluralism, the increasingly positive appreciation of religious diversity on theoretical and practical levels, and the issues this raises for Christian theology generally but particularly for christology. The first of the three, entitled "Catholic Pluralism on Religious Pluralism: Rahner and Schillebeeckx," aims straightforwardly at showing that the question of the relationship between Jesus Christ and other religions or religious mediations is an open question. That means that there is no clear answer commonly held within the Christian theological community. This is shown by illustrating the pluralism on this question within the Roman Catholic Church as that is exemplified by two theologians, Karl Rahner and Edward Schillebeeckx, who are arguably the two leading Catholic theologians of the twentieth century. Although the essay is short, it seeks to show how each of these two different positions are deeply rooted in coherent and comprehensive theological visions that share much in common but are also quite different and at certain points contrary to each other.

Missions and missionary activity mark out a traditional area of church life and theology that is strongly and deeply affected by religious pluralism and a new, positive evaluation of it. Vatican II reaffirmed the conviction that the Christian church is intrinsically and by its very nature a "mission" and hence missionary. Yet people of other religions are threatened and profoundly distrustful of a missionary church which, in seeking conversions, undermines their existence. Not a few Christians themselves are newly suspicious of missionary activity. For decades these questions have occupied missiology where the discussion is intense and nuanced and comprises many different views. Chapter 6, entitled "Jesus and Church Mission," does not resolve the many issues at stake in this extensive conversation, but it achieves the limited goal of preserving the missionary character of the church by rooting it in the universal relevance of Jesus, while at the same time broadly characterizing the immediate goals of missionary activity with the metaphor of dialogue. "Dialogue," as a symbol containing rich valences, releases in turn a view of Jesus Christ and the church that justifies mission in a noncompetitive way and at the same time helps to open up in a simple but transformative way a new vision of the role of the church in history.

Chapter 7, entitled "Outline for an Orthodox Pluralist Christology," was written in the context of an interfaith conference involving representatives from many different religions. The deliberately schematic form enabled a clarity of presentation necessary for it to fulfill three functions at once. In the first place it is intended to explain to Christians, who are innately conservative regarding christology and skeptical about this thesis, how a pluralist christology can be orthodox. In the second place it is intended to explain to members of other religions, who are innately suspicious of Christian absolutism, how Christians may be both truly

Christian and genuinely open to and supportive of other religious traditions. A third intention of this essay in its interreligious context is to provide an invitation to analogous thought among all the religions about how they can balance absolute commitment and loyalty to a tradition in a noncompetitive way that remains open to other religions.

Chapter 8, whose title is intentionally drawn from a major essay of Karl Rahner, moves in a direction other than his.[3] He defined two methods of christology; this essay defines two christologies in terms of content drawn directly from the New Testament, namely, a Spirit christology and a Word christology. Along with chapter 1, this essay shows in a second instance how interaction with New Testament scholarship directly affects development in systematic christology. In this case the chapter opens up today's theological imagination to the viability of different ways drawn from scripture of portraying Jesus' divinity.

The final essay, chapter 9, entitled "The Future of Christology," is a response to an invitation to think about the direction in which christology as a discipline seems to be headed. The essay envisages a Christian audience and reflects on how a shrinking world with increasing interaction between religions is expanding the horizons of Christian consciousness. It represents an attempt to articulate and appraise the developments in christological thinking that are actually occurring among educated people in the mainline churches.

To these essays is added an Epilogue entitled "*Jesus Symbol of God:* Criticism and Response." The title summarizes its content. *Jesus Symbol of God* elicited a good number of reviews, which can be grouped into four categories: Some reviews were quite positive, others were quite negative; the greater number were composed of reviews that were positive but proposed some basic questions regarding various positions that were taken. A fourth group was noncommittal — reviewers described the work without comment. The Epilogue enters into conversation with the criticism and questions that were addressed to *Jesus Symbol of God.* Of course it is difficult if not impossible to respond adequately to some of these issues, but perhaps this whole collection of essays may be taken as a more expansive reply.

---

3. Karl Rahner, "The Two Basic Types of Christology," *Theological Investigations* 13 (New York: Seabury Press, 1975), 213–23.

I am grateful to many who were involved along the way with the development of these essays by providing the occasion for their writing. But I am especially indebted to Otto Hentz, S.J. and Kevin Burke, S.J., who carefully read the manuscript of this collection and offered many suggestions for improving the argument and clarifying various positions. Such expert advice is invaluable and is reflected in the final form of this work. I am also especially grateful to Frank Oveis of Continuum International, who as editor of the work made specific suggestions for revisions of the initial manuscript that greatly improved the final version of the text, and who negotiated its appearance. A special thanks to Gerard Jacobitz for his keen eye as a proofreader and for a comprehensive index. Finally, looking beyond the professional assistance, I feel privileged in the experience of the solid support of students and friends from around the world, of most of the many members of the American theological community, and of the Jesuit Community at America House in New York City.

Chapter One

JESUS RESEARCH AND
FAITH IN JESUS CHRIST

᭴᭴

I BEGIN with an incident. I taught an introductory course on the church, and one of the early considerations of the course dealt with the relationship between Jesus and the origins of the church. Historical study of the New Testament has raised the question of whether and in what sense Jesus founded a church similar to what had actually taken shape by the beginning of the second century. In the course of a discussion of this material a student made a statement to this effect: "I wonder if others found this material paradoxical. On the one hand the Catholic doctrine affirms that Jesus is God. On the other hand here we are asking whether Jesus intended a church or knew one would arise."

This incident which occurred within the boundaries of the faith-filled community is a version of the perennial tension between the historian and the believer which became acute during the nineteenth century but has remained a fruitful and generative topic of discussion. What is the relation between the knowledge gained by the "objective" historian through critical research into Jesus of Nazareth and the faith of the believer, including the public belief structure that gives expression to that existential commitment? The tension between these two kinds or differentiated formalities of conscious engagement with Jesus of Nazareth is so basic that it must be seen as part of the elemental structure of Christian faith itself.[1]

---

1. Terrence W. Tilley has gone a long way in resolving what may have been taken as an intrinsic theoretical problem between understanding reality historically and understanding transcendent reality theologically. See his *History, Theology and Faith: Dissolving the Modern Problematic* (Maryknoll, N.Y.: Orbis Books, 2004). By contrast I am describing what may be called a tension

13

A vigorous interaction between historical science and christological belief has been going on for the last two centuries. This history has generated a variety of different methods of construing and appropriating this active relationship, and I shall consider two of them in the course of this chapter. The issue is particularly pressing at present for a number of reasons: one is the enormous output of and interest in the historical reconstruction of first-century Christianity generally and, more particularly, the focus of this research on Jesus. Another is the fact that this material has become available to a broad audience that transcends theologians. Still another is the potential confusion that is generated by the results of this historical research as indicated by the anecdote.

A tension, and at times an open conflict, marks the relation between two ways of thinking about Jesus of Nazareth, or between two distinct languages about Jesus, the doctrinal and the historical. Doctrinal language interprets Jesus of Nazareth on the basis of an encounter of faith, or the experience of salvation that Jesus mediates for the Christian. The doctrinal language of faith portrays Jesus in transcendent terms as being intimately related to God and, finally, in his own person, divine. Historical language also interprets Jesus, but in this-worldly fashion, in order to portray him in terms of his life in this world. Today an enormous output of historical Jesus research very frequently presents Jesus in a way that seems at odds with doctrine. A particularly striking example is provided by John Hick: What does it mean to say, on the one hand, doctrinally, that Jesus is an incarnation of God and, on the other, with historians, that Jesus was unaware of his divinity?[2]

The issue that I wish to address can be focused by the following question: How does historical study of Jesus of Nazareth, that is, Jesus

---

of a more practical nature that usually consists in some kind of confusion between or failure to sort out the differences between a theological affirmation and a historical affirmation. The two kinds of judgment are distinct because they concern different levels of reality and rest on different grounds. Historical judgments appeal to historical evidence; theological judgements rest on faith. But these two are intrinsically related because all human concepts of the transcendent order are drawn from the finite or worldly sphere and are thus historically mediated and symbolic in character. This intimate relationship accounts for what I call a tension between these spheres of cognitive activity when they overlap in specific faith statements.

2. John Hick, *The Metaphor of God Incarnate: Christology in a Pluralistic Age* (Louisville: Westminster John Knox Press, 1993), 68.

research, influence faith in Jesus Christ, including theological understanding of Jesus Christ? How does Jesus research come to bear upon and influence a doctrinal construal of Jesus? From that point of view I will try to define a connection between the two languages.[3]

This straightforward question would not yield an equally clear answer across the discipline of christology. Christology is pluralistic in both method and content. However, the thesis, method, and framework for my discussion of the topic are all contained in the following proposition: a way of understanding and measuring the influence of Jesus research on christology lies in the category of the imagination. I propose that by looking at imagination as playing a key role in understanding, one will also find in it a common ground, in some instances a battle ground, in and through which these two languages are interacting. However, I do not conceive the goal of these reflections as breaking new ground. The new ground is being broken by the steady interaction between these two languages. More modestly I intend simply to use the category of imagination to describe what is going on in this interchange in such a way that it will be clarified and thus seen as not destructive but constructive and salutary.

I will be able to do this in a five-part development. I begin by presenting the framework of the discussion, including an account of the imagination. I shall then consider possible imaginative construals that attend some of the classical christological doctrines. How do people imagine Jesus in the light of christological doctrine? In the third section I will consider the premises and the content of Jesus research and how they are reshaping the imaginative portraits of Jesus. Then, fourthly, I will compare two theologians who deal with this issue and measure them in terms of the thesis proposed here. And as a conclusion I will draw out the impact of Jesus research on christology in a few theses that show some of its positive consequences.

---

3. It may be useful simply to note the questions that are not being directly addressed here. I am not asking whether or how one can get to faith from history. Nor am I asking what faith adds to history, or how religious questioning engenders a distinctive religious interpretation of historical data. Rather I am presupposing faith as a given and asking about the way it is influenced by historical research. In this way I hope to reveal something about the structure of faith and thereby also shed some light on these other questions even though they will not be formally entertained.

THE FRAMEWORK FOR THIS DISCUSSION

Let me begin by describing briefly the framework of this discussion. Our pluralistic theological situation makes it necessary to lay out some of the presuppositions and premises of any particular discussion. In this case, the main premises can be reduced to two: the conception of imagination being enlisted in these considerations and, second, the christological framework that underlies the discussion. In both instances I will be operating loosely within the context of a Thomistic Aristotelian tradition.

Imagination

The imagination is the subject of an enormous literature in a wide variety of disciplines announcing innumerable theories of its nature and function. My goal has nothing to do with establishing a theory of the imagination but in simply laying down a number of axioms that may be confirmed by common experience. In Thomas's faculty psychology, the imagination is a fairly discrete inner power of the human spirit that, as it were, warehouses or stores up the concrete sensible images that are received through the external senses.[4] In what follows I consider the imagination not as a discrete power of the human spirit, but as one of many functions or activities of the human mind that is mixed up with and implicated in other cognitive processes. And rather than describe an integral picture of imaginative activity, I will limit myself to three propositions that will be useful for this discussion.

The first of these is that all human knowledge enters the mind through the mediation of sense data and the imagination. This view reflects the empiricism of Aristotle. According to Thomas, in terms of objective content the human mind is born like a clean slate upon which nothing is written.[5] It stands in relation to the whole of reality as a pure potency

---

4. Thomas Aquinas, *Summa Theologica: Complete English Edition in Five Volumes,* trans. Fathers of the English Dominican Province (Westminster, Md.: Christian Classics, 1961): Part I, Question 78, Article 4. For a brief account of Aquinas's theory of the imagination, see Ray L. Hart, *Unfinished Man and the Imagination: Towards an Ontology and a Rhetoric of Revelation* (New York: Herder and Herder, 1968), 318–34. Also Jacques Maritain reviews Thomistic psychology and epistemology with an eye to imaginative artistic creativity in *Creative Intuition in Art and Poetry* (New York: Pantheon Books, 1953), 95–145.

5. Aquinas ST, I, 79, 2. This discussion has become much more complex in the light of empirical, prenatal research. The "slate" is not as "clean" as it appeared in the classical Greek or medieval periods. But this does not undermine the role of the imagination in human knowing.

ready to be filled with content. This content comes to it through the five senses which mediate external reality to the human spirit. The sensible images from the material world are processed in the mind by what Thomas calls internal senses, two of which are imagination and memory. These provide the immediate resources for intellectual or conceptual knowledge. It is finally the active, spiritual intellect itself that discerns within these concrete and particular images immaterial and universally relevant ideas. Thomas calls this process abstraction, a drawing out of universal truth or meaning from a material, sensible datum.[6]

Second, this foundational empiricism yields the proposition that "the intellect knows nothing but what it receives from the senses."[7] And this can be expanded to include the imagination: all human knowledge is drawn from the material world through the senses and the concrete images that are formed and stored up by the imagination. Thus it follows that there are no concepts, or words, or, more generally, languages that do not also bear with them an imaginative residue. Abstraction of a universally relevant idea from a particular imaginative datum does not mean leaving physical, sensible reality behind. Rather it means discovering and grasping universally intelligible meaning within the concrete and specific. I am suggesting that even our most abstract ideas and propositions always carry along, or imply, or create some concrete imaginative construal.

Third, imagination in Aquinas has a passive and an active dimension. It is passive in the sense that it receives and stores images of the external world. It is active in the sense that it divides and combines received images and constructs new ones. For example, from the received image of gold and the image of a mountain the imagination can construct the picture of a golden mountain.[8] On this basis one can speak of a twofold function of the imagination: it is both conservative and creative. The passive storing of images to which all knowledge is bound keeps our speculative reasoning in touch with reality; it prevents imagination from becoming fancy or fantasy. The active dimension of imagination is the principle of creative discovery and invention in poetry, in art, and in the breakthroughs of science.

---

6. ST, I, 79, 4.
7. ST, I, 78, 4, obj. 4.
8. ST, I, 78, 4.

Christological Framework

The christological framework within which I am operating here builds on a philosophy of religion which shares deep resonances with the Aristotelian empiricism of Aquinas. This empiricism rules out an immediate contact with God. All our knowledge of God is mediated through the world, through some finite, historical medium; one can find no universal nonmediated religion. Human knowledge clings to a particular time and place in history in such a way that even universally relevant knowledge is conditioned by unique, specific, and individual images. This rules out a single religion based on reason alone or a universal natural theology. Reason itself is historically conditioned in its operation, even though it shares certain invariant patterns. All religion, therefore, arises out of historical mediation. The central medium that defines Christianity is the event and person of Jesus of Nazareth. Christianity is the religion in which faith in God was and is mediated by the external historical medium of Jesus of Nazareth.[9]

Given this fundamental understanding of the historical ground of Christianity, christology developed out of the specific experience of the disciples of Jesus, more specifically the experience of salvation from God being mediated or made present and available to them through Jesus. My purpose here does not allow going into detail in describing this experience nor how it developed within faith's recognition that Jesus was raised by God. It is sufficient to say that the New Testament bears witness to various interpretations of how Jesus is savior and how he is to be understood relative to us and relative to God. Moreover, this interpretation continued as Christianity spread into the Greek and Roman worlds and their intellectual cultures. The classical christological doctrines of Nicaea and Chalcedon are public interpretations referring back to Jesus of Nazareth that also respond to specific historical problems that were raised in those particular historical contexts. Beneath them, as the ground and rationale for their intelligibility, is the same ground that underlies the New Testament witness, namely, the experience of Jesus as the mediator of God's salvation.

---

9. For an account of the necessity of historical mediation for all our knowledge of God, see John E. Smith, "The Disclosure of God and Positive Religion," *Experience and God* (New York: Oxford University Press, 1968), 68–98.

Let me sum up the first part of this discussion, which lays the groundwork for what follows. I am working within the framework of a theory of knowledge and of religion that takes our contact with the sensible world as the starting point and basis of all knowing, including religious knowing. This means that the imagination will have an important role in the way we construe things, even the personal, spiritual, eternal, and transcendent reality of God. All knowing in this world involves the imagination. This anthropology and epistemology lead to the view that Jesus is the concrete historical foundation of Christian faith and that the history of christology is the history of interpreting Jesus of Nazareth. In the next two parts I will consider the imaginative understandings that accompany the classical doctrinal interpretations of Jesus and the imaginative understandings that are being proffered by Jesus research.

CLASSICAL CHRISTOLOGICAL DOCTRINES AND THE IMAGINATION

I turn to a brief outline of the imaginative construal of Jesus of Nazareth that is implied in the classical christological doctrines of Nicaea and Chalcedon. The goal here is not to prove anything but to point to common Christian experience. The premise of this description consists in what was just discussed, that all language and concepts have an imaginative residue. I shall not analyze the genesis of the classical doctrines, which would be necessary if one wished to uncover their historically generated theological meaning. I am less interested in their technical meaning, and more interested in the imaginative understanding that accompanies them.

The Council of Nicaea, in the year 325, affirmed that what is incarnated in Jesus, namely God's Word or Son, is not less in stature than God the Father; it is rather of the very same stuff as God. Jesus, then, is truly and properly divine. So great was the stress on Jesus' divinity, however, that Jesus' humanity seemed to get lost in some conceptions of him. This resulted in controversies that led the Council of Chalcedon in the middle of the fifth century (451) to declare that Jesus Christ is truly divine and truly human, of the same nature as God and of the same nature as human beings. Jesus Christ is one proper individual, but this individuality unites within itself a distinctly human and divine nature.

In one sense one could say that this formula righted the imbalance left in the wake of Nicaea, for Jesus was declared to be consubstantial with us human beings. But from another perspective Jesus' divinity still held the upper hand. For the theology surrounding the formula allowed certain forms of speech that are paradoxical. Because the one person Jesus Christ had two integral natures, one could affirm of him that which pertained to either one of the natures. One could say, for example, that Jesus suffered, because he did so in his human nature. One could also say that Jesus in his earthly life was God incarnate. One could affirm of Jesus' knowledge and consciousness what was proper to God. Thus, although one could read the classical doctrine as simply a confession of faith that Jesus is simultaneously and integrally divine and human without any explanation, still the theology of the time allowed one to say undialectically that Jesus was divine. The portrayal of Jesus left by the council was that Jesus was a divine individual who also bore an integral human nature.

If this is an accurate representation of these classical doctrines, what is the imaginative portrayal of Jesus that they communicate? Overwhelmingly, the most significant image the doctrines portray is that Jesus is God. This does not imply that a direct image of God is available, which is then predicated of Jesus; God is known negatively, that is, through this-worldly images by a denial of all limits in the positive images and qualities that are predicated of God.[10] But once the language is in place, these characteristics can now be predicated of Jesus. Jesus is really infinite being, all knowing, all powerful. In himself he is substantively, or hypostatically, God.

Originally it was Jesus who supplied Christians with their images of God. Such is the point of many of Jesus' parables, for example. But when the classical doctrines are the starting point of one's christology, one is introduced to Jesus by way of the doctrine. "Jesus is God" provides an imaginative framework that controls the reading of the gospel accounts of Jesus. From this perspective it is not surprising that Jesus worked miracles, although one can recognize the astonishment of those who experienced them for the first time. When one is in possession of the doctrine, it is less amazing that Jesus cured from a distance, or walked on water, or calmed the storm, or raised people to life, for he was himself

---

10. Aquinas, *ST*, I, 13, 2.

the agent of creation. The doctrinal imagination, once it is internalized, forms a kind of master pattern that reinforces itself by a literal construal of the miracle traditions in the gospels. One may at this point recall the anecdote that began this discussion. It was a doctrinal imagination that caused the surprise that Jesus, being divine, could have been ignorant of the movement that would develop after his death and evolve into a church.

JESUS RESEARCH AND THE IMAGINATION

We pass now to Jesus research and ask about the bearing of the imagination upon the quest for the historical Jesus. I have divided this discussion into three simple points: first, the role of imagination in historical reconstruction; second, the content of Jesus research; and third, the effect of Jesus research on the imagination of those who read it.

How does imagination enter into the process of reconstructing the past? R. G. Collingwood, historian and philosopher of history, responded to this question in the first half of the twentieth century. History, he said, is not written on the basis of collecting and collating authoritative witnesses. Rather the historian assumes a certain autonomous responsibility for reconstructing the past by selecting, adding to, and amending the sources.[11] First of all, negatively, by the principle of analogy, historians reject what appears to be impossible according to commonly accepted laws of nature.[12] And positively, historians exercise autonomy by constructing an integral, in some measure unified, and plausible picture of a specific part of history and a coherent narrative. This is done by what Collingwood calls an a priori or necessary imagination that interpolates into the evidence. This imagination is not freewheeling fancy but bound to the evidence by necessity. For example, if the sources say Caesar was in Rome, and later in Gaul, one must interpolate the journey even when the sources do not mention it. If a ship appears on the horizon at one point and some time later at a different point on the horizon, we are "obliged to imagine it as having occupied intermediate positions

---

11. R. G. Collingwood, *The Idea of History* (New York: Oxford University Press, 1956), 235. John McIntyre, *Faith, Theology and Imagination* (Edinburgh: Handsel Press, 1987), 109–15 provides a synopsis and commentary on Collingwood.

12. Collingwood, *The Idea of History*, 239–40.

when we were not looking."[13] We necessarily imagine "the under side of this table, the inside of an unopened egg, the back of the moon."[14] When the historian considers Jesus as a human being, the humanity of Jesus presents another example of an instance that requires all sorts of necessary imagined data about him.

Generalizing on Collingwood's analysis one will have to say that the imagination that controls interpretation is *both passive and active*. On the one hand, if it were not objective and passive, keeping close to the evidence received, imagination would turn into fancy, and in that measure stray from the truth. But, on the other hand, if it were not subjective, active, and creative, one could not assemble a coherent and continuous account of this truth. Therefore both the passive and active dimensions of imagination that were noticed by Thomas have an essential role in historical reconstruction.

This plainly appears in the contents of Jesus research today where there are two distinguishable but overlapping kinds of research. The one focuses on the overall portrait of Jesus and relies more on an active imagination; the other focuses more on Jesus' teachings and actions, and remains more closely dependent upon the sources. Regarding the first, however, there is no single portrait of Jesus that is beyond dispute. A great diversity in the pictures of Jesus emerge from the relatively limited sources the historian has to work with. Much of the diversity comes in trying to decide the "genre" of Jesus, that is, the basic historical role he assumed or projected, the type of character he appeared to be. Most admit that because Jesus was a Jew he should be understood in the terms of some position or role known in the Jewish world of his time. For example, negatively, the Galilean Jesus was probably or surely not a priest, or an Essene, or a Zealot, or a scribe, or a lawyer.

Positively, three major generalized portraits of Jesus are currently being exploited in Jesus research: Jesus was a prophet, or a holy man, or a philosopher-poet. A strong case has been made by many that Jesus appeared as a prophet, or the eschatological prophet, and presented his teaching in an apocalyptic way. Others depict Jesus as a healer, an exorcist, and a wonder-worker who proffered forgiveness of sins. Still others

---

13. Ibid., 241.
14. Ibid., 242.

see Jesus as a wandering, Cynic-like, philosophical figure who taught a countercultural message and dramatized it by a simple life of poverty. As the judgment about the genre of a text gives a first interpretation of the data contained in it, these large interpretations of Jesus shape the content and meaning of his message in different ways. It is probable that all of these types contribute something true about Jesus and one should not judge between them too quickly.

There is more consensus when the imagination stays closer to the evidence about the basic message of Jesus: that he preached the kingdom of God, that he went around teaching, healing, and doing good, that he associated with the poor and the outcasts of society, that he criticized structures and practices that were dehumanizing, that he told parables and performed symbolic actions that dramatized the kingdom of God, that these dramatizations reversed everyday patterns of thought, and that his ethics of the kingdom of God were radical. However one depicts Jesus, one should take into account that he was publicly executed as a criminal. Jesus was a public figure who rubbed authority the wrong way.[15]

Finally, what is the impact of these imaginative historical reconstructions of Jesus on the imaginations of those who read and study them? The answer to this question is simple and blunt: one cannot but be impressed by the humanity of Jesus. Negatively, the historian as historian and not as theologian can present to us nothing more than Jesus as a human being. Epistemologically, the divinity of Jesus is a datum of faith and not empirically evident. Moreover, on the supposition of Jesus' humanity, the imagination can and must interpolate all sorts of data that are not explicitly supplied by the texts but which are necessarily implied by them, namely, the implications of being a human being. In doctrinal terms, these are the characteristics that attend upon Jesus' being "consubstantial with us as to humanity, like unto us in all things but sin (cf. Heb 4:15)."[16] In sum, historical research presents us with a Jesus who overwhelms our imaginations as being thoroughly human. What then is the impact of this upon christology?

---

15. The rich harvest of the quest for the historical Jesus is summarized in Roger Haight, *Jesus Symbol of God* (Maryknoll, N.Y.: Orbis Books, 1999), 55–87

16. Council of Chalcedon, *Enchiridion Symbolorum,* ed. H. Denzinger and A. Schönmetzer (Freiburg im Breisgau: Herder, 1963), 108, no. 301.

TWO VIEWS ON JESUS RESEARCH
AND CHRISTIAN FAITH

Before turning directly to an analysis of the impact and significance of Jesus research relative to Christian faith I want to compare two views on this matter and relate each to this understanding of the role of imagination in the encounter with Jesus Christ. The two theologians are Schubert Ogden and Jon Sobrino.

Schubert Ogden

Schubert Ogden approaches the relationship of Jesus research to Christian faith in Jesus Christ by first establishing that the question that is addressed to Jesus, the christological question, is an existential and religious question. It is not an objective question aiming at knowledge about Jesus as he is in himself; it is a question about God, about ultimate human self-identity and destiny, and about Jesus as the medium of an answer to these two deep issues.[17] Given the nature of the christological question, he then asks about the subject matter of christology, the object that is the referent of the term "Jesus" when Jesus is accepted in faith as the Christ. Is this Jesus the object of Jesus research, "the actual Jesus of the past insofar as he is knowable to us today by way of empirical-historical inquiry using the writings of the New Testament as sources?"[18]

Ogden's response to the question revolves around two distinctions. The first is between what he calls the "empirical-historical Jesus" and the "existential-historical Jesus." The empirical-historical Jesus is Jesus insofar as Jesus can be reconstructed by empirical-historical method, whereas the existential-historical Jesus is Jesus insofar as Jesus engages human subjectivity existentially as mediating a response to the religious question. The distinction is similar to H. Richard Niebuhr's distinction between external and internal history, which is illustrated by Lincoln's reference to the birth of a nation at the beginning of his Gettysburg Address. The bringing forth of the nation is of interest to Lincoln and any patriot because it is "the origin of a nation so conceived and so dedicated, and hence the primal authorizing source of their own as well as all

---

17. Schubert M. Ogden, *The Point of Christology* (Dallas: Southern Methodist University Press, 1992 [orig. 1982]), 20–40.
18. Ibid., 44.

other authentic Americanism."[19] Analogously, the existential-historical Jesus authorizes human existence. It is important to note that this is not an "adequate" distinction; Jesus as a historical figure is common to both terms.

Secondly, Ogden distinguishes between a "Christ kerygma," which is the developed message of the meaning of Jesus Christ as found, for example, in Paul and John, and the "Jesus kerygma," which is "accessible through critical analysis of the synoptic gospels."[20]

On the basis of these distinctions, Ogden can state his basic thesis as follows: "I contend that the Jesus to whom the earliest witnesses point as 'the real locus of revelation' is the existential-historical Jesus, and therefore neither the empirical-historical Jesus nor their own witness of faith, save insofar as it is solely through their witness that this event of revelation is now accessible and continues to take place."[21]

The implications of these distinctions are several. First of all, the distinction between the existential-historical Jesus of faith and revelation and the empirical-historical Jesus means that "what can or cannot be inferred concerning the empirical-historical Jesus has no bearing whatever on the point of christology."[22] The subject of christological assertion is not Jesus in himself or as merely a historical figure, but Jesus' meaning for us as a medium of God. But this is supplied by the Jesus kerygma which is the earliest existential-historical witness to Jesus. On the one hand, there may be empirical data about Jesus that can be retrieved by historical research, but this has no decisive bearing upon the claim that Jesus is the Christ. On the other hand, christological formulations too have to be controlled and normed by a historical study of scripture. But this historical quest for the norm of christology is not a quest for Jesus but for the Jesus kerygma or earliest witness to Jesus as the Christ. In this way Ogden implicitly embraces the new quest for the historical Jesus, but he makes it clear that, insofar as it is relevant to christology, what this quest reaches is not an empirical-historical Jesus but the existential-historical Jesus of the Jesus kerygma.

---

19. Ibid., 57.
20. Ibid., 51.
21. Ibid., 59–60.
22. Ibid., 60.

Jon Sobrino

In *Jesus the Liberator* Jon Sobrino defines the idea of the historical Jesus in such a way that it corresponds to what Ogden calls the existential-historical Jesus. The gospels presuppose and were written out of faith in Jesus as the Christ. But this faith needed to hold on to its historical referent: "it was not enough to confess Christ; it was necessary to refer back to Jesus, and to the reality of Jesus."[23] Two things, then, must be held together. Ogden calls these two the existential faith and Jesus; Sobrino calls the two theology and Jesus. Sobrino describes the gospels as history and theology simultaneously. They are not factual information but theology; but they are theology that is historicized. No history of Jesus without theology; and no theology of Jesus without writing a history of him.[24]

Sobrino offers an analytic account of how the historical Jesus functions in his christology. He contrasts Latin American liberationists with other European theologians and then sums up his position in three or four points. First, by the historical Jesus Sobrino means "the history of Jesus," the words, actions, attitudes, and spirit that make up his history.[25] And the core of what is important in this history of Jesus is Jesus' "practice with spirit." By practice he means "the whole range of activities Jesus used to act on social reality and transform it in the specific direction of the Kingdom of God. The 'historical' is thus primarily what sets history in motion, and this practice of Jesus, which in his day set history in motion, is what has come down to our time as a history set in motion to be continued."[26] To "practice" Sobrino adds the phrase "with spirit," designating the attitudes and intentions with which Jesus did what he did: his spirit of mercy, his concern for others, his partiality for those who suffer. "Practice with spirit" highlights the formality or aspect of the historical Jesus material that Sobrino makes central.

Then, second, within this practice with spirit one can discern the person of Jesus: his practice provides a framework for organizing the

23. Jon Sobrino, *Jesus the Liberator* (Maryknoll, N.Y.: Orbis Books, 1993), 59.
24. "Presenting the history of Jesus, however theologized, is the best way of giving truth and substance to believers' faith and encouragement to their lives. And this is, in my view, the permanent value of the specific way of going back to Jesus that the Gospels offer." Ibid., 60.
25. Ibid., 50–51.
26. Ibid., 51.

various elements of his ministry. The way to understand Jesus the person is through a consideration of the various aspects of his practice. And, third, the link between the historical Jesus and faith in him as the Christ is also mediated through practice. The practice of discipleship, of following Jesus, defines a prior condition for faith's appreciation of him as the Christ. "It is, in the last resort, a matter of affinity and connaturality, beginning with what is most real in Jesus."[27] To get to faith in Jesus as the Christ, one needs a prior experience or prior affinity. This is discipleship, a participation in the practice of Jesus. "In the case of faith in Christ, the prior objective phenomenon necessary is the phenomenon of the historical Jesus and the prior subjective experience is being his disciple."[28]

Finally, Sobrino describes liberation christology as gospel christology. He has a good appreciation of the critical limits of Jesus research. But his interest lies more in using the results of Jesus research within the context of faith and presenting Jesus as the Christ narratively. This means telling how Jesus is the Christ in story form, in a history that of course opens up to following him: to discipleship, practice, and ethics.

Role of the Imagination

Both Ogden and Sobrino affirm that the basis of christology, insofar as it is christology, is not an objective, empirical historical account of Jesus of Nazareth. Such will never generate what Christian faith recognizes in Jesus; faith transcends what history can determine. What is preserved for us in the New Testament as the norm of christology is Jesus perceived as the Christ, a mixture of empirical datum or historical reconstruction and faith's appreciation, a duality of history and theology, or a kerygmatic Jesus. This distinction between the transcendent and gratuitous character of faith's appreciation of Jesus and the empirical details about Jesus which appeal to the imagination grants faith a degree of autonomy and protects it from being jerked around by the latest historical hypothesis.

But no matter how much one presses this side of the distinction, and it is crucial that one do so, it does not break an intrinsic bond between

---

27. Ibid., 54.
28. Ibid., 55.

Jesus in his "empirical," historical actuality and the faith's appreciation of him. One must distinguish between subjectivity and objectivity, but one cannot sunder their continuity completely. The distinction between an existential-historical Jesus and an empirical-historical Jesus is a formal distinction in the way the knower knows the object; the material object, Jesus, is common to both. The existential-historical Jesus is still Jesus; internal history is an appreciation of external history; theology cannot be separated from history. Therefore the results of empirical historical research on Jesus enter into christological construal, even though they do not by themselves control it. The way this occurs is through the imagination.

The role of empirical history can be explained in terms of the role of the imagination in faith's construal of Jesus. All subject-object encounter entails the imagination. Christian faith is encounter with God mediated through Jesus of Nazareth, so that the Christian conception of God is not confirmed by Jesus, but is mediated by Jesus. Negatively, one cannot say that Christian faith would remain the same if Jesus of Nazareth never existed. Nor could one continue to maintain the faith assertions mediated through Jesus if in fact Jesus were the opposite of all that the Jesus kerygma attributed to him. On the contrary, the dynamic of Christian faith, even though its object is God mediated through Jesus, assumes a continuity between what is asserted of Jesus and the empirical historical reality of Jesus. This is shown in the natural curiosity to know more about Jesus upon which Jesus research feeds. The role of the imagination in knowing correlates with this intrinsic bond between understanding and concrete historical mediation. Knowing is never separated from concrete images of the object known. But this means that the implicit imaginative portrayal of Jesus will either remain naive and unreflective, as in a dogmatic imagination that is exclusively nurtured by doctrine, or will itself be the object of critical reflection. It is precisely the task of theology as critical reflection on the witness of faith to develop a critical understanding of faith. But this includes a critical image of Jesus, and this is done by the discipline of history. In sum, the role of history is to establish within faith a critically reflective image of the existential-historical Jesus.

THE IMPACT OF JESUS RESEARCH
ON CHRISTOLOGY

Let me conclude this discussion by outlining the impact of Jesus research upon christology generally. The pieces are in place and need only be drawn together. I will do this by presenting four propositions which I will also briefly explain.

First, there will be a tension between the historical reconstruction of Jesus and the transcendent and doctrinal aspects of christology. Where a doctrinal christology has generated a docetic and monophysitic imagination, this tension will amount to a clash of opposition.[29] Docetic and monophysitic christologies do not include a reckoning of Jesus as absolutely human like all other human beings; Jesus is imagined as God on earth in human clothing. This imaginative view of Jesus Christ will be directly challenged by Jesus research. This is a significant observation if Karl Rahner was correct in asserting that the heresy of monophysitism is widespread among Christians today.[30] But even in a balanced or orthodox christology there must be a tension between the humanity and divinity of Jesus.

Second, historical research that tries to reconstruct the figure of Jesus provides a starting point and a structure for relating the humanity and divinity of Jesus. This research makes it clear that Jesus of Nazareth is the subject matter of christology, even though he is only the subject matter of christology when he responds historically to the existential religious question. Epistemologically, the existential response to Jesus or to God through Jesus leads back to Jesus. We do not, for example, have any content for a risen Christ apart from Jesus of Nazareth. As was said, knowledge of transcendence begins with the world, history, and sense data. The divinity of Jesus, therefore, must be imagined as *within* or as a dimension of the integral human being Jesus of Nazareth. Another way of putting this is that the human being Jesus cannot be

---

29. Docetism refers to the early heresy that held that, although Jesus appeared to be a real flesh and blood human being, in reality he was not. Monophysitism is the name given to the christological position that Jesus had only one nature, a divine nature, as distinct from a "two-nature" christology. Such a position usually slights Jesus' integral humanity. In both instances I am using these designations loosely to signal a kind of imaginative fixation on Jesus' being God.

30. Karl Rahner, "Current Problems in Christology," *Theological Investigations* 1 (Baltimore: Helicon Press, 1961), 160.

left behind in the affirmation of Jesus' divinity. Jesus of Nazareth is a sacrament or symbol or concrete medium making God present to history. An imaginative, historical construal of Jesus cannot be neglected or even played down in a critical christology. Rather doctrinal christology should assume into itself an imaginative historical portrayal of Jesus' human career.[31]

Third, Jesus research functions as a negative norm in the fashioning of an integral christology. By a negative norm I mean that one cannot affirm of Jesus what is positively excluded by a consensus of history. For example, a necessary imaginative judgment recognizes that as a finite human being Jesus was limited by his historical particularity; he had limited insight, judgment, and knowledge. This is confirmed by the historical evidence. Thus any christology that depicts Jesus as essentially constituted with God-like knowledge is false by the criterion of history. Or again, it is the consensus of Jesus research that the idea of the kingdom of God was central to Jesus' preaching and action; it formed a center of gravity for his public ministry. A christology that fails to give any attention to this dimension of Jesus is less than adequate. Here one sees the conservative role of the passive dimension of the imagination. The passive imagination stores the historical images of Jesus, and doctrine about Jesus is bound to stay close to the imaginative memory of him.

Fourth, Jesus research provides a positive guide for christological interpretation. Here the active dimension and the creative role of imagination come to the fore. Jesus as he is imagined to be in his historical life provides a guide for Christian understanding of God and of human existence. This is what it means to say that Jesus reveals God. His teaching and his person open up the imagination for its encounter with and construal of God. Jesus also mediates to the Christian imagination a way of understanding human existence. Since Jesus was a figure of the past, this requires imaginative and creative interpretation today, not rote or literal imitation. But it is Jesus of Nazareth who is the subject matter of this hermeneutics.

---

31. This cannot be escaped on the basis of the pluralism of the reconstructions of Jesus, because in fact all christologies imply some conception of the character of Jesus. A critical christology will recognize this implicit necessity and lay out its implied image of Jesus in dialogue with historians.

In sum, in these four ways Jesus research is having a dramatic influence on christology today.[32] This historical research is not something to be feared, but to be welcomed as enriching knowledge of Jesus and the impulse to discipleship.

---

32. Elizabeth Johnson reaches a similar conclusion through an analysis of the corporate image, or the "memory image," of Jesus passed on by the church. "The image of the historical Jesus, formed by the coalescence of historical knowledge about him, is not properly utilized if it becomes a verification or proof of faith. It is, however, theologically relevant for faith in that it gives concrete content to the faith confession, corrects faith images of Jesus, and, most crucially, carries the element of the free, divine 'given' in the Christ event, the actuality of God's self-gift in history to which Christian faith is a response." Elizabeth A. Johnson, "The Theological Relevance of the Historical Jesus: A Debate and a Thesis," *The Thomist* 48 (1984): 1–43 at 35.

Chapter Two

THE LOGIC OF CHRISTOLOGY
FROM BELOW

❧

A NEW MILLENNIUM encourages the feeling that we are entering a new period of history. True, numerical markers of time are arbitrary, and there are few sudden changes in global history. But at the same time it is only now for the first time that the human race can begin to think of itself in terms of a truly global history, a consciously common history of all, bound together by political, economic, and cultural ties. The human race in the twenty-first century has embarked upon a new age of world solidarity. This in turn should cause Christians to expect shifts and changes in their self-understanding. The church in the West has gone through several major changes over its two-thousand-year history that can be correlated with changes in society and culture. No reason impels us to think that Christian theology has ceased to develop. But such development is most crucial at the core of Christian faith itself, namely, the mediation of Christian faith in God through Jesus Christ. It is no surprise, therefore, that few areas in Christian theology are as vitally active as christology. In the animated discussions within the discipline one can begin to see the broad contours of a new Christian consciousness beginning to take shape.

The developments in christology are occurring piecemeal in areas that are sometimes quite independent of each other. I will enumerate some of them further on. When one draws them together and measures their cumulative effect, one begins to see the depth and far-ranging scope of the christological discussion. How can one begin to bring all these investigations and inquiries into a coherent statement? How can they be integrated into a unified christology? One way of doing this is to propose a consistent method. In the essay which follows I want to outline such a method under the well-known phrase "a christology from below." My goal is to represent clearly and schematically the logic of a christology formed in response to the new situation in which we find ourselves.[1]

The phrase, "the logic of christology," carries a double meaning. First, the logic of christology when taken formally or abstractly refers to the suppositions and method of its development. The logic of christology is like the grammar of a language; it is the underlying set of rules that govern usage. In this formal sense, the logic of christology simply refers to the method by which a christology is generated. Second, in a more material sense, the logic of christology refers to the content of the christology but in a schematic, abbreviated form similar to an outline. After a formal account of a method, I will lay out the fundamental line of interpretation and understanding that could be assumed by such a christology. The term "logic" is used to underline the fact that the intention here is not to develop this christology fully, but merely to point holistically to the strategy by which a christology might respond to our new situation.

The designation "from below" refers to the distinctive quality of the christology that is being described here. Everyone has a vague idea of the meaning of christology from below since Karl Rahner described it positively for Catholic theology decades ago.[2] I use the term here in an epistemological and not an ontological sense. Two things are signaled by a christology from below. First, such a christology is one that begins here below on earth: it begins with human experience, with human questioning, with the historical figure Jesus of Nazareth, with disciples who encountered Jesus and interpreted him in various ways. The word "from" in the phrase "from below" thus indicates a point of departure in our christological thinking. "From below" does not indicate the end, goal, or result of christological thinking which, by contrast, is a "high" christology. "From below" does not negate or minimize the ontology of grace, or God's initiative "from above," for this initiative of God can be experienced according to the common testimony of Christians.[3]

---

1. Behind this essay is my *Jesus Symbol of God* (Maryknoll, N.Y.: Orbis Books, 1999). With this essay I intend to cut through the large size of that work and present the method that provides the key to its interpretation. This work is referred to as JSG.

2. Karl Rahner, "The Two Basic Types of Christology," *Theological Investigations* 13 (New York: Seabury Press, 1975), 213–23.

3. "Experience" here does not refer to direct apprehension of transcendent reality. Its meaning may be discerned in contrast with a theology that is based exclusively on the authority of objective statements which are not explicitly correlated with existential self-consciousness.

Second, this beginning epistemologically from below sets up, or constitutes, a structure of thinking and understanding that remains consistent.
Epistemologically, christology is always ascending; it is always tied to
human experience as to its starting point. It is always searching for transcendence. And when its conclusions are reached, they must always be
explained on the basis of the experience that generated them. But this
will become clearer during the course of this chapter.

I have divided the discussion into five parts. The first describes the
historical consciousness that marks contemporary intellectual culture. I
also reach back to chapter 1 and locate the quest for the historical Jesus
described there within this context of a sense of historicity. The second is
a formal statement of a method in christology that proceeds from below.
The third characterizes the genesis of christology during the period represented by the New Testament. The forth generalizes the structure of
christology on the basis of an analysis and theoretical interpretation of
its genesis. And the fifth section simply enumerates some of the classical
loci of christology that would be interpreted by being drawn into this
interpretive structure and method.

THE SITUATION OF CHRISTOLOGY

A discussion of the discipline of christology should begin with a description of the situation or human context in which it unfolds and to which
it responds. One could develop this at length. At this point I focus on
historical consciousness as a key feature of a postmodern culture that
will be explained in chapter 6.[4] The supposition of this thin description
is that readers will recognize it because they participate in it, and also
that Christian theology must adjust to it, just as it adjusted to the Greek
and Roman worlds as it moved out of Palestine.

Historical Consciousness

The term historical consciousness refers to a conscious awareness of the
historicity of human existence. As such it functions as an expression
into which are encoded a whole host of experiences and insights that

---

4. At this point it is sufficient to define the idea of "postmodernity" redundantly as pointing
to features that appear genuinely new relative to the modern. Chapter 6 contains a more specific
indication of what some of those features are. See pp. 127–30.

accompany a sense of being in history. For example, science estimates that human existence has graced our planet for a hundred thousand years or more. History and cultural anthropology have enabled us to reflect upon the wide variety of social and cultural forms humanity has assumed in recent periods. People who have come to appreciate cultural pluralism that stretches across the history of the human race have learned to accept as well the situated character of all knowing, the contextual bias in all value judgments, the relativity of all human conceptions. In its concrete content the process of reasoning itself is historically conditioned. These are some of the implicit background data that are connoted by the term "historical consciousness."

The roots of historical consciousness are both epistemological and ontological. As knowers human beings are tied to the material world of sense data. Humans do not possess in their genetic code a packet of preformed concrete images and a priori knowledge of information, even though a good deal more programming goes on before birth than was formerly recognized. What humans know explicitly is for the most part learned, and it is learned from sensible and experiential sources. In the Thomistic tradition as outlined in chapter 1, knowledge is understood to be drawn forth from the world of sense data; in Rahnerian language, because human existence is spirit in the world, the physical world becomes the medium for our experience and reflective knowledge. The human spirit is also self-transcending; it can appreciate the general and the universal, and even becomes aware of reality that transcends the finite. But because every manifestation of human existence is circumscribed by space and time, our ideas of what transcends the particular are also bound by the particular. We both transcend the sensible media of our knowledge and are bound to them. We have only a relative grasp of what it means to be human, of the nature of authentic virtue, of the character of ultimate reality.

The essential theme of historicity, then, consists in individuality and particularity.[5] Even when we transcend ourselves to appreciate classic formulations of universal truth, our very appreciation of them is individual and particular at the same time. It is typical of historical consciousness to

---

5. Ernest Troeltsch, *The Absoluteness of Christianity and the History of Religions,* trans. David Reid (Richmond: John Knox, 1971), 45–47, 63–65, 85–106.

recognize that affirmations can be both relative and true, and that even seemingly contrary insights might be equally true, because they are pronounced from different historical interests and perspectives, and thus are not really meant in the same respect or sense.

Another aspect of the world of experience that is summed up in the phrase "historical consciousness" is an appreciation of the openness of history. If the term "postmodern" has any distinct and commonly appreciated meaning it lies in this sense of the openness of reality: the future is not predictable in any detail. In the words of John O'Malley, "history can never repeat itself, for the same contingent concatenation of human factors can never be reassembled. Each word, document, event is historically and culturally conditioned, radically individualized, and understandable as history only insofar as it is unique and the result of man's more or less free action and decision."[6] We are learning new things and creating new things and growing more humble in the process because of what we do not know, because of the vast horizon of unknowing.

This historical consciousness thus comes to bear on theology and how one is to understand Jesus Christ, the church, and its mission. The initial thesis proposed here is that historical consciousness should be considered the framework within which Christians must think today. If theology is to be intelligible to the world, it must be correlated with and inculturated into a historically conscious world. Historical consciousness describes an aspect of the context within which our questions arise. It describes the intellectual culture or world into which theological answers must be appropriated.

This historical consciousness has come to bear on christology in two distinct and powerful ways over the past two or three decades. Historical consciousness dictates that to understand anything human in this world one must know how it arose historically. There can be no adequate understanding of a historical phenomenon without an analysis of its origin. The other area where historical consciousness influences today's thinking can be perceived in the measure in which we expect and appreciate pluralism. Recognition of the individuality and relatedness of all expressions of truth and value extends to the religions. This has resulted in an

---

6. John W. O'Malley, *Tradition and Transition: Historical Perspectives on Vatican II* (Wilmington, Del.: Michael Glazier, 1989), 75.

enormous interest in interreligious dialogue and how this in turn reflects back on our appreciation of the status of Jesus Christ and missionary activity.

Christology Begins with Jesus

We have seen that the recent past has witnessed a continuous output of research into Jesus. This is both a symptom and a cause of the increasing impact that historical consciousness has had in christology. Historical consciousness as cultural awareness and the fact of Jesus research have combined to determine that the starting point for christology must be Jesus.

A starting point in christology, as it is for a systematic understanding of anything, is important because it reveals assumptions and a method. It is axiomatic within the framework of a historical consciousness that if one wants to understand a phenomenon of history, such as the rise of Christianity and christology within it, one must understand its historical origins. One begins christology with a consideration of Jesus of Nazareth, therefore, because in a context of historicity the appearance of Jesus is the origin of everything that came after it. The event in history of the human being Jesus is the subject matter of christology; christology is based on and refers to Jesus. The risen Jesus, the one who is alive, with God, and of God today, and the one who relates to us in the present moment, is none other than Jesus of Nazareth. We do not have any knowledge or data about this risen Jesus that does not originate and have some connection with his earthly appearance. All knowledge of Jesus Christ, then, all the doctrines and theology, refer back to Jesus of Nazareth. This simply draws out what many people today feel instinctively, that one must begin with Jesus to understand Jesus Christ.

But the fact that one should know something about Jesus in order to do christology does not mean that he is immediately available to us in the pages of the New Testament. In fact the critical historical attempt to reconstruct Jesus within the context of the relationships that defined him has been called a "quest" with good reason; this quest has been filled with controversy for over a century. On the one side there are those who believe, or at least seem to act with a tacit assumption, that the synoptic gospels are like conventional historical sources from which one can construct a narrative and psychological biography of Jesus. On the other side are those who hold that the gospels have no strictly historical value so that it is impossible to depict the historical Jesus as he was. Moreover, theology does not need this quest, they say, because theology is based sheerly on the kerygmatic message about God acting in Jesus. A third view, which was represented in different ways by the positions of Schubert Ogden and Jon Sobrino in chapter 1 and is reflected here, argues that one can know something about Jesus on the basis of the memory of him that is preserved in the faith-filled, existential-historical accounts of him in the synoptic gospels especially. The results of this investigation is a vague and diffuse kind of knowledge that is substantially sound, although not in any great detail. But this knowledge is sufficient to focus the imagination on the person who was Jesus. This seems to be the dominant view today.

What is perhaps most important about Jesus, however, and this is implied in all that has been mentioned, is the God of Jesus.[7] For Jesus it seems did not put himself forward with explicit claims but preached the kingdom of God. Who is the God that Jesus reveals and whose reign he mediates by living and dying for it? This is a God who is personal, and whom Jesus called Father. This God is also one who is benevolent and loving. The creator God of Jesus is also savior, one who is set upon the well-being of all human beings because all of them are God's own. Moreover, Jesus believed in the resurrection of the dead, something that was confirmed for his disciples in their Easter experience of Jesus alive and with God sometime after his crucifixion.

In sum, the situation of christology on the level of intellectual culture is dominated by historical consciousness, and this reinforces the relevance of the focus on Jesus that has accompanied Jesus research.

CHARACTERISTICS OF A CHRISTOLOGY FROM BELOW

I move then to a formal description of the method of christology. This method is not idiosyncratic: implicitly or explicitly the characteristics enumerated here qualify the efforts of most theologians attempting to address the contemporary situation. Only the way in which they are put

---

7. See Haight, *Jesus Symbol of God*, 88–118.

together may be distinctive. It is important to lay out these various elements of method because they explain to a large degree the content contained in the rest of this book. Simply stating a method, as distinct from mounting an extensive argument to justify it, may raise many questions without answering them. But these arguments have been presented in other works, and the point here is to present the case in a direct, straightforward, and holistic way.

An Apologetic Method

Our situation as Christians in a world that is not homogeneously Christian or even religious demands an account of our self-understanding and thus an apologetic method. By that I mean a way of doing theology that does not presuppose Christian doctrine as an accepted set of principles, but rather sets out to explain and communicate those very doctrines in a language of commonly shared principles and values. The Apologists addressing the Roman empire in the second century are instructive for our day. This apologetic dimension defines a style of theology that also has a bearing on Christian self-understanding, that relates to those inside the church insofar as they participate in and have internalized a postmodern culture, or any other culture that does not take Christian truth for granted.[8]

Christology from Below

I explained briefly what I mean by "from below" at the top of this chapter as indicating a point of departure and not the goal of christology, and as defining a structure of thought that epistemologically is rooted in this-worldly experience. Let me add a further precision: constructively christology from below begins with a consideration of the historical Jesus. This is demanded by our historical consciousness. Jesus of Nazareth is the object of christology and there can be no consideration of Jesus in any other state apart from the only Jesus that we know from history, because "from below" points to a structure of understanding in which this historical Jesus is always present as a criterion for christology.[9]

---

8. Edward Schillebeeckx, *Interim Report on the Books Jesus and Christ* (New York: Crossroad, 1981), 10–19.

9. I have simplified a complex discussion. There are many factors prior to a turn to Jesus: for example, religious experience and interest, perhaps membership in the Christian community,

A Genetic Method

The phrase, "a genetic method," describes how an apologetic christology from below proceeds. It begins with Jesus and, after his death and the Easter experience of his disciples that Jesus is risen, follows the development of christologies in the New Testament. It traces and then analyses the genesis of christology "for the first time." On the basis of this development, and through an analysis of its structure, this genetic analysis discovers the structure or logic of christology itself. In other words, an analytical appreciation of how the Christians represented in the New Testament interpreted Jesus of Nazareth as the Christ provides the model or paradigm for the structure of christology as a discipline.

A Hermeneutical Method of Critical Correlation

The genesis of christology can be understood in terms of interpretation theory. In this case I appeal to the tradition of hermeneutics stemming from Schleiermacher and exemplified today in the writings of Heidegger, Gadamer, Ricoeur, and Tracy.[10] Just as the genesis of christology consisted in the interpretation of Jesus as the Christ in the light of the encounter of God in his life and the conviction of his exaltation by God, so too, analogously, christology today is interpretation of Jesus in the light of those same experiences. But as a formal discipline in today's historically conscious world, this interpretation takes on certain technical qualities of method. These are referred to with the terms hermeneutical, critical, and correlation.

A hermeneutical method is a method of interpretation. The structure for this interpretation is indicated by the term "correlation." Correlation means placing the data of the tradition of Christian faith, in this case going back to Jesus of Nazareth, in conjunction with the world in which

---

a preliminary conception of God, a notion of theology as a discipline. There are questions of whether and how Jesus may be known historically through documents that are expressly interpretive and confessional. What I wish to stress here is a structural point: epistemologically, in the inseparability of the mutual subject-object relationship within the knowing subject, the object impresses itself upon the subject as over against it and as distinctively that which is being interpreted. However the various debates I have just mentioned are settled, Jesus still emerges as the object or referent of Christian interpretation.

10. See the three essays of David Tracy, "Part Two," in Robert M. Grant, *A Short History of the Interpretation of the Bible,* 2nd ed. (Philadelphia: Fortress Press, 1984), 151–87 where he draws out the implications of the hermeneutical theories of Gadamer and Ricoeur for method in systematic theology.

one lives at any given time. Interpretation occurs within a dialectical or a dialogical going back and forth between the past and the present, the witness of faith from the past and the forms provided by the culture of any given present situation. Finally, this conversation must be critical in several senses. It must involve the mutual questioning implicit in any dialogue, and thus the mutual listening to and criticism of each interlocutor of the correlation, the past and the present. "Critical" refers to self-conscious epistemological reflection on the dynamics of knowledge, religious knowledge, and faith. "Critical" also implies "social critical," or an attentiveness to the sociology of knowledge and, more generally, the social construction of thought and cultural bias. Interpretation in Christian theology usually unfolds within the tradition. But at certain points the tradition itself should be placed in critical dialogue with "the world" so that traditional "blind spots" may be discovered.

In sum, the basic genetic structure of christology consists in tracing the initial and ongoing interpretation of Jesus. Today, the formal discipline of christology incorporates the critical tools of present-day intellectual culture into its interpretation of Jesus.

Other Principles of Interpretation

Other elements of a critical appropriation of a religious tradition enter into theological method and thus into christology. I indicate some of these here without developing them.

A first and very significant element in theology generally, and especially in christology, is *the symbolic character of religious language*. The category of symbol plays a central role in the christology outlined here. The idea of symbol, of something that mediates another reality, is used in two analogous senses: a *conceptual* symbol refers to a symbolic idea, or word, or other device of consciousness; and a *concrete* symbol refers to some thing, an object, event, or person which mediates and makes present something other than itself. The category of symbol is used frequently to reinforce an awareness of the symbolic character of all knowledge of transcendent reality.[11]

Some other terms and categories that have a bearing on method include *a distinction between meaning and truth*. Meaning, or a unity of

---

11. Religious symbols and their function in theology are discussed in Haight, *Dynamics of Theology* (Maryknoll, N.Y.: Orbis Books, 2001), 127–66.

intelligibility, or the "sense" of a text, may be distinguished from whether or not this construal actually exists or existed. Truth, in its traditional definition of mental representation corresponding to objective reality, adds to meaning the dimension of reference to external reality. In conjunction with the distinction between meaning and truth, hermeneutical theory insists that, in affirming the truth of the past, of past texts, for example, one must draw that meaning into the present. Affirming the truth of something, as distinct from a nonreferential meaning, is an act of responsibility to the evidence that cannot escape the conditions of what one knows to be true in a given time or place. This gives rise to *the principle of analogy*. The principle of analogy says that one affirms the truth within the context of what one knows to be true in one's present world. Within an ontologically unified world, analogy with what one experiences as true in the present operates as a criterion for affirming truth generally. Ordinarily one cannot affirm as true in another historical context what one knows to be ontologically impossible within one's own.

I want to underline a principle of interpretation that was mentioned earlier in passing, namely, that one must interpret the meaning of the past in correlation with both the *personal experience of individuals* and the more objective *social condition of human existence*. The degree to which the public social conditions of human existence shape the individual is a relatively recent discovery that has contributed to the formation of postmodernity. Interpretation, in its quest to uncover the meaning of the past in its relevance to the present, cannot avoid its social conditions and its social implications. Paul's aphorism regarding equality in Christ is an example: "There is no longer Jew or Greek, there is no longer slave or free, there is no longer male or female; for all of you are one in Christ Jesus" (Gal 3:28). It is hard to avoid the sociocritical significance of this Christian identifier.

The Criteria of Christology

What are the criteria to determine whether a certain christology is adequate or not? It is clear that a pluralism of different understandings of Jesus Christ obtains within the greater church and within particular churches as well. Such a pluralism is not necessarily a bad thing. Therefore, the criteria for christology must be fluid enough to allow for a certain pluralism at the same time that they establish limits to what is acceptable: every christology is not adequate. I propose three criteria as central but not exhaustive: the first is fidelity to scripture and the landmark interpretations of Jesus Christ from the history of the community, such as the Councils of Nicaea and Chalcedon. The second is intelligibility to a present-day community. Christology must make sense in the language of today's world. The third is an ability to empower a Christian life in the contemporary world. A christology unable to do this is irrelevant and lacks a moral credibility.

To conclude this part, these reflections lay out the broad framework for a method of christology that responds to the situation at the beginning of the third millennium. This represents a first and purely formal description of a logic for a christology from below that is both historically conscious, in some measure systematic, and attentive to our cultural situation. I now move to an account of the genesis and structure of christology.

THE GENESIS OF CHRISTOLOGY

I have already described a genetic method in christology. In this section I want to add some content to that formal description, while at the same time remaining on a somewhat abstract and general level of discussion. I analyze the genesis of christology in three phases: Jesus, the Easter experience of his disciples after his death, and the development of christological interpretations of Jesus in the light of his resurrection. I shall indicate briefly how each of these phases enters into the development of christology.

Jesus

Frequent reference has been made to the quest for the historical Jesus which has been pursued vigorously over the last decades. There are several debates concerning this research that have bearing on christology itself. One concerns what we can know of Jesus historically and how we know it. Another issue is the bearing of such knowledge on a theological appropriation of Jesus. A third issue regards the measure and degree to which this research is attended to by christology and integrated into the discipline. Chapter 1 dwelt on this aspect of Jesus research and how it reschools an overly dogmatic imagination with concrete images of the person of Jesus of Nazareth.

Still another role of an initial attention to Jesus of Nazareth and what can be known of him through Jesus research is so deeply embedded in the genetic logic of a christology from below that it could be overlooked. Beginning with Jesus allows the person of Jesus as he is defined by his teachings and actions, his parables and his ministry, to settle in as the initial subject matter of christology. It has already been established that christology as a part of theology is not exhausted in its attention to the human being Jesus; as theology deals with God, so christology deals with Jesus as the icon, symbol, or sacrament of God. The writers of the New Testament present a faith-filled portrait of the existential-historical Jesus, and the christologist as such approaches this source material in faith. But Jesus the human being remains the historical symbol and medium of this particular quest for revelation of God. What Jesus was portrayed as saying and doing make a difference in the character of the symbol, Jesus, and the witness to him. The person of Jesus, therefore, fills the ground floor of the building of a christology.

The Easter Experience

I shall not outline a theology of the resurrection here, but simply enumerate a few principles that will be at work in an approach to Jesus' resurrection "from below." First, a historical approach to Jesus' resurrection proceeds through a consideration of what the disciples experienced that led them to the dynamic conviction that engendered the Christian mission, that Jesus is alive and was raised by God. The question of the exact character of the Easter experience cannot be decisively answered, and one finds many theories about it. But it remains an important hypothetical question that reveals the structure of one's thinking. Also, the principle of analogy plays a role in this consideration. I agree with Edward Schillebeeckx that despite the differences of proximity to and knowledge of the earthly Jesus, one should not conceive an enormous difference between the disciples' experience of Jesus raised by God and alive and our own Christian experience of the same thing.[12] However

---

12. Edward Schillebeeckx writes as follows: "There is not such a big difference between the way we are able, after Jesus' death, to come to faith in the crucified-and-risen One and the way in which the disciples of Jesus arrived at the same faith." *Jesus: An Experiment in Christology* (New York: Seabury Press, 1979), 346.

one explains this analogy in its degree of difference and sameness, an apologetic christology must make some appeal to experience to make sense of the disciples' conversion from disillusion to a robust faith in Jesus' resurrection.

Interpretations of Jesus

The third moment in the genesis of christology consists in the interpretations of Jesus as the Christ that were formulated by the followers of Jesus who themselves thus became Christians. In my own analysis of these christologies three things assume a certain importance. The first is that there is a wide variety of different interpretations of just who Jesus-now-risen was and is. This corresponds nicely with the fact that these are historically conditioned interpretations by different communities in different situations. The second is that one can discern a certain unity or sameness in all of these interpretations: they are based on and witness to the experience that Jesus is the bearer of God and God's salvation. Jesus the "mediator of salvation from God" is as it were a common denominator of all New Testament christologies. Third, this pattern can be raised to a level of principle: christology is a function of soteriology or at least the experience of salvation. This in turn provides a foundational conception of the structure of christology and one of the most salient features of its logic. The pattern will also provide christology with its most fundamental criterion of adequacy. Whatever else a christology must do, it must explain why or how Jesus Christ is savior.

THE STRUCTURE OF CHRISTOLOGY

In the genesis of christology, that is, beginning with Jesus, and in the light of the experience of him as raised by God and the interpretation of him as the bearer of God's salvation, one can discern the structure of christology. I summarize that structure around the category of symbol as in the phrase *Jesus Symbol of God*. I have to give a brief account of that central title for Jesus since it carries a good deal of weight. Some may prefer the term "sacrament" over "symbol": I take them as equivalent in the religious domain.

The Historicity of All Religious Experience

I relate the structure of christology to a general theory of the mediated character of all concrete human experience of God and hence the mediated character of all religion. This corresponds neatly with Karl Rahner's view of revelation and knowledge of God, and with the Aristotelian-Thomistic tradition of epistemology as well. All knowledge of God is historically mediated, that is, through nature or through the events, persons, or constructs of history.

Jesus Symbol of God for Christian Faith

In his philosophy of religion, John Smith refers to the worldly and historical media through which all positive revelation or religion receives its content.[13] His descriptions of such media, however, make it clear that they are synonymous with what other authors, such as Paul Tillich and Karl Rahner, call symbols. On this general understanding of revelation and religion, it becomes clear that Jesus of Nazareth is the concrete historical symbol around which Christian revelation and faith are centered. Christianity is structured by and around Jesus of Nazareth as the Christ or Savior from God. Placed in the context of history the notion of symbol explains why Jesus is at the center of the Christian religious imagination.

The Dialectical Structure of Symbol

Because of the epistemological power and the ontological density of the symbol, however, it can also play a central role in a systematic understanding of Jesus Christ. First of all, symbols are often called into play in the knowledge of things that transcend other ordinary ways of knowing. For example, one finds in psychology and the arts areas of knowing that can only be opened up by means of symbols. The same is true of the transcendent sphere of religion where objects of faith transcend knowledge of this world. Conceiving of Jesus as symbol of God, therefore, opens up a form of participatory knowledge that exceeds what is communicated by univocal or literal speech. Second, through a phenomenology of symbolic communication and participatory knowledge, one can speak of an ontological mediation by symbols. A most common example of this is the mediation of human personal presence to another through bodily

---

13. John E. Smith, *Experience and God* (New York: Oxford University Press, 1968), 68–98.

gesture. Even though the self, insofar as it is spiritual, transcends matter, it still requires matter for its self-actualization and self-disposition. Such communication is not automatic, because gestures may also be used to dissimulate. But ordinarily they communicate one's self outside oneself. In short, concrete symbols render present and available the being of something other than themselves.

Both the epistemological and ontological functioning of symbols reveal a dialectical structure. By dialectical here I mean a tension between two forces or dimensions of a symbol that move in opposite directions or pull against each other in a manner that remains unresolved. For example, in the conception of my body being the symbol of my self, the body both is and is not the self. Generalizing, in the case of some concrete symbols, one must say that the symbol both *is* and *is not* what it symbolizes. This unresolved dialectical structure characterizes all religious symbols, so that to remove it would be to destroy their symbolic character. In christology, this dialectical structure is reproduced in the classical christological doctrine finally forged at Chalcedon after years of debate: Jesus both is not and is divine; Jesus both is and is not merely (that is, restrictively) human. Calling Jesus symbol of God, therefore, is a way of depicting the role of Jesus Christ in the historically distinctive Christian faith. Symbol is also a systematic concept that is analogously common among other forms of human knowing and academic disciplines. And, finally, the category of symbol offers a way of explaining the basic classical doctrines of how Jesus saves (soteriology) and the characterization of the status of Jesus as a person (christology).

LOCI IN CHRISTOLOGY

A number of fundamental questions about Jesus Christ make up the classical loci that would have to be considered in any adequate christology. Some of these questions are relatively new, and together they act like a lever to move christology slowly forward. Others are less the focus of attention but, because of the interrelated character of all of them, are also undergoing reinterpretation. In what follows I will simply indicate how the logic of a christology from below subsumes these questions without developing specific positions.

Classical Soteriology and Christology

It seems impossible to me for an adequate christology to jump over the period which generated the classical doctrines, as some evangelical theologians tend to do. The basic doctrines on how Jesus saved and the person of Jesus Christ are written into current liturgical, devotional, and catechetical language about Jesus Christ in the mainline churches. A christology from below, by dealing with the genesis of christology, will by definition analyze the biblical witness on these questions. It must also trace the further development of christology in the classical patristic period. The passage of Christian faith into the Hellenistic world is filled with instructive lessons. The more classical theology is compared with the theology of the New Testament, the more it will become apparent that within the continuity of the tradition major shifts in understanding and appropriation occurred during the patristic period. These shifts are of major import to those who think patristic christology is identical to the New Testament witness, that it represented no significant change in the interpretation of Jesus Christ. They are equally significant for those who think that the New Testament witness does not need to change its form but is as intelligible to present-day intellectual culture as it was in first-century Mediterranean culture.

One way of appropriating both the New Testament and classical theology from below would be through the use of a hermeneutical method of critical correlation. This would roughly consist in bringing to bear three kinds of analysis. First, it would begin with a strictly historical analysis of the genesis and development of doctrines within the context or horizon of their historical situation. Second, it would subject these doctrines to various forms of critical analysis from the point of view of our present horizon of understanding. Among these would be analyses that try to characterize the human experiences which generated the doctrines and which they therefore crystallize. And, thirdly, it would seek to appropriate and reinterpret the experiences that are latent in these texts as possibilities for self-understanding and living in the present. These possibilities that are opened up by the theologies of the past must be reformulated within the context of our own present and future life situations. These constructive reinterpretations are not automatic, and theologians use a variety of hermeneutical devices to reappropriate traditional symbols into a present-day framework of understanding. "Correlation" is no more than a general name for analogous procedures of interpretation. What is crucial in the process of correlation is that the critical analyses of the second phase be understood as opening up constructive possibilities for the present and future however that constructive move is made.

Salvation Theory

By salvation theory I mean what is often called theories or theologies of redemption, that is, of what Jesus Christ did to accomplish human salvation. Most educated Christians would probably agree that some of the language of the tradition, including the language of official liturgical prayer and devotion, has become embarrassing to Christian faith. The mythical and symbolic languages of the past no longer function positively in a historically conscious culture, especially when their symbolic character is forgotten. A hermeneutical method of critical correlation, when applied to the traditional characterizations of what Jesus Christ did for human salvation, points in the direction of a *reductio ad simplicitatem*. The following four points might at least serve as a groundwork for understanding salvation, or provide a foundation for interpreting more fully how Jesus Christ saves. First, Christian faith in God mediated by Jesus is at the same time an opening up of the imagination in a way that allows Jesus to be a parable of God. Second, in existential terms this means that Christians encounter God in Jesus. This phrase represents the absolute foundation and point of departure for a christology from below. Thirdly, within this encounter Jesus reveals God, that is, mediates God and makes God present in a more conscious, intense, and personal way. Fourth, Christian salvation consists in the encounter with the saving God in and through Jesus, so that Jesus saves by revealing and making God present. Much more could be said about the content of Jesus' mediation, especially as it relates to ever different situations of human captivity.[14]

Social Salvation and Christian Spirituality

By itself the language of personal individual salvation is inadequate in our present context. Given our sense of human historicity, social solidarity, and social constitution, one must show the meaning and truth

---

14. The topic of salvation is addressed at greater length in the following two chapters.

of Christian salvation for our lives in common. We need a theology of the appropriation of salvation that is simultaneously a theology of history, society, and our natural habitat. Liberation theology, which is in some respects the first Roman Catholic postmodern theology, has contributed a theology and spirituality of salvation that addresses the negativities of social history and describes the possibility of the salvation of history.

Appreciation of the significance of a liberationist construal of salvation and spirituality requires an appreciation of the questions to which it is an answer. These are generated by distinctively historical experiences of negativity: Is there any ground for affirming the dignity of the human subject in the historical world we experience? Does human history have any meaning-giving direction? Does human freedom have any overarching or metaphysical purpose that may provide a norm for human self-actualization and self-direction? These three questions, in many different guises, are questions of salvation, here and now and in the long term. As such they influence the form that the Christian answer will take. When Jesus of Nazareth is interpreted as symbol of God in response to these questions, he presents a God who is concerned with these issues and, concomitantly, proffers a possible salvation in response to them. That possible salvation must be read primarily in the ministry of Jesus, through his death, into resurrection. Human salvation has a narrative structure. Such a salvation will become an actuality in a person's life, however, only in the measure in which it is internalized in a freedom and praxis that in turn address the problems of human suffering. The possibility of salvation in and of history can only be experienced as an actuality within praxis. Salvation must negate the negativities to which it is a response by being acted out. In sum, Jesus Christ becomes actual savior in history in the measure in which people take up and practice his liberating revelation of God. Salvation does not exist apart from spirituality or the Christian life; and eschatology without faith-praxis has no existential content.

Jesus and Other Religious Mediations

Our historical situation makes the question of the place of Jesus Christ among other religious mediations a new question, despite the fact that it has been asked and answered in its literal form from the beginning of the Christian tradition. In other words, present-day contextual experience is coded into the question itself making it genuinely new. More specifically, today's consciousness, with its sense of historicity and expectation of religious pluralism, views religious pluralism positively, and this in turn puts severe pressure on the tradition's absolutistic understanding of Jesus Christ. Even the now common Christian understanding that Jesus Christ's salvation potentially includes all people so that all may share in Christ's saving grace is called into question by a new theocentrism. It is precisely such totalizing, that is, all-embracing and exclusionary, meta-narratives that are suspect. They short-circuit the historical character of human existence and the narrative structure of salvation and christology.

A position that in some measure respects the reservations of post-modernity and at the same time guards the substance of Christian tradition might be outlined in the following manner: To begin, it would insist that the encounter with God mediated by Jesus is both universally relevant and true. That is, God really is the way Jesus reveals and actualizes God's presence. This God is precisely one that is intimately close as loving creator to all human beings. Therefore, one must expect that God's gracious presence will be reflected in all religions, despite the many and sometimes serious ways in which it is also concealed. Jesus is thus normative because he is a universally relevant mediation of the truth of God. But this very revelation implies that God is universally active and graciously present in other religions which, in the measure in which God's grace is efficacious, are also true and therefore normative. In other words, the normativity and truth of Jesus Christ do not undermine other mediations of God; the religions need not be competitive, but may enter into dialogue; and the Christian can affirm the substantial truth of other religions on the basis of the revelation of Jesus Christ.[15] What is becoming more difficult to hold today, however, and it is an open question among theologians, is that the saving grace in other religions is caused by the historical event of Jesus.

The Divinity of Jesus

The distinctiveness of a method of christology that consistently proceeds from below is most apparent in dealing with the questions of Jesus' divinity and the theology of the trinity. The reason for this is that christology

---

15. This line of reasoning within the framework of Christian faith itself will be developed at greater length in chapter 7.

from above has dominated the tradition and thereby shaped the imaginative structure of Christian self-understanding. A major part of the justification of the need for a thoroughgoing christology from below will depend on the recognition that, at least for many, the basic problem of christology has shifted. By its assumptions and method, christology from above faces the problem of the humanity of Jesus: What is implied in the construct by which Jesus Christ truly had a real human nature? With the deepening of historical consciousness, and especially through the influence of Jesus research, the problem of christology has been fundamentally altered.[16] With Jesus of Nazareth at the center of one's historical imagination, the question becomes the following: What does it mean to say that this human being, who came to be worshiped by Christians, is to be called divine? What is the meaning of divinity when it is predicated of the prophet who stands at the head of the Jesus movement? Jesus the historical figure, the human being, is the supposition or a "given" in this question; there is no question here of accommodating a human nature in a divine actor in history.

A christology from below cleanly correlates with the new christological question. It begins with Jesus. It traces the various New Testament interpretations of him in the light of the experience that he was raised and exalted by God. The vast majority of these interpretations of him do not depict him as a divine figure in the sense that that came to be understood in patristic theology, that is, "of the same substance as the Father." But all of them recognize God's saving action through him and God's presence and power in him. Amid this pluralism of christologies two in particular are apt for characterizing the person of Jesus himself as divine, namely, a Spirit christology and a Logos christology. Is this Spirit or Logos language capable of portraying Jesus as a truly divine figure in history? Yes it is, and I will explore these two christologies further in chapter 8. But this language, and the theo/ontological way of construing the person of Jesus with it, must be set within the broader framework of symbolic mediation of God; it cannot cease to be symbolic and dialectical. The truly dialectical character of this language consists in the fact

---

16. John P. Galvin, "From the Humanity of Christ to the Jesus of History: A Paradigm Shift in Catholic Christology," *Theological Studies* 55 (1994): 252–73 analyzes this new situation.

that the tension it maintains between affirmation and negation cannot be smoothly resolved. In christology this is its virtue and its truth.

Trinitarian Theology from Below

In a historicist and religiously pluralistic context, Christian language about God is most credible when it confesses God's absolute mystery. Historical consciousness declares the end of religious triumphalism, of full possession of final truth, of anything but a fragmentary grasp of the ultimately real.[17] These newly experienced convictions do not conflict with some of the deepest strains of Christian spirituality which are now raised to the status of being the conditions for credibility. In this situation, how can the language of trinity about God, that seems to claim some knowledge of the inner life of God, be made to appear plausible?

Several dimensions of a trinitarian theology from below can be brought to bear on this issue. First of all is the recognition that trinitarian theology depends historically and logically on christology. "Trinity" is not a name for God, but a doctrine about God that is a function of christology and not the other way around. Second, however, an account of Christian salvation is unimaginable without trinitarian language. For Christian salvation is a narrative of God's saving action in history, and this story cannot be told without reference to God creator, Jesus Christ savior, and God as Spirit at work in the church and in the world. Trinity is the shorthand symbol of this Christian story of salvation. Therefore, third, the point of trinitarian language is salvation. This is born out at the junctures of the definition of the doctrine. The arguments for the divinity of the Word of God and the Spirit were made on the basis of salvation: "only God saves; therefore Word and Spirit cannot be less than divine." Fourth, from this salvific point one can make the trinitarian affirmation that God truly is as God is revealed to be in creation, and in Jesus, and in the Spirit experienced at work in the community. Does this entail real differentiations into distinct "persons" or "subsistent relations" or "hypostases" or "modes of being" in the Godhead? It may. But one ought explicitly to underscore the speculative character of such a reach into the interior of God's absolutely mysterious being.

---

17. Fragmentary is not opposed to true and passionately held. It characterizes the inner realization of the transcendence that is affirmed in an authentic encounter with *God* as measured against the narrowness of every human perspective.

Conclusion

Does the logic of a christology from below as it has been laid out here amount to a paradigm shift in christology? Does it entail a substantially new method of christology that finds its basis in new premises and assumptions so that the conclusions reached in a former way of thinking are drawn up into a distinctively new synthesis?[18] The characterization of this christology from below as a paradigm shift would depend on that with which it were contrasted. The turn to history and experience in Christian theology during the modern period seems to qualify as a paradigm shift with reference to the premodern period. This turn, which occurred dramatically with the theology of Schleiermacher, was countered in the Protestant world by Neo-orthodox theology, and that debate is nearing its close.[19] In Roman Catholic theology, when the turn to history and experience was attempted in the modernist period at the beginning of the twentieth century, it was simply silenced by authority. Although Catholic theological discussion was reawakened by Vatican II, at the present time discussion of christology that begins with history and experience seems once again to be threatened with authoritarian censure. In the measure that this authority repeats a premodern christological tradition, this christology from below represents a paradigm shift. But by being confronted with authority, instead of alternative postmodern theologies analogous to *Neo*-orthodoxy, it lacks the debate that is necessary to prove its viability. A serious theological discussion between a variety of views of how to adjust to our current intellectual situation is needed before one could characterize this christology from below as something radically new.

---

18. The idea of a "paradigm shift," indicating a revolutionary new framework for understanding data, is drawn from Thomas Kuhn, *The Structure of Scientific Revolutions* (Chicago: University of Chicago Press, 1970).

19. It is passé and no longer fruitful; it has been transcended.

Chapter Three

HUMAN FREEDOM AND A CHRISTIAN UNDERSTANDING OF SALVATION AS LIBERATION

ᶜ·ᵔ

T HE LANGUAGE OF SALVATION expresses the core of Christian faith and the believer's self-understanding. For Christians, Jesus is the savior. How should the process of such a salvation be understood? If human existence is understood fundamentally as a form of freedom, it is this very freedom that is saved. This chapter begins with that premise and discusses the meaning of salvation from the perspective of its relationship to human freedom and human liberation. It unfolds in two parts: the first lays out a number of attendant problems that set the context of the question that is engaged and the method of approach used to address it; the second outlines a theological interpretation of the Christian meaning of salvation that also responds to the noted problems or issues. The result is a holistic interpretation of the Christian idea of freedom and salvation formulated into a relatively concise outline.

FRAMING THE DISCUSSION

Flourishing in the late eleventh and early twelfth centuries, Anselm of Bec in Normandy and then Canterbury, following Augustine of Hippo in North Africa in the fourth and fifth, proposed that the discipline of theology be conceived as "faith seeking understanding." The phrase stuck in the West, and most Christian theologians can appropriate it. It involves a generative ambiguity in the tension between faith and reason, what the believer receives from what he or she takes as an ultimately transcendent authority and what the corporate human mind can critically discern with all the tools of observation and logic. Theological conviction lies somewhere between fideistic assertion of incomprehensible mystery and reduction of mystery to psychological, sociological, or rational mechanism. If it is to be genuine theology, it must preserve the two languages of transcendent mystery and natural explanation in tension: one truth in two languages.[1]

Various different styles and methods dot the theological landscape, and it makes some difference which method is employed. Since theology unfolds as a hermeneutical discipline, the method of the interpretation, with its premises and suppositions, largely controls the content of the interpretation itself. But different methods suit different problems; taking a wrench to the class on water colors will not help. I shall begin then with a set of issues that define the concerns operating behind this essay before turning to an outline of a suitable theological method.

The discussion is set within a framework shaped by four problems. Each one seems to call into question the intelligibility of the Christian language of salvation. The perspective from which they arise originates in present-day, late modern or postmodern intellectual culture. From this perspective several Christian teachings connected with salvation seem archaic and surely complicate communication of this profound reality to those looking to learn about it.

One problem that arises with the Christian language of salvation concerns a background conception which stipulates a division between two spheres of human existence, natural and supernatural, that accompanies Christianity as a religion based on revelation. Early on, perhaps in the course of the development of christology in the second century, Christians became convinced that something happened in Jesus that not only changed history but altered human nature itself. The event of Jesus Christ set up a new human order of reality. Although his context was limited, Cyprian of Carthage asserted in the mid-third century that no salvation was available outside the church. Augustine could not conceive of people outside the historical influence of Jesus being saved, because if they were, the whole point of the divine drama in Jesus would be voided. In the theology of the schools in the Middle Ages, the appropriation of Aristotle's philosophy of nature facilitated the conception of two distinct spheres

---

1. Edward Schillebeeckx, *Church: The Human Story of God* (New York: Crossroad, 1990), 110.

of God's interaction with the world and human history, the one natural and the other supernatural, each with its distinct economy and teleology. "Human nature" was that which constituted the human as such, and it provided a basis for specifically human activity that led to the goal of human existence, its ultimate happiness or fulfillment. But since human beings in Christ were called to the higher goal of intimate personal communion in God's own life, this required a higher supernature to generate the proper actions of faith, hope, and love to achieve the higher proportionate goal.[2] In a variety of ways, in theological thought and ecclesial society, this distinction risks separating Christian identity from the rest of the world, often setting itself above or against the world. Yet human beings do have experiences of contingency, gratuity, and gift that signal a transcendence that breaks into the natural order. The language of spirituality portrays both a depth and a height in human existence, neither of which is fully accounted for by an inner-worldly historical causality or a flat two-dimensional worldview. The question of the two orders of reality plays a major role in the Christian conception of salvation, and it faces major challenges from contemporary conceptions of the continuous character of all finite reality.

Another problem lies in the basic story that as children Christians learn of creation, sin, the need for redemption, the saving appearance of Jesus Christ and the promise of everlasting life. One of the factors of this story, the conception of an original sin and a fall of humankind, portrays a pervasive negativity; Christians are taught to have a consciousness of sin. Most educated Christians accept the mythic character of the story of Adam and Eve, and surely it has more power understood as such than as a literal narrative. The same is true of the event of a fall. Once people begin to appreciate the human race as a product of evolution, they simultaneously put aside the idea of a human fall portrayed in terms of a picture-book narrative. The story in the end does not and is not meant to explain; as a symbolic narrative it expresses the sense of guilt of the religious person before the holy God.[3] This doctrine is often defended

---

2. Thomas Aquinas, *Summa Theologica: Complete English Edition in Five Volumes,* trans. Fathers of the English Dominican Province (Westminster, Md.: Christian Classics, 1961), Part I–II, Question 109, Article 2; also I–II, 112, 1.

3. Paul Ricoeur, *The Symbolism of Evil* (Boston: Beacon Press. 1960), 242–43.

as the one with the most empirical evidence: a dark side does seem intrinsic to human freedom. The symbol effectively places in full view not only the whole range of human depravities, but also tendencies inside us. Such a consciousness need not be disordered; it can reflect a proper internalization of the Greek maxim, "know thyself." But Christian realism can also mediate a heavy, negative view of human existence that cripples freedom and is almost as destructive as the evil it portrays. The Christian religious symbol of salvation has to preserve the power of the ancient symbol in a credible way, but without a simplistic or destructive residue; an account of this doctrine should also energize and not diminish human freedom.

A third problem area emerges with the idea of a redemption occurring at a precise moment, as if it were a historical transaction. Almost immediately, disciples of Jesus who were caught up in the Jesus movement that confessed Jesus as savior asked themselves exactly what Jesus had done for their salvation. The New Testament contains many answers to that question, but some have become standardized in Christian language: Jesus Christ is a sacrifice or a ransom victim for human sin. Athanasius of Alexandria comes close to affirming that human nature itself was altered by the incarnation of the divine Son. In the mid-fourth century, he wrote: "the incorruptible Son of God, being conjoined with all by a like nature, naturally clothed all with incorruption, by the promise of resurrection."[4] Augustine developed the idea that Jesus' death was a sacrifice to God, atoning for human sin, thus winning salvation for all who would accept it.[5] He also developed a theory of Christ's death as a ransom in a negotiation with Satan.[6] Anselm, again borrowing from Augustine, developed the most influential of all theories: Jesus the God-man, by his free self-offering of his life to God, satisfied for the injury done to God by the sins of humankind.[7] True, educated Christians today recognize that these descriptions of a metaphysical transaction between Jesus and God in a point of time are symbolic representations and not to

---

4. Athanasius, *On the Incarnation of the Word,* in E. R. Hardy with C. C. Richardson, *Christology of the Later Fathers* (Philadelphia: Westminster Press, 1954), 63.

5. Augustine, *The Trinity* (Washington, D.C.: Catholic University of America Press, 1963), 144–64.

6. Ibid., 384–404.

7. Anselm, *Why God Became Man?* in Eugene R. Fairweather, *A Scholastic Miscellany: Anselm to Ockham* (New York: Macmillan, 1970), 156–64.

be taken literally; and they also see God's salvation as available across the whole range of history, however that may be explained. But at the same time Christians consistently look back to Jesus of Nazareth as the one who provides the answer to the religious question of ultimate meaning. Something happened in him; something raises him above the horizon and commands attention as mediator of God's saving grace. Christian theology has to give an account of this pervasive Christian attitude.

A fourth issue concerns freedom itself. In the second half of the twentieth century, a number of analogous liberation theologies arose across churches and continents and interpreted Christian salvation in terms of liberation. By and large, what was meant was some form of social liberation for large groups of people who were marginalized and oppressed. Liberation theology in Latin America and beyond focused on the poor; black liberation theology fought racism with Christian symbols of saving, of resistance, and of construction; feminist liberation theology brought forward new meaning to Paul's dictum: "There is neither Jew nor Greek, there is neither slave nor free, there is neither male nor female; for you are all one in Christ Jesus" (Gal 3: 28). But the secular citizen questions whether one needs God or religion to settle social problems, and many people of faith seem to agree: What does God and God's salvation have to do with politics? But if human freedom is socially constituted, one will have to find the connection between salvation and the public order lest religion be reduced to an individual and private sphere. If personal religion entails privatization, the loss of all public relevance, then religion also surrenders all claim to truth.

The central issue that these cumulative questions pose to Christians and also to those who inquire from outside the circle of Christian faith regards the intelligibility of this salvation in a period marked by a heightened sense of historicity, by the social construction of consciousness, and by the sheer diversity of religious beliefs. Historicity means that all human ideas and values are particular to the specific time and culture of their expression. Social consciousness recognizes the social component of all individual thought and behavior. Both convey forcefully the relative dimension of human thought and largely explain the multiplicity of religions and religious beliefs. This means that a view of salvation that claims universal relevance to human freedom must be explained in a way that takes account of this pluralism and the intellectual culture that it has generated. Theology has to widen its scope and present a view that can be appreciated universally.

I turn now to a discussion of an appropriate theological method for addressing the meaning of salvation against the background of these issues. One can no longer just start "talking theology" and expect to be understood by ordinary people, nor by academics in other disciplines, not even by all Christian theologians, so pluralistic has the field become. In the arts and sciences it has become customary constantly to recall that method shapes the logic and affects the intelligibility of any discourse dealing with theoretical issues. In theology the situation becomes infinitely more complicated because to many theology appears to be "data-free" analysis. Explanation of exactly what one is talking about is crucial, and this is a question of method. In what follows, then, I propose brief statements about, first, the nature of theological language as intrinsically symbolic but not "merely" so and, second, the method of theology that is employed here.

On the Nature of Theological Language

"Theology" is often transliterated as "talk about God." But if God is really God, God must be utterly transcendent, and thus not available to human knowledge as it is ordinarily understood. Since God can only be reached or contacted by faith, theology has to be viewed as having its base in some form of religious experience resulting in religious faith. Actually the idea of "talk about God" is far too restricted in its object to be adequate to actual theological discourse whose range is practically speaking unrestricted. A more adequate description of theology might take a cue from Thomas Aquinas, who defines the object of what he called "sacred doctrine" as the whole range of reality from the perspective of Christian doctrine.[8] Adapting that point of view, theology is understood here as interpretation of reality, the same reality as is mediated by any other discipline, but through the lens of the symbols used by Christians to express their faith. Theology is a hermeneutical discipline. It interprets reality out of faith experience. It employs symbolic language.

Innumerable theologians across the span of Christian history discuss the symbolic character of religious language. But no one explains the

---

8. Aquinas, ST, I, 1, 7.

logic of the religious symbol better than a mysterious Greek writer, probably a Syrian monk, of the late fifth and early sixth centuries, who wrote pseudonymously as Dionysius the Areopagite, the name of a disciple whom Paul is said to have won over in Athens (Acts 17:34). His thought influenced the theology of the icon of Eastern Christianity and the theological epistemology of medieval Western theology. For Dionysius this world is interpenetrated by a divine sphere which can only be perceived through symbols. A Platonic distinction between above and below, the divine and the creaturely, is bridged by the symbolic. Because the world is suffused with God's creative power, the "below" participates in the "above" and symbols are mystagogic, that is, they lead or draw human consciousness into divine mystery. Symbols are perceptible images by which human beings "are uplifted as far as we can be to the contemplation of what is divine."[9] The reference of religious symbols is transcendent reality; thus they do not yield a kind of knowledge that can be translated into objective data or information. They mediate a kind of transcendent consciousness and participatory or contemplative knowledge that, indeed, exceeds the empirical or the literal. The mechanics of symbols unfold in a manner analogous to symbols in the spheres of other disciplines. A symbol mediates access to something other than itself, and is especially significant when that other thing can be reached in no other way. Symbols play a major role in areas ranging from psychoanalysis, to literature, and to the hard and the social sciences. As in all disciplines, when the reality that is disclosed by symbols cannot be known in any other way, the realism of symbols cannot be demonstrated outside of the very experience that they mediate.

On Method in Theology

What theological method will be appropriate for the interpretation of the symbols that constitute the language by which Christians interpret salvation? One such method that takes historical consciousness into account owes a debt to hermeneutical theorists such as Hans-Georg Gadamer, Paul Ricoeur, and David Tracy.[10] It operates under three imperatives.

9. Dionysius the Areopagite, "The Ecclesiastical Hierarchy," in Colm Luibheid, *Pseudo-Dionysius: The Complete Works* (New York: Paulist Press, 1987), 197.

10. Hans-Georg Gadamer, *Truth and Method* (New York: Crossroad, 1982); Paul Ricoeur, *The Conflict of Interpretations* (Evanston: Northwestern University Press, 1974); David Tracy,

First, the interpretation tries to be faithful to the tradition that defines the symbols of the Christian community's language. It must be especially attentive to the New Testament and the Bible generally as the normative source for Christian theology. But in attending to past symbols, attention focuses to the extent possible on the experience that is contained within them, that generated them, and to which they give expression. Second, in order to be intelligible in today's world, interpretation must attend to the common human experience and knowledge that defines present-day culture. Without such a correlation with contemporary thought and experience, theology would be unintelligible. These two, traditional symbols as they were established in the past and present human experience, are the two principal sources of theology. The first source makes the language of theology Christian, the second makes it credible. These two sources for reflection are brought into conjunction with each other, each criticizing and illumining the other, often under considerable tension, thereby generating an interpretive discussion.

But these two criteria are also modified or controlled by a third, the imperative that theology open up, to those who pursue, read, or study it, a certain way of viewing the world and of living and behaving. Not only the past and the present have a bearing on theology, but also the future makes a demand for a distinct praxis. Religion can hardly be reduced to a system of understanding; religious communities also integrate a way of life into the cultural system that constitutes them. Theology thus implicitly bears an intimate relationship with ethics, so that the vision of reality contained in religious texts opens up a possible way of acting in the world. An appeal to or empowerment for a certain set of values or mode of living implicitly directs theological discourse.

SALVATION AS LIBERATION
OF HUMAN FREEDOM

I turn now to a constructive interpretation of salvation as liberation of innate human freedom. This interpretation unfolds in four stages. Each of these stages takes a classical Christian symbol and elicits its symbolic meaning through a brief phenomenology of human experience. The four

"Part II," in Robert Grant, *A Short History of the Interpretation of the Bible* (Philadelphia: Fortress Press, 1984), 149–87.

are: creation, sin, salvation, and heaven. The intent is to be faithful to the essential dimensions of what is revealed by the symbol. When the theologian fails in this, the community he or she represents will not accept the interpretation. But at the same time the interpretation has to make sense more generally to people who live in the world today, for we live in no other world. The description of experience thus implicitly or overtly appeals to common dimensions of meaning and value that guide human life in today's world. In other words, I use Christian symbols here to construe what is going on in the human realm as such. The theological affirmation, "Jesus saves," has to be a statement referring to what is going on universally if it is to be considered a universally relevant statement. The appeal to common human experience therefore ironically becomes intrinsic to unpacking the meaning of specifically Christian theological statements.

Creation

I begin with the symbol of creation because it is an absolutely primal religious understanding of reality. The Christian creed begins: "We believe in God...creator of heaven and earth." The point in treating these foundational Christian symbols, however, cannot be to unfold fully the doctrines contained in them, but only to make one or two relatively fundamental points that help advance a fuller understanding of salvation relative to human freedom. With respect to creation, three points seem important: the meaning of creation, what God has fashioned in the human, and God's presence to the human.

The symbol of creation refers primarily not to something that God did "in the beginning" but to the permanent power of being that holds finitude in existence and on which all things are absolutely dependent. The Christian concept of creation contrasts with some Deist views that God built the world system and left it to run "on its own," so to speak. Such a distant and uninvolved God is not the object of Jewish and Christian faith or discourse in the Bible. Rather, God "creator" means God always actually "creating." But at the same time, that which God creates is other than God. Creation is not some form of emanation of the divine that ultimately entails pantheism. Various concepts have been adopted to distinguish and relate the influence of God's causality to intraworldly causality, such as the primary causality of God as distinct from the whole system of secondary causes that are observable. But the coherence of such distinctions is less important than the fundamental experience and conviction that God must be the power behind all powers — the power of being itself that holds reality up against the void of nonbeing.

What is it that God has wrought in the creation of the human? Before providing an answer to that question in a paragraph, let me explain how one might attempt such a thing. I presume that ultimately the human is a mystery just short of the mystery of God. The mystery of human existence provides much more workable data, but it still remains impenetrable in its ultimate why and wherefore. As a product of history, the meaning of the human will not be complete until the end. The arena within which this history unfolds and in which the human is to be understood has so vastly expanded in terms of time and space, that humanity seems dwarfed in the cosmos; the many sciences that study the human continually reveal new dimensions. It can only be with a sense of absolute humility that one points to what God through time and evolution has created in the human: namely, spirit, whose very nature is freedom. This idea is consistent in the Christian theological tradition of the West and finds a clear modern proponent in Karl Rahner.[11]

The symbol "spirit" points negatively to nonmatter; this is manifested primarily to human existence itself as self-consciousness. That which distinguishes the human is the power of reflection, the ability to bend back upon the self and know the self as knower. The human "knows it knows." The grounding meaning of freedom, then, is not choice or even existential commitment, although these important dimensions do help define it more fully. Rather, I use freedom here as a symbol that runs parallel with spirit and points to the defining characteristic of the human: self-transcendence. Far from being separable from matter or the physical in which it is embedded, human spirit — freedom — is the self-transcendence of matter itself, or matter transcending itself as self-conscious knowing and willing.

The doctrine that God creates reality "out of nothing" implies that there is no "space" and no thing between God and the physical world.

---

11. Karl Rahner, *Foundations of Christian Faith: An Introduction to the Idea of Christianity* (New York: Seabury Press, 1978), 26–39.

This conception spills over into anthropology: God is direct and immediate presence to human existence. For Edward Schillebeeckx finitude and contingency are the inherent characteristics of creation. They are not negativities to be transcended: "...we do not need altogether to transcend our contingent or finite nature and to escape from it or regard it as a flaw."[12] God is present to finitude; creation is creation out of nothing, and this means that nothing lies between creation and the creator. God is totally present to creation: "From a Christian perspective, the world and man are totally other than God, but within the presence of the creator God."[13] The God-world relationship depicted here implies that all creation subsists within the power and personal presence of God who creates and sustains it as something other than God. This provides the radical ontological basis for the symbol and language of God as Spirit at work in the world. The fuller doctrine of God represents God as personal, benevolent, and loving, the active lover of what God has created out of love. It is hard to imagine God as less than personal, and no other divine motive can account for creation except self-transcending or altruistic love. God is present not only in power but also in love, a personal love that is appropriate to personal creatures. The doctrine of creation by a loving creator entails a divine will for human flourishing and fulfillment.

To conclude: this symbol of creation can overcome the various dichotomies between the so-called different orders of creation and redemption, or the natural and the supernatural, that have so plagued the Christian imagination over the centuries. The meaning of God as lover of humanity, or savior, or redeemer are all entailed in the conception of God as loving creator. No reason necessarily demands a distinction between a natural and a supernatural relation of God to humanity; as many theologians today deny such a distinction as affirm it. This does not mean that such a distinction is incoherent and not useful at some points. These may be regarded as alternative theoretical frameworks, each of which has a consistent logic and highlights different particular aspects of the God-human relationship. But given the history of how such a distinction has narrowed the Christian vision, the expansive power of the doctrine

---

12. Edward Schillebeeckx, *God Among Us: The Gospel Proclaimed* (New York: Crossroad., 1983), 93.
13. Ibid.

of God as creating Spirit, by contrast, seems to promise a world of new meaning.

Sin

Despite the positive creative power of the creator, creation is marked by finitude and headed toward death. More will be said in response to those features further on. What is of concern here is that human existence also seems intrinsically marked by an inability to "get it right." One cannot avoid the doctrine of sin. This symbol, too, points to ultimate mystery, but I want only to draw two points forward: sin infects freedom itself on a personal level; but even more powerfully, sin as social wraps individual human freedom in a near total bondage.

The symbol of sin refers not to objective evil; rather, as Augustine and more recently Paul Ricoeur have shown, it points to a condition of human freedom itself prior to the exercise of choice and decision. The term "original" has several specific references, but let it stand here for this a priori character which I will discuss broadly on a personal and then on a social level, although these two dimensions of human freedom cannot be separated.

In the course of his life, Augustine developed a full-blown doctrine of sin, especially in his controversies with Pelagius and the Pelagians in the last twenty years of his life. But earlier, in the late 390s when he was engaged in writing his *Confessions,* one can observe him wrestling with the mystery of sin's manifestation in the will itself. The spiritual will can move the body; the will commands and the hand obeys. But the will cannot will itself; spirit does not obey but resists itself.[14] Paul's words struck home: "I do not understand my own actions. For I do not do what I want, but I do the very thing that I hate" (Rom 7:15). Augustine's introspective phenomenology of the mechanism showed that this inability to transcend the self affected the human spirit: spirit or will so to speak curved back and in on itself and could not transcend a clinging self-interest. Over time the inner self buttressed itself with the muscle of habit and custom and reflexive response. The self continued to enjoy freedom of choice, for this is the elemental self-transcendence that is constituted with the human as such: the human as spirit is a

---

14. Augustine, *Confessions,* trans. and intro. Henry Chadwick (New York, Oxford: Oxford University Press, 1991), 8:8 and 10. Reference by book and chapter.

freedom that can self-consciously choose. But it lacked what Augustine called liberty, the desire for truth and value outside and above the self and requiring self-transcendence of a different sort: transcendence of a concern for the self. Spirit was thus trapped within the prison of self-interest. Freud and the discipline of psychology have given us a fuller language to characterize what Augustine referred to on a psychological level. Yet for Augustine himself, the distinction of liberty from freedom of choice was a matter of putting the human self in a right relationship with ultimate reality.

But an even higher wall confines the human spirit. It may be called, paradoxically, social sin. Social sin consists in an arrangement of a society or culture in which one or more groups of people are systemically excluded, oppressed, or violated in their humanity. Such a situation is evil because it diminishes or destroys human being as measured against the intrinsic value of the human person. It is sin because we know that ultimately the arrangement of society depends on human freedom and can be changed. In other words, human beings are responsible for this situation. But this responsibility is precisely social and not individual. The paradox consists in sharing some measure of responsibility for a social situation as a member of a society, while not having any controlling individual freedom or power relative to the same situation. Frequently this intrinsic tension is either not experienced or simply denied in highly individualistic cultures.

How can such social sin be diagnosed since moral and ethical standards are precisely socially determined? One such way is through a negative experience of contrast, a corporate moral perception borrowed from social theorists and described by Schillebeeckx.[15] Such an experience is like a corporate intuition in which a person, but more importantly a group, comes to the intuitive realization that a certain situation is simply wrong because it appears implicitly against the background of something like a Platonic idea or ideal of what can and should be. Such experiences can be quite powerful as in the reaction against the Holocaust, against racism in the United States, against systemic poverty in much of the Third World, against a system that discriminates against women, and so on.

---

15. Schillebeeckx, *Church*, 5–6. I say more about this distinction in the following chapter in reference to a reaction to Jesus' cross.

Although such systems rest on the stuff of socially organized freedom, not an individual's freedom, still the individual person is through and through socially constructed and thus becomes part of the system. The helplessness of the individual before various groups and society at large indicates how society and culture can constitute structures constricting human freedom and closing off transcendence in the person's disposal of the self. This analysis of sin helps to provide a context within which the notion of salvation can be meaningful.

Salvation

The symbol of salvation refers to the flourishing wholeness that the doctrine of creation affirms is the will of the creator. It seems thwarted on two levels: in this world human freedom seems to be held in a bondage of sin and self-interest that prevents both personal and social fulfillment. On a broader scale, finitude and death threaten existence itself with final annihilation and senseless insignificance. I deal with these two aspects under the two symbols "salvation" and "heaven," the latter being an aspect and projection of the former. The meaning of salvation has been portrayed as liberation: liberation in this world discussed in this section and final or eschatological liberation discussed in the next section.

The Christian symbol of salvation draws its meaning from the basic religious questions of why human existence is at all and what it is for. So dense and illusive are these questions that more and more people are simply surrendering to their mystery and giving up any attempt at an answer. Yet because of their basic and comprehensive character they continue to press in and call our own existence into question. In fact, one cannot avoid answering such questions because human behavior itself carries a conscious or unconscious response. Christians are unanimous in looking to Jesus of Nazareth for an answer. But no single construal of that answer exhausts the issue. What follows is one interpretation among several. It attempts to be responsive to the problems raised in the first part of the discussion.

I began with the principle that if Jesus is to be considered as relevant for all, he must reveal something that is going on universally in the world. Application of this premise to the question of what Jesus did for human salvation militates against reading that salvation as a transaction that Jesus negotiated with God in a point of time to the advantage of his disciples.

It can also shift the way one conceives the relevance of Jesus. Instead of considering his earthly career as a particular transaction with God, one may regard it as a concrete symbol revealing the intrinsic character of the primal relation between God and human existence. From this perspective one would read in the actual teaching, ministry, and final outcome of Jesus a pattern revelatory of God, human existence, and the relationship between them. Jesus saves by revealing what is going on generally in the world and in history from the very beginning. This outlook in broad terms is found in John's gospel where Jesus is presented as revealer of God; this perspective serves well to open up the revelatory power of Jesus and his message. It provides a possibility for all people to read in them, as in a classic, a direct relevance to their own actual experience. The task of Christian theology in such a framework would be to analyze how Jesus reveals salvation going on within human freedom itself on both the personal and social levels.

On the level of individual persons, salvation may be interpreted as liberation of human freedom from internal bondage of various forms of egoism, and the release of freedom toward altruistic values. Jesus reveals that God as Spirit is at work in human hearts opening up freedom closed in upon itself through self-transcending love. I turn once again to Augustine for an analysis of this phenomenon because he addresses it at a primal level. No one analyzed more minutely or brilliantly the logic of grace than the dour theologian of sin. Most people are partially scandalized when they ask the question: Why is there evil in the world? Why, especially, do human beings prey upon each other? Augustine reversed the question: "From what source is there in people the love of God and of one's neighbor?"[16] Given the sin of the world, one has to marvel at the phenomenon of genuine self-transcending love. Where does it come from?

In the light of this second question, Augustine analyzed the human condition in the following way: everyone has the power to choose freely. But from where comes the liberty that allows one to break out of self-enclosure in a delight for what is of transcendent value or truth. For Augustine, this could be only from the power of God as Spirit at work

---

16. Augustine, "On Grace and Free Will," in Whitney Oats, *Basic Writings of Saint Augustine*, I (New York: Random House, 1948), 763.

within the human spirit, illumining the mind with attraction, and empowering the will to action. "It is certain that it is we that will when we will, but it is He who makes us will what is good.... It is certain that it is we that act when we act; but it is He who makes us act, by applying efficacious powers to our will."[17] For Augustine the first time this happens marks the beginning of an "ascent" toward absolute truth, goodness, and being. What is absolutely crucial for our times, however, is that we be more faithful to Augustine's primitive intuition than he was. For Augustine, the drama of salvific grace was relatively rare, and where it seemed to occur outside the Christian sphere, he considered it a mere illusion. The virtues of the pagans only appeared to be such. In effect, he underestimated the universal scope of the revelation in Jesus Christ. On the basis of the universal relevance of Jesus Christ, one should be open to seeing the power of God's grace more abundantly, indeed universally, in individual human life.

On the social level, salvation is no less real and can be discerned as operative within or through various forms of human solidarity that enhance the freedom of groups and support a common good. In other words, social grace or social salvation is the negative image of social sin: it negates the negation. In themselves, social structures appear as inanimate things, as routinized patterns of human behavior. But they rest on freedom, and they canalize it in specific directions. They act as a kind of second material nature that materializes, or concretizes, action of the human spirit and will. In the measure in which these structures build up and nourish the common good, they bear the marks of gratuity and come as gift; as such the religious imagination construes them as grace, as salvation.

In this view of salvation, Jesus of Nazareth is not considered its efficient cause but as its revealer or exemplary cause, a view which among others is supported by the New Testament. Jesus promised that the power of God's Spirit would work in groups and communities. The kingdom of God that Jesus preached is precisely a symbol for social grace and social salvation. The kingdom of God is also that for which Christians pray with the prayer that Jesus taught his disciples. It is an object of prayer because ultimately peace and reconciliation in justice in this world is a

---

17. Ibid., 759–60.

gift that transcends human ability. Few leaders in the world today would fail to recognize that every breakthrough of reconciliation and peace is a "blessing" which has to be embraced in gratitude. All who long for social grace and salvation and accept it in gratitude when it appears in fragments are implicitly praying.

How did Jesus save? As revealer Jesus preached and actually mediated in his ministry the kingdom of God. This means that Jesus is an invitation to look for this process going on within the whole of human life and history. Movements aimed at advancing justice, reconciliation, and peace in the world, at resisting social suffering, have a sacrality marked with religious depth. They can hardly be taken for granted.

Heaven

The second aspect of salvation points to an ultimate or final salvation in an end time. It is symbolized by "heaven" and its equivalents. As an eschatological symbol, heaven expresses and appeals to hope. Heaven is not a place, since the sphere of God, whatever it may be, precisely transcends finite place. People do not spend time in heaven, because eternity precisely transcends time. Rather, heaven is a symbol for the sphere of God into which Jesus was raised; it gives direction to human existence, mediates openness to an absolute future, and offers an "object" of hope.

It is important that there be clarity about the epistemology of faith and hope. Neither faith nor hope is the equivalent of knowledge; although both have cognitive aspects. William James has documented a certain cognitive immediacy to religious experience that is self-validating.[18] Hope is that same religious experience reaching into the future. Although the future remains absolutely unknown, it is imagined or constructed on the basis of a projection of faith experience in the present. Hope for the future can only have meaning that is based on faith that is rooted in contemporary religious experience. Although hope lacks the clarity of the religious experience of faith in the present, it lives off the latter's conviction and shares in its realism. For historical beings, in fact, some form of hope is just as necessary for human existence as is faith; one cannot live without some form of faith and hope, for each is integral to the elemental self-transcendence that defines human existence as such.

18. William James, *The Varieties of Religious Experience: A Study in Human Nature* (New York: Vintage Books/Library of America, 1963), 55–74.

All human beings live on the basis of some faith into some future that they hope for, even when the object of that faith and hope is not fully known to them and only manifested indirectly in their actions.

On this logic, heaven and its equivalents — the kingdom of God, for example — have two functions, and both are essential to the salvation of human freedom. The one has to do with the eschatological future; the other with the role of that future in life today.

The first function is to express the final fulfillment of human freedom in the absolute future. That meaning includes but ultimately transcends the fulfillment of my personal freedom. Since we are social creatures whose existence and fulfillment are unimaginable outside of social relationships, our ultimate salvation must be a social reality. It must also be real and comprehensive, drawing the whole of human life up into itself. Lacking either reality or comprehensiveness, it would not be ultimate salvation. Salvation in the absolute future, in order to be such, must draw the present and the past into a wider horizon of meaning that promises to redeem the negation of life, the innocent suffering, the evil of the whole past, present, and temporal future into absolute meaning. The alternative is total meaninglessness, and only the fool would hope for the death of meaning.

But hope in heaven and the ultimate kingdom of God has another function without which it would be an opiate. Jesus' life and ministry did not sedate. Rather, this utopic symbol and vision of resurrection bends back from the absolute future to criticize life in this world, life in its sinful actuality. Jesus Christ saves by being the catalyst for the negative experience of contrast that simultaneously unmasks sin and reveals what can and should be. The absolute future of heaven measures finitude as finitude, not as an absolute in any of its forms; it deabsolutizes the finite and the relative, and unmasks idolatry in all its many guises. It also judges sin as sin and not as what ought or has to be. Finally, it empowers resistance to evil with the promise of coherent meaning which, in the measure in which it is absolute by the promise and power of God, is also saving.

God entrusts history to human creativity. The Christian humanist asks why God would have created human freedom if God did not trust it. Jesus is an expression of God's trust and the proper human response. And Jesus' resurrection is testimony that God's trust will not be put to shame: "In Jesus, both God's trust in man and man's response of trust in God take on their definitive historical form."[19] In Jesus, one sees God's entrustment to human freedom of the struggle against evil. Jesus is to be interpreted as "the man in whom the task of creation has been successfully accomplished, albeit in conditions of the history of suffering. The consequence of this is that trust in this man is the specific form of belief in God, creator of heaven and earth, who reposes unconditional trust in man through his active creation. Without this divine trust in man, creation would in fact make no sense!"[20]

In sum, these four symbols are interlocking, and when they are interpreted as they have been presented here, they meet the four challenges to their credibility. Setting the Christian story of salvation firmly within the framework of a theology of creation overcomes the various possible and actual dichotomies that people have set up between a natural and a supernatural order. Such a distinction, while surely possible, is not at all necessary. A unitary, theocentric framework of the creator God bent in love on human salvation conveys more clearly the power and the universal relevance of the Christian story of salvation. It is true that sin pervades the whole of human history from the beginning: there is no break between a before and an after, and no ultimate explanation for its existence. But in no way does sin become the focus of the Christian imagination. Sin is the pervasive background, the context, the situation in which human existence must make its way, but the nature and goal of this existence is the freeing of freedom from the bonds of sin for creativity. Creation means that, in a certain sense, God is in God's world and human existence unfolds in this one — ours. Resisting and overcoming suffering in this world is the human task: "It is not a matter for God, except that this task is performed in his absolute presence and therefore is a human concern which also is close to his heart."[21] Salvation then is not an event that happened all at once, but a process that has been going on with the dawn of creation and the appearance of the human species. God as Spirit is the within of cosmogenesis, the immanent power of being in the development of the human, and the personal presence of

---

19. Edward Schillebeeckx, *Interim Report on the Books Jesus and Christ* (New York: Crossroad, 1981), 109.

20. Ibid., 111.

21. Schillebeeckx, *God Among Us,* 96.

God to a human self-transcendence that can respond to God's presence by responding to the suffering of God's creatures. This is the potentially universal dialogue which is revealed in the life and ministry of Jesus. Salvation, which symbolizes the fulfillment of human existence, is no private reserve of any religion, but the inner telos of creation itself which in Christian language is called the *eschaton* and was designated by Jesus the kingdom of God.

The question of whether this salvation should be the public language of a society cannot be answered in the abstract. There is simply no formula that can regulate the relation of all religions to all societies. But it is just as sure that the energy released by the Christian symbol of salvation is not private; that in its authentic form it necessarily has a bearing on the way society works. The problem arises not with religion but with hegemony in a pluralistic society. But the Christian view of salvation offered here clearly indicates that the power of salvation is going on in religions other than the various forms of Christianity, and that in principle they have an equal voice in public affairs. Centering Christian salvation in creation makes its representation in different religions, again in principle, noncompetitive.

The four symbols of creation, sin, salvation, and heaven together constitute the essential structure of the Christian vision of reality. Their ultimate credibility before the world depends on the degree to which the whole body of ordinary Christians actually redeem ultimate meaning for human freedom from an alternative of sheer contingency by the way they live.

Chapter Four

NOTES FOR A CONSTRUCTIVE THEOLOGY OF THE CROSS

⌇⌐

THAT JESUS DIED on a cross can be taken as a historical fact. But the symbol of the cross for Christians portrays considerably more meaning than what can be reconstructed by the historian. It contains layer upon layer of meaning, and for some it penetrates to the heart of being a Christian. It is only with great care that one should approach what is frequently referred to as the mystery of the cross. One cannot begin adequately to penetrate such a profound symbol in a single essay; one only risks muddying the waters with questions and distinctions that ultimately do not serve, help, or support. But at the same time the language of the cross, even as it occurs in liturgy and the common Christian language of piety, is filled with problems. When such language appears alienating and scandalous to not a few, these problems have to be regarded as serious.

The following essay is written to clarify what for some was an overly brief treatment of the cross of Christ in the work *Jesus Symbol of God*.[1] I shall not review what was said there, but turn directly to the topic in the following way. In the first part, I want to raise some of the difficulties that attend a theology of the cross. These serve as a background for what is proposed positively as a way of reflecting on them. The second part begins a constructive statement with some methodological considerations. In many ways, issues of presuppositions, points of departure, and method constitute the field in which problems and solutions grow and positions are tacitly decided. One cannot avoid what frequently read as abstract and merely formal topics. In the end, they rule. In a third part, which is directed by the problems and builds on the methodological

---

1. Roger Haight, *Jesus Symbol of God* (Maryknoll, N.Y.: Orbis Books, 1999). Cited hereafter as JSG.

premises, I will suggest some theses that address the difficulties connected with a theology of the cross. These are put forward tentatively,
not as clean solutions to the problems, but as viable ways of dealing with
them. Offering a series of theses or propositions that come to bear on
the cross of Jesus Christ, rather than a fully developed theory, explains
the word "notes" in the title; it connotes their exploratory character. In
a topic as deep as the Christian theology of the cross, there can be no
single exhaustive understanding. The theses are meant to provide some
road markers along one way to arrive at the Christian theological desti-
nation of integrating Jesus' historical suffering and death into an overall
understanding of his person and his title, savior.

PROBLEMS IN SOME THEOLOGIES
OF THE CROSS

What follows is a list. It is not meant to be exhaustive. Nor are the
problems raised here new. The theology of the cross has carried these
questions with it almost from the beginning. But the questions take on
new qualities in new times and perhaps an increased urgency in our day.

1. What is the meaning of "the cross?" and a "theology of the cross?"
These innocent questions introduce the depths and richness of a religious
symbol. The cross refers to the wood upon which Jesus was crucified.
More expansively and historically, the word refers to the whole event
of the suffering and death of Jesus. Beyond these clear designations of
meaning the secular and Christian theological interpretations of the symbol become overwhelmingly complex. On the one hand, the theological
interpretations of the cross that allowed early Christians to reconcile it
with Jesus' being Messiah are subtle and wide-ranging. On the other
hand, completely innocent of the horrors of a death on a cross, a Christian may symbolize his or her Christianity with a stylish cross worn as a
piece of jewelry. For many the crucifixion is the single symbol which goes
most deeply to the essence of Christianity. There can be no question of
simplifying this symbol. But one can be clear about a particular usage of
the terms "cross" and "theology of the cross." In this essay the primary
meaning of the symbol "cross" is its reference by metonymy to the passion and death of Jesus of Nazareth, or the suffering of Jesus in the cruel
way he was executed. This primary meaning, then, is not limited to the

fact that Jesus died, but includes especially the fact that he was executed in a manner that included a great deal of physical punishment. "Theology of the cross" refers to an interpretation of that historical given, frequently with a fixation on it, and yielding an integral theory of its meaning.

It may be significant to note here that the cross of Jesus causes some confusion in Christian consciousness. This is so because Jesus is perceived as innocent, pure goodness, the bearer of salvation from God, and divine. Thus consideration of or meditation on his cross may be accompanied by feelings of sadness, mourning, and sympathetic pain of various intensities, coupled with recognition of the deepest of paradoxes: the physical suffering of God. Yet by the time of Paul salvation was associated with the way Jesus died. These two vectors of religious affection can be conflicted, and a certain parallel dissonance may be discerned between what the first disciples experienced in the immediate aftermath of Jesus' death and the structure of the experience of all subsequent Christians. As historians reconstruct it, the original followers of Jesus were shocked, confused in the sense of being disoriented, and set loose and adrift from the moorings of their expectations. Only with some time, the light of an Easter experience, and a good deal of discussion were they able to regain religious composure and begin the process of integrating the cross into some intelligible, salvific framework.[2] This mix of emotions, negative and positive, often characterize the worship on Good Friday. It leads to the next issue.

2. Is or was Jesus' cross, the punishment he underwent and the execution by which he was killed, a good thing? When the question is put so bluntly, it is hard to imagine it receiving a positive response. But gradually and by indirection, the association of Jesus' death with the way he won salvation for the human race seems to have given his suffering and death positive meaning.

It is possible to imagine that the attention to and interpretation of Jesus' death as the specific way in which salvation was mediated by him began as a reaction against embarrassment at Jesus' death. For his followers this kind of death could only have been a disaster, a colossal failure. How could someone who died such a death at the same time be

---

2. Hans Küng, *On Being a Christian* (Garden City, N.Y.: Doubleday, 1976), 397.

hailed as Messiah? An implicit question such as this stimulated study of the scriptures and elicited various reinterpretations of messiahship that incorporated the manner in which Jesus met his death. The New Testament contains a variety of interpretations of Jesus' death that involve the cross as an essential ingredient, and patristic and medieval theology develop the tradition. Jesus was slain "for us"; he died for our sins; his death was a ransom, a price paid; in a cultic framework, Jesus' cross was a sacrifice for sin; his death constituted a satisfaction of the demands of justice; Jesus' suffering substituted for ours and thus made us whole.[3] These theories make Jesus' suffering and death, his cross, the instrumental cause in his saving activity. In an objective, narrative transaction that goes on metaphysically or metahistorically, human beings are saved, and in the light of this result or outcome the cross becomes bathed in positive value. This language has warrant in the New Testament, pervades liturgy and piety, and has structured Christian experience over the ages.

The problem is that salvation through the cross indirectly makes Jesus' death something good, not directly but by implication and consequence. Spiritualities that are contemplative or meditative are encouraged by such a theological logic to fix attention on Jesus' suffering and death. I have read spiritual writers who proposed a conception of Jesus' knowledge that allowed him to be conscious of all the sins of the world, and awareness of these psychologically compounded the physical pain expended "for us"; the more the pain, the more Jesus' love for us, and the more compunction is demanded of us. This kind of spirituality involves a certain fascination that is intensified by a tension between what repels and what attracts. Fixation on Jesus' path of suffering to his death engenders horror on one hand, and on the other, since this pain is endured "for me" and merits my salvation and absolute identity in God's embrace, it draws me in and gives me absolute metaphysical comfort.

This fascination and the spirituality it engenders can also lead to scandal. One reason for this is that the conception extends beyond the case of Jesus. Since Jesus is the model of Christian life, the revealer of what human life should be from God's perspective, suffering is turned into a kind of negative *bonum,* an ascetic ideal that should not only be imitated

---

3. I develop some of these salvation theories, many of which amount to a theology of the cross, in JSG, 152–84, 213–43. See too Küng's straightforward pastoral theological reflection on these interpretations of Jesus' death or cross in *On Being a Christian,* 419–36.

but made into the ideal pattern of human existence. The framework becomes individualist: to follow Christ is to follow his path of the cross; the truly good life is one of self-negation and even suffering. If this is where the "scandal" of the cross lies, then many among the most sincere of people will indeed be scandalized and have none of it. Is this a proper reaction? Or is this spontaneous reaction communicating that something has gone wrong?

3. Did God will or intend Jesus to suffer? Part of the logic of the theologies of the cross that are implicit in the theories of salvation mentioned above seems to entail a view that God willed or intended Jesus to suffer. Certain phrases from the New Testament, which also recur in liturgy and formulas of prayer, reinforce the conception to the point where it has become ingrained in Christian language and a spontaneous way of speaking. In Galatians Paul speaks of Jesus who "gave himself" for our sins "according to the will of our God and Father" (Gal 1:4). In Romans, he characterizes God as one "who did not spare his own Son but gave him up for us all" (Rom 8:32). John's gospel provides this testimony: "For God so loved the world that he gave his only Son . . ." (John 3:16). Phrases such as these are expressions of a deep conviction that does not necessarily entail a naive sense of God's design that Jesus suffer; they bear a larger religious meaning than their literal sense deploys. But the point here is whether the overt meaning of such language is admissible or whether it orients Christian consciousness in a fundamentally wrong direction.

4. Was the cross "necessary?" Did Jesus have to suffer and die as Luke implies (Luke 24:26)? Could Jesus have been savior if he had died of natural causes, of a heart attack, or during his sleep as an aged person? Did he have to be killed in a manner that involved torture and execution?[4]

In point of fact, Jesus was punished and executed by crucifixion. Most scholars take the way Jesus met his death as a historical certainty. It may seem to do little good to ask hypothetical questions about what might have happened because one has to return to the data. But the response to such questions reveals the kind of thinking or logic by which the given facts are understood. Once the suffering and painful execution of

---

4. Jon Sobrino, *Jesus the Liberator: A Historical-Theological View* (Maryknoll, N.Y.: Orbis Books, 1993), has an extensive discussion of this question at 195–211.

Jesus has been drawn into an "explanatory" metaphor and developed into a theory, this theory bends back and legitimates the whole event in a higher scheme of things. It is given a historical, cosmic, and divine logic or rationale. "Explaining it" justifies it. Once it makes sense, it becomes part of the larger metaphysical narrative, and as part of this narrative the historical events of the passion and execution of Jesus become in some measure necessary. This necessity itself can have different meanings or rationales: it is "fitting" according to this or that way of thinking. Perhaps Jesus' execution was necessary by some perverse pattern of human nature, as when all prophets who speak God's word are resisted and sometimes killed.[5] Necessity according to a concept of the transcendent order of justice, an equilibrium that required recompense or restitution in response to a breakdown of God's order of the universe, played a part in Anselm's thinking about "satisfaction."[6] One cannot say that the sinfulness of the human race or even individuals does not make any difference in the large scheme of things.

But critical reflection has to ask whether these various rationales are no more than attempts to assign some logic to what cannot be explained, or at least not in any simple way. They do have some logic in themselves, but it is impossible to fit the mystery of God's dealing with human existence into the narrow framework of any single logic. The New Testament always says more. For example, one can ask how and in what way Jesus Christ mediates the religious conviction of salvation from God into actual Christian lives. When one asks that question of the New Testament witness, one finds a large variety of different answers, many of which do not dwell on Jesus' suffering and painful death.[7]

---

5. Ignacio Ellacuría, "The Crucified People," *Mysterium Liberationis: Fundamental Concepts of Liberation Theology,* ed. I. Ellacuría and J. Sobrino (Maryknoll, N.Y.: Orbis Books, 1993), 586–87. Ellacuría calls this the "historic" necessity of Jesus' death, one which does not exempt it from human responsibility. For a discussion of Ellacuría's position, see Kevin Burke, *The Ground Beneath the Cross: The Theology of Ignacio Ellacuría* (Washington, D.C.: Georgetown University Press, 2000), 177–80.

6. R. W. Southern says that in Anselm's view of "satisfaction," "God's honor is simply another word for the ordering of the universe in its due relationship to God." *Saint Anselm: A Portrait in a Landscape* (Cambridge: Cambridge University Press, 1990), 227.

7. Jesus Christ is savior in different ways in the synoptic gospels, in John, and in Paul. The concept of how Jesus saves correlates with the conception of the predicament in which the human race finds itself. The New Testament authors worked with particular conceptions of the sin and bondage that hold human existence prisoner (Frank J. Matera, *New Testament Christologies* [Louisville: Westminster John Knox Press, 1999], 250–52). Our own day gives witness to other

5. What is needed to constitute a "theology of the cross?" In fact Jesus of Nazareth was put to death in a violent and painful way. No account of Jesus can prescind from this, and all theological portrayals of Jesus as the Christ have to take this fact into consideration. One cannot very well pretend that the ministry of Jesus was not interrupted in the way it was. Thus every full account of Jesus' life includes his death and integrates this into a theological consideration of his being Christ and savior. But these last two titles are central to the Christian interpretation of who Jesus is. Christology proposes a theological interpretation of the person and work of Jesus of Nazareth for our salvation, and his death has to be included in this account. But does one need a specific "theology of the cross," or is this simply a subset and component of one's understanding of Jesus Christ? There can be no doubt that "the cross" and a "theology of the cross" have in some christologies become the heart of the matter, because they conceive salvation as having been accomplished precisely in or by or through his painful death. But it is not certain at all that such a particular salvation theory and christology should be made the standard for christology as such. It would rather seem that the burden of proof for such a primacy lies with the claim itself, for throughout its course the history of christology has witnessed a good deal of emphasis on victorious resurrection and glory that did not ignore Jesus' painful death but drew it up into a higher synthesis without dwelling on it.

This raises the question of the implicit expectation contained in the question about the presence or absence of a "theology of the cross" in any given christological synthesis. What is too much or too little emphasis on the torture and pain inflicted upon Jesus? What is the standard or measure by which one can assess the adequacy of a given christology? It is usually the case that, when such judgments are made, a tacit norm is possessed by the critic, and the grounds and adequacy of such implicit norms may not be stated or even critically appropriated.

PRELIMINARY CONSIDERATIONS

Christian theology that deals with fundamental doctrines has grown into a complex discipline. The topics have been discussed across the two

---

radical human dilemmas, so that the salvation Jesus wrought will be accommodated to them in various different ways according to the paradigm of the New Testament itself.

millennia of Christian history and the language has become increasingly nuanced. The pluralism within the discipline correlates with a variety of different methodological options, and someone approaching the discipline for the first time might rightly be confused. One cannot presume a common framework of understanding, or set of presuppositions, or method in any given essay on basic Christian matters. On the one hand, this requires that theologians in some measure declare their background theories, premises, and ways of proceeding. This was done in a general way in chapter 2. On the other hand, even when these presuppositions are explained, much misinterpretation of or lack of appreciation for what is being said may stem from a lack of sympathy for theological perspectives that are prior to the discussion itself. I thus begin this discussion by singling out some specific elements of the perspective from which the constructive section of this essay is generated. The four points which follow summarize points made at considerable length in previous essays and bring them to focus on the topic under review.

First, several phrases may be used to characterize the method used in this essay, for example, a critical, hermeneutical method of correlation or a method "from below." Another phrase that gets to the heart of things is "a genetic method." A genetic method as it is conceived here supposes that Jesus did not teach his disciples christology, but the values of the kingdom of God. Christology was something that developed most pointedly after his death and in the light of an Easter experience, although not without reference back to Jesus of Nazareth. The story told by Luke of the experience of the two disciples on their way from Jerusalem to Emmaus can be read as an allegory depicting the extended experience of the community of Jesus' followers interpreting the person and ministry of Jesus by reflecting on the Jewish scriptures within the context of a eucharistic experience of him risen.[8] The background for christology, then, is made up of a set of givens such as these: the historical data concerning Jesus' life and death, which can be historically retrieved, not in much detail, but with sufficient historicity to ensure a historical referent in the person of Jesus; an Easter experience in which Jesus was perceived in faith and hope to be alive and raised into the life of God; and a developing effort to understand and appreciate who

---

8. Haight, JSG, 136–39.

Jesus was in his deepest being, something that had started in his lifetime, but grew with urgency in the light of the experience of his death and resurrection.

The point of these three premises is that christology, as the effort to understand the person of Jesus Christ, is a product of historical development. It began with Jesus himself who is the object of the reflection, and it proceeded to gain "christological" depth and transcendence as Jesus was interpreted to be the Christ, the Messiah. But if christology as a specific kind of human reflection with particular contents is a product of development and has a historical life, it follows that the only way to understand it critically and adequately is to chart its genesis and development. Without that kind of reflection, one will risk working with premises that have not been tested, or presuming something as commonly accepted that in fact is limited and esoteric, or taking for granted something that scarcely transcends partisan opinion.

One could also describe what is intended by the term "genetic" with the concept of development: thus a developmental method. Because the period that is reflected in the New Testament represents the privileged period in which the community's normative scriptures were written, one can say that christology was generated during the course of this period. This does not imply that no development occurred thereafter, for surely it did, especially in the great councils but also in theology. However, one can retrieve in the writings of the New Testament all the basic principles that constitute the dynamic structure of christology. That is, one can read the genesis of the discipline of christology in the New Testament and find in it the major moves or principles of theological interpretation applied to Jesus. In this way one critically appropriates the discipline of christology itself.

A second major presupposition that lies behind the constructive effort of this chapter is the thesis that one can pinpoint a primary Christian experience "behind," "beneath," and "within" all the interpretations of Jesus Christ and thus all christologies. This common experience consists of a recognition that salvation from God has been offered and experienced as being made concretely present in Jesus of Nazareth. While this may seem a contentious premise, it is meant in a way that can be understood as commonsensical and yet full of significance.

Such a view makes common sense when some of the possible objections to it are removed. An "experience" here does not refer to the perception of an overt object, but to a human existential awareness, however its object may be conceived or expressed in language, that is prior to whatever language is used to describe it. Priority in this understanding should not be taken temporally as though there were language-free experiences, but as a deep dimension of awareness that "searches for" and can sustain more than one form of expression. Applied to the salvation mediated by Jesus, a common religious appreciation of Jesus is shared on a deeper level than linguistic construal, and it can support different articulations. The following questions show that such a structure is at work in the New Testament: if such an experience were not there, why would the witnesses that make up the New Testament appear at all? It is in fact precisely such an experience that unites the many different conceptions of what this salvation is and that in turn makes up the New Testament confession of faith. The conceptions of who Jesus is and what he did for our salvation are plural; what holds them together is a common conviction that Jesus is the instrument of that salvation however "salvation" is construed.

The significance of this common sense observation, now raised to the level of theoretical principle, is that it supplies the final criterion of christology. In a context of christological pluralism, the adequacy of statements about the content of Christian faith and hope in Jesus Christ cannot in the end be judged on the basis of comparison with other propositions. The norm must lie in their relative adequacy to the community's experience of Jesus as the bearer of God's salvation. This undercuts the procedure of criticizing a christological interpretation by merely citing some proposition as a single adequate norm, instead of measuring adequacy against the existential faith of the community that is witnessed to and contained in a rather large and pluralistic pool of statements of belief and theologies from both the scriptures and the tradition of the church. It seems self-evident that Christians both possess the truth of salvation from God in Jesus Christ, because they have been claimed by it, and that this mystery completely escapes their full comprehension, so that no language can exhaustively control it. What all Christians share and can talk about in different languages is the experience that Jesus is savior because he communicates God's salvation.

Third, religious language that refers to a transcendent object, thus Christian language of faith and all statements that are strictly theological, are symbolic and iconic; they do not adequately represent their object, but lead the mind from things readily known in this world into something transcendently other. In this logic of the symbolic, Jesus himself is symbol of God, and all theological language is symbolic language. Does this construct in itself solve most of the problems raised by the Christian theology and language used to describe the cross of Jesus? Yes and No.

On the positive side, two features of a theory of the symbolic character of religious and theological language go a long way in solving many of the problems with a language that seems overly fascinated and fixated on the death of Jesus and its relevance for our salvation. The first is that, because theological language is symbolic, it should not be taken as literal or univocal or representative according to its earthly meaning. Christian theology should not be imprisoned by propositions that are understood in their overt, empirically derived meanings and imposed as the juridical boundaries of the community. Rather, and by contrast, symbolic language is precisely not literal or univocal, but leads the mind by analogy into mystery. Notice that such language also marks the boundaries of the community; communities identify themselves by the language they speak. But the language of radical mystery does so in a religious way. Religious language bears reference to a transcendent order which is discerned in a deep, common experience of God and shared by the community. But the very "object" of that experience is transcendent and always invites new language about itself. Transcendent mystery confined by univocal and literal language becomes mystification.

On the negative side, however, symbols cannot work if they appear incomprehensible in their first or overt meaning. Symbols which aggressively attack intelligence or experience and go begging for some rationale cannot succeed. The appeal to the past alone, to a tradition that lacks intelligibility in the present, or an appeal to authority alone, with no interpretation of how its word fits coherently into common human experience, cannot expect a hearing. It is quite another thing to assault prejudice with the steady reasonableness of discussion, to bring socially and culturally ingrained bias up short with an alternative coherence, to appeal to a way of life that carries its own authenticating credentials. Making the cross a true symbol today requires work; no theology of the cross today can be effective as mere assertion within a reflective or critical culture.[9]

Finally, it is important to note that this constructive theological interpretation is not offered as the only possible appropriation of Jesus' suffering and death. Several reasons explain why the account that follows cannot claim to exhaust or control this subject matter or provide an exclusive interpretation. Jesus' suffering and death contain a mix of negativity and positivity that runs so deeply in Christian experience that one cannot hope to account for Christian faith experience with a single theological representation. These experiences and thus the theological conceptions that try to catch up with them unfold at various different levels of construal, from the psychologically unconscious and conscious to such metaphysical concepts as creation, nature, history, and the ontological structure of existence. Christian experience is in principle so complex at these levels of basic religious response that a single theological account is absolutely unable to absorb and encompass it. Just as there is no one christology in the New Testament but many, so too are there many theologies of the cross. And so it is today. Thus other theologies of the cross that in many respects run counter to this construal may appear to be quite reasonable. These "notes," therefore, are not offered as a polemical reflection, except insofar as some language concerning the cross of Jesus turns suffering into a good, scandalizes faithful Christians, and renders the Christian message absurd. This is what is at stake in some of the problems attached to current language describing Jesus' passion, death, and work for human salvation.

NOTES FOR A CONSTRUCTIVE THEOLOGY OF THE CROSS

The reflections that follow are too schematic to be anything more than an outline for an argument. They loosely form a line of reasoning that

---

9. Another premise that will not be developed here is the need of a holistic christological framework or theory of which a theology of the cross is a part. Such a christology would integrate Jesus' punishment and execution, what we know of his actual death, into a holistic understanding of the person of Jesus and what God did in and through his life. While such a christology cannot be developed or even outlined here, the constructive effort that follows fits into the framework of JSG.

addresses the problems described in the first part of this essay and pre-suppose the premises enumerated in the second part. The reflections are stated in the form of theses or propositions in order to help keep the line of reasoning clean. By so narrowing the discussion I hope that I will succeed in demonstrating that there is much more to be said about the beliefs surrounding this profound Christian aspect of the mystery of Jesus Christ, that these are indeed notes, but that they point to a coherent and viable theology of the cross.

The physical suffering in the crucifixion inflicted upon Jesus was not good; it was an evil.

The cruel torture of Jesus cannot be turned into a good or made into something positive. We shall see that the subject of this suffering and death, Jesus, can be subsumed by God into God's own life by resur-rection, and in that measure his suffering and death are rescued from complete meaninglessness, but suffering and death in themselves can-not be transformed into a good. I take this as a kind of "bottom line" criterion by which to test a theology of the cross and the language of piety and prayer used by the church to channel devotion. On this basis it would have been better for Jesus and for us if he were not tortured or crucified. We shall also see that this line of reasoning will be able to accommodate Jesus' suffering into his work of salvation, but it will require dialectical reasoning and language: Jesus saves in and through his being tortured, but also despite it. In other words, the negativity of Jesus' being physically punished can itself be saved by God, and its being saved bears positive meaning for the many, that is, all human beings. But this drama, which will be described more fully in the course of these notes, does not and cannot turn Jesus' actual death into something good. Torture of anyone, not only the innocent, is evil.

Because the suffering inflicted on Jesus is evil in itself, it cannot be the basis or object of Christian devotion.

Jesus' suffering and death are, like all humanly inflicted innocent suffering and killing, a profound cause of scandal. To regard his tor-ture in itself as a focus of devotion harmfully compromises Christian faith.[10] The various ways of justifying a focused attention on Jesus' physical suffering as though it contains some religious value are counterproductive. Jesus' suffering was imposed upon him; he did not voluntarily choose or accept it as a good. This action of others in killing Jesus in itself saved nothing; it was rather part of the massive surd of evil whose meaninglessness threatens existential meaning and coherence itself and hence calls out for some salvation.

What then is or should be going on at commemorations of Jesus' death as on Good Friday? Indeed, is Good Friday good? The most obvious explanation for the commemoration of Jesus' execution should run in parallel with the sympathy and mourning for the death of a family member or friend who was unjustly condemned and then tortured and executed. Such an event carries tremendous existential power and is a cause of grief. But if torture is evil, one would not after the fact venerate the instruments of torture. One has to ask what is going on in the veneration of the cross by Christians. This appears to be one of those strange reversals by which what is intrinsically repugnant has somehow been turned into a good. Only an exercise of sharply dialectical thinking can save any kind of reverence for the means of Jesus' physical suffering. In sum, the gathering to commemorate Jesus' death in Holy Week seems to require a horror at what was done to Jesus mixed with a religious sympathy and grief analogous to a response to the cruel torture and killing of an innocent friend. It is an experience intrinsically filled with deep questions.

But Jesus' going to his death was the final act of Jesus' life which drew his innocent suffering into the logic of his whole ministry and life.

I begin this thesis with the adversative "but" in order to signal further reflection that will ultimately be dialectical in character. It begins with Karl Rahner's thought on the theology of death.[11] Rahner underlines how, when one dies consciously and intentionally, the facing of death actively draws one's life to a close. Such an encounter with one's own death is an action, a self-disposition that, because of its ultimacy, in

---

10. The phrase in this thesis, "in itself," is significant because it opens the way to the more expansive, dialectical view that will be explained further on. In it the cross is considered precisely not in itself but within the larger context of an already accomplished resurrection.

11. This thesis is inspired by Karl Rahner's theology of death, but these reflections are not intended to reproduce his thinking historically. See Karl Rahner, *On the Theology of Death* (New York: Herder and Herder, 1961), 35–39.

profound ways recapitulates one's life. In the case of Jesus, his being symbol and sacrament of God in the course of his whole life thus comes to a recapitulating climax in the way he faced his death.[12]

But there is more: throughout one's life the conscious spirit which constitutes the self is constantly drawing one's whole self, one's body, one's whole physical self, and all one's actions, into the synthesis of the person. Moreover, one consistently draws the world by one's interactions with it into the self so that one is constantly being fashioned by other people, of course, and by the physical environment in which one lives as well. This means that as the self is part of the world, the world is also part of the self. This consideration allows one to see how Jesus' torture and death, in all of its negativity, becomes part of Jesus' self and identity. This provides one reason why his death as a criminal was such an embarrassment to his disciples. It helps explain why those who began to formulate his messiahship with various interpretations of his death had to make that death integral to his life and person. And, finally, it also explains why Jesus' actual death entered not only *in fact* but also *intrinsically* into his actual saving activity. We are what we do; we also are what is done to us, especially when what is done to us is consciously appropriated and we respond to it. Jesus' meeting his cruel and unjust death became part of who he was. Thus one can say with Jon Sobrino that what was pleasing to God was not Jesus' death in itself, or even as one element alone in his life, but Jesus himself. Jesus' life as a whole was pleasing to God. "The cross, as a historically necessary component of love, is part of its historical fullness, and what God was pleased by was this fullness of love."[13]

God saved Jesus by resurrecting Jesus from death; through death Jesus was drawn into the life of God.

Jesus did not die naturally but violently as one crucified. But God did not leave him in death, but raised him from death into the eternal life of

---

12. That Jesus is symbol or sacrament of God is the burden of the christology presented in JSG which has to be presupposed here. Of course we do not have any access to the actual consciousness of Jesus in a psychological sense during his lifetime. But neither does any historical evidence contradict the resolute character of Jesus' steadfastness to his mission through his passion and death. The whole New Testament is witness to that fidelity and obedience to the cause of the kingdom of God.

13. Sobrino, *Jesus the Liberator,* 228.

the creator God. This thesis states bluntly the Christian belief in Jesus' resurrection which is a topic that cannot be developed here.[14] Rather the focus shifts to the topic of salvation because the understanding of Jesus' suffering and death enters into the Christian imagination through the framework of what he did for our salvation.

> *One can understand how God saves human beings through Jesus, in the sense of Jesus' relation to that salvation, in two distinct ways: in the one Jesus is involved in the process of salvation as cause, in the other he is the revealer of this salvation.*

A commentary on this distinction will help shed light on this subtle topic because each of these two distinct ways of understanding Jesus' role in salvation tends to place a specifically different valence on Jesus' suffering and death.

A single, generalized conception of salvation can be shared by each of the alternatives which follow. Salvation may be understood as a condition of being united with God, and in and through God a being united with other human beings and at peace in one's existence.[15] This salvation from God is metaphysical, that is, a condition that transcends empirical existence in this world by involving God. Although human beings may participate in it in this life either consciously or unconsciously, it will be fully realized only in an absolute future. This condition of being saved is complex; it has the character of "salvation" because it releases human being from negative structures of existence. According to the witness of the New Testament and Christian tradition it involves being accepted by God's love in such a way that one is freed from sin and guilt and made righteous before God. At the same time it entails the victory of life over death, a being freed from the ultimate condition of annihilation, so dramatically represented by death, and being raised to eternal life within the sphere of God.

---

14. The meaning of resurrection, of Jesus' resurrection, and the epistemology of how the disciples came to faith's appreciation of this resurrection are treated in JSG, 119–51.

15. Salvation may be understood as the condition of being saved. Seen from that perspective, Gustavo Gutiérrez offers a broad but remarkably suitable characterization of it in these words: "Salvation — totally and freely given by God, the communion of men with God and among themselves — is the inner force and the fullness of this movement of man's self-generation which was initiated by the work of creation." *A Theology of Liberation: History, Politics and Salvation* (Maryknoll, N.Y.: Orbis Books, 1973), 159.

The question, now, pertains to the relation between this salvation from God and Jesus' life, death, and resurrection. The first of two distinct ways of construing this relationship is that Jesus was the instrumental cause of this condition. On this view, God's salvation of the world is constituted by Jesus, so that without him there would be no salvation available to humankind. The New Testament and the history of Christian theology provide a variety of different redemption theories which express how Jesus negotiated this salvation or it was negotiated through him. Many of these are expressed in a drama that goes on "behind" or "within" the overt events of history as a transaction between God and Jesus that accomplished the salvation of humankind. These "theories," if they may be so called, are based on such metaphors or analogies as a sacrifice, a scapegoat, paying a ransom, or making satisfaction for sin. If these were taken as literal expressions of what happened in Jesus' life, death, and resurrection, they would exemplify how Jesus' death might be construed as a cause of human salvation.

Another way of conceiving the relation of Jesus' life, death, and resurrection to human salvation takes these pascal events as revelatory of the nature of God and of human destiny. On this view, Jesus is not the cause of human salvation generally but its revealer. This conception begins with a historical perspective. What has been revealed to Christians in the ministry, death, and resurrection of Jesus regards the very nature of God as savior. But this means that God has always been savior and that salvation has been going on since "the beginning." There never was a time when God was not savior, nor a period in human history when God's salvation was ineffective. But this saving activity of God is not accomplished only secretly in the private life of each person, through reason or private inspiration, but reaches people through the public means of external history and society. In Israel salvation is experience in Torah and the prophets. In Christianity it is experienced in the encounter with Jesus Christ. In other religious places salvation is mediated by other names through the religious symbols that respond to the questions of ultimate meaning and destiny of human existence and the world. Since this was going on before Jesus Christ, and continues to go forward apart from Jesus Christ, one cannot consider Jesus the exclusive historical mediator of this salvation. Rather God causes salvation through a variety of historical mediations.

Although Jesus is not the cause of human salvation as such, for God alone is that cause, Jesus functions as the medium or symbol of God who defines for Christian existence who God is, God's nature, and how God relates to human beings generally. Moreover, Jesus as the revealer and sacrament of God's salvation to Christians causes the consciousness of God's salvation that in turn shapes the common life of the Christian church. Through Jesus the Christian community and each one in it ultimately gains the consciousness that he or she is united with God and that this God preserves human life against death by drawing it back into God's life out of love. To be caught up in that faith in such a way that it is acted out, not privately but in one's public life in the world, is salvation rendered conscious and active here and now. For the Christian, God alone saves and has been saving since the initial act of creation, because such is the nature of God as God has been revealed in Jesus. For the Christian, Jesus is the parable of this God, so that the acceptance of sinners by Jesus and the resurrection of Jesus by the power of God correspond with the saving nature of God who saves all human beings according to the pattern revealed in Jesus. In sum, according to this second view, the life, death, and resurrection of Jesus does not cause but reveals what has been going on from the beginning of the creation of human existence. God the author of life accepts life even in its sinfulness and guilt and protects and guarantees it through death. God the author of life is also the finisher of life by acceptance and resurrection.

Both of these views find support in the New Testament. The first places high value on the passion and death of Jesus as intrinsic to the causality by which he won universal human salvation. In the second, the suffering of Jesus is not causally or constitutively linked to human salvation as such.

In a revelational conception of how Jesus saves, the cross does not save, but God saves in spite of and in the face of the cross.

This proposition sums up the direction these notes have taken up to this point before they move to another stage of the argument. It appears from what has been said that the formula of salvation by or through the cross is gravely misleading. It subtly turns something intrinsically evil into a good and may reflect the confused sentiments that have made the cross in itself an object of veneration. Ordinarily the instruments of the torture and execution of Jesus should stimulate something between shock, disgust, and confusion, analogous to a reaction to the relics of a genocide, an outrightly negative emotional response. They are not instruments of salvation. Of course, there is much more going on here that is complex and difficult to sort out. But it should not be immune from reflection.

Throughout the Jewish and Christian scriptural tradition the author of salvation is God. In the New Testament God saves, and one should rather say, first, that God saved Jesus and, because the cross became an integral part of Jesus' whole life, it was "saved" with and in him. In order to see how Jesus' suffering enters into his saving activity, one has to transcend the passivity by which this suffering was imposed on Jesus, and look to Jesus' activity and the manner in which he appropriated these sufferings into the positive commitment of his whole life to the kingdom of God. This is what God resurrected from death. In this action of saving Jesus God was acting as God is. The ground of salvation, therefore, is first of all the loving goodness of God that lies behind and within God's creativity or creating. In a second sense, revelation of this saving nature and action of God, once appropriated and internalized, becomes salvation here and now by forging union with such a God. In the light of this revelation life is lived on the promise and in the hope of eternal life.

I now turn to a slightly different level of consideration, namely, how the cross, that is, Jesus being tortured and executed, fits into or shapes the Christian imagination. What role does the cross play in Christian life? Here I want to stress again the dialectical logic of the cross and then appeal to some of the well known constructs of St. Paul which will, in turn, exemplify the dialectical mind-set.[16]

The existential place of the suffering and death of Jesus, that is, the cross, in the Christian experience of salvation mediated by Jesus can be explained in terms of a negative experience of contrast.

I have already given an account of the dialectical way in which the cross became part of Jesus' life for the kingdom of God to the end, an end

---

16. It will become apparent from the discussion that the term "dialectical" is not used here in contrast with either an "analogical" imagination, as that phrase is used by David Tracy, in *The Analogical Imagination: Christian Theology and the Culture of Pluralism* (New York: Crossroad, 1981) or with a "sacramental imagination," as that phrase is frequently used with reference to Catholicism. The term "dialectical" here means holding together qualities or aspects of a reality that are in tension with each other without relief; the tension cannot be resolved.

that entailed torture and a cruel execution. The evil inflicted upon him had no redeeming power whatsoever apart from its being absorbed into his total commitment to the truth and reign of God's values.[17] In other words, his death cannot be understood adequately apart from its place in the whole course of Jesus' life as it is reflected in his public ministry. The same dialectical structure characterizes the *experience* of salvation which is mediated to human beings in this life through the revelation of the God of life implied in faith in Jesus' resurrection. This thesis tries to make sense out of language which, if it were taken literally, would be seriously questionable. Examples of such language are found in the ideas that "the blood of Jesus . . . cleanses us from all sin" (1 John 1:7), or the idea that we "were ransomed . . . with the precious blood of Christ, like that of a lamb without blemish or spot" (1 Pet 1:18), or that Jesus is the one who "freed us from our sins by his blood . . ." (Rev 1:15), or the conception that Jesus gave "his life as a ransom for many" (Mk 10:45). Granted that this is searching, symbolic language of people striving to express the paradox that God was somehow manifested as savior in the cruel fate of Jesus; but how can one perceive the self-revelation of God and salvation in such a death and not more reasonably be scandalized by it? Why would not God's self-revelation be more evident in a life lived out in its full course and according to its full potential?[18] How can the height of divine revelation be imagined to occur in the dark depths of evil punishment and innocent suffering? This is the crucial question for a theology of the cross that often seems to be begged by revelational positivism and a facile assertion of various formulas.

I draw again on the common structure of a negative experience of contrast formulated by Edward Schillebeeckx as an explanation of how Jesus' life, death, and resurrection reveals salvation.[19] The structure of

---

17. Life according to God's values is synonymous with "the kingdom of God," which is not a place, but the quality of human existence as it was willed by the creator. The Christian has an insight into what the creator considers important or "values" by accepting Jesus as the revealer of God, for Jesus' preaching and life were dedicated to portraying and acting out the kingdom of God.

18. Irenaeus quite reasonably thought in the terms that became an axiom: what was not assumed, was not saved. The Word in becoming flesh took on life in its full range in order that the full range might be redeemed. Thus Irenaeus thought that Jesus must have lived to old age before he was crucified, otherwise the full life cycle would not have been the subject of the incarnation.

19. Edward Schillebeeckx, *Church: The Human Story of God* (New York: Crossroad, 1990), 5–6. See chapter 3, p. 67.

this common experience has three components. One is the experience of something that is wrong or bad, so patently evil that its negativity appears as something self-evident and known more or less intuitively as such. One needs no demonstration that a carefully planned and implemented program of genocide is evil. But, second, the spontaneous knowledge of the evil of the given situation or event or condition cannot be known as evil without some background awareness of what should be, of the good that it distorts or the positive situation it corrupts. Dialectically, evil could not be known as evil without some horizon of a perception of the good. This need not be a clear concept, but its presence is absolutely necessary for negativity to be perceived as such and not simply as the way things are. Third, however, the perception of the negative against what is good and should be in place spawns a desire to right the wrong, to at least escape the evil, or, better, do what is in one's power to overcome the negativity and replace it with what should be. This fundamental logic plays itself out in big things and small; it can be seen at work in world-wide movements of reaction against dehumanizing situations, as well as in individual, personal appraisals of common everyday situations. Such a fundamental moral perception could be developed into a technical epistemology of ethical awareness. But what is important at this juncture is the recognition, first, that this structure is really quite basic and operative on an almost instinctive level of response to reality and, second, that it has an intrinsically dialectical character. The negative and the positive inform each other in generating an impulse to action, but the negativity is never transformed into a good, except by its being negated.

This negative experience of contrast offers some help in explaining the attention to the suffering of Jesus contained in faith in him and the salvation mediated through him. Focusing on the suffering of Jesus is focusing on evil in the world, the sin of the world and in particular political situations, in the hearts of human beings, in the ability to destroy another human being, and in a whole world of innocent suffering. These things cannot be made good or explained away; they confront us. If one can explain how it could happen that Jesus was crucified and destroyed, one has not explained away the evil as a mistake but has revealed it as an evil. But in the very measure in which Jesus' suffering and death are perceived as evil, one also knows that it should be otherwise and hopes that it could be so. Innocence and good intention should live; human existence should flourish; the works of love should last forever. Metaphysically, salvation from God in the form of resurrection rights the wrong, and recognition of that resurrection in faith provides a saving hope that suffering and death will not have the last word, but will be transformed into life everlasting. In this way the fact that Jesus was tortured and crucified remains evil, and the experience of this scandalous event is never turned to good, but it is transformed in the hope of resurrection. In faith's recognition of the resurrection of Jesus by God there is a meeting, a fit, a correlation of a drive for meaning in the face of its real negation and the discovery of positivity from God that transforms or redeems the negativity by overturning and negating it.

Some of Paul's reflections on the resurrection correlate with this dialectical pattern for understanding the meaning of the "cross."

Certain Pauline texts can be correlated with the direction suggested by these notes. But before citing any of these texts, it is imperative that the rationale of this exercise be clear. The point does not lie in any attempt at proving from scripture a theological interpretation that excludes other possible interpretations. I am not bringing to bear an exegetically sophisticated representation of Paul's theology, for that step is not necessary for this discussion. The point here does not consist in an appeal to hermeneutical theory for an argument that Paul's texts open up the imagination for this interpretation, even though this may be true. Nor do I contend that the theology of the cross developed here is a development of Paul's position. I am simply proposing that there is a certain correlation and thus continuity between the theology of the cross offered here and isolated positions or statements of Paul. The presence of this language in Paul and elsewhere in the New Testament sets up a situation in which one can look back and see affinities between the position that has developed in our contemporary situation, that is, the theological construal and formulas that are being offered here, and some of Paul's classic language.[20]

Paul makes a significant comment on the resurrection when he says: "if Christ was not raised, your faith has nothing in it . . . " (1 Cor 15:17).

---

20. For a background theory of the development of doctrine and tradition that gives warrant to this kind of interpretation and use of scripture see John E. Thiel, *Senses of Tradition: Continuity and Development in Catholic Faith* (Oxford: University Press, 2000), 84–95.

This frequently cited text of Paul suggests that the resurrection of Jesus is what makes the cross of Jesus salvific. Without God's raising Jesus from death, the cross in the end or ultimately would not have been or be salvific. To state this role of the resurrection in Jesus' work for our salvation in its bluntest form, the cross of Jesus bears no salvific value at all. In itself, as that which was imposed on Jesus, its value is completely negative. The radicality of Paul's statement is that, by a thought experiment, a contrary to fact hypothesis, and a radical alternative, he sorts out the logic of the paschal mystery. It is so radical that it seems to devalue all the positive things that Jesus did in his public ministry by word and action in service of the kingdom of God and make them conditional upon the resurrection. Are these not of value in themselves? Yet such is the devastating power of death; it annihilates. Without the final action of resurrecting Jesus, God's action in Jesus as Word and Spirit would have been annihilated and drained of ultimate meaning, as distinct from finite and temporal meaning. The either-or of Paul's aphorism contains a powerful and decisive alternative. But the positive side of the alternative, that Jesus was raised, is now in place and is equally radical. It retroactively floods the whole life of Jesus and of anyone dedicated to God's values in history with meaning that will itself be resurrected, and therefore have absolute and eternal meaning. Resurrection thus validates an already intrinsically meaningful existence with the absoluteness of eternal life.

This theology of the saved, nonsalvific value of the cross correlates with Paul's equally dialectical view of life through death.

According to Wayne Meeks, the idea of a crucified Messiah stands at the center of Paul's Christianity. But the idea contains a basic paradox, the paradox of life through death, that represents the fundamental structure of Pauline thinking. "The belief in the crucified Messiah introduces a new and controlling paradigm of God's mode of action."[21] It allows for the paradoxical and antithetical style of Paul's thinking. Meeks goes on to describe how this center blossoms out into a cosmic view of reality in the light of the salvation wrought by Christ. Its structure is dialectical, as

---

21. Wayne A. Meeks, *The First Urban Christians: The Social World of the Apostle Paul* (New Haven: Yale University Press, 1983), 180.

salvation must be. It consists in bondage and liberation, guilt and justification, estrangement and reconciliation, deformity and transformation.
After the pattern of Jesus Christ, one can now understand death as issuing
into life. This pattern of death to life, of self-negation to self-fulfillment,
has multiple applications, making it a fundamental framework for seeing
reality, for interpreting human life as it is lived in this world, and for
understanding the ultimate destiny of human existence.[22] "The most
important observation is that at the center of Paul's hortatory rhetoric
is an expandable set of analogies, some explicit, more often implicit in
metaphorical speech, between the story of Jesus' crucifixion and resurrection and the desired dispositions and behavior of believers. This
transformation of what was for Paul the basic message of Christian faith
into a malleable, polysemic trope was perhaps the profoundest and most
enduring contribution that Paul made to Christian speech and thought."[23]
This fundamental symbol of life through death to life, the dialectical
tension between death and life, functioned in many contexts: a theology
of baptism, the eucharist, the essence of Christian morality, the Christian
life of following Christ. It seems plausible to associate this foundational
theme of Pauline Christianity, what Meeks calls paradoxical and antithetical, with the dialectical understanding of the cross that is proposed here.
Paul's theology of the cross does not make the negative into something
good, but explains how the saving power of God draws the subject
through what is negative into something that is purely positive.

*Another frequently exploited concept from Pauline theology, that of
kenosis, also fits within a dialectical framework.*

The passage from Paul's letter to the Philippians in which he cited
what was probably a current hymn to Jesus Christ from a cultic context is a good example of the idea of kenosis (Phil 2:6–11). The term
means "self-emptying," or "self-denying" (Phil 2:7). This self-negation
is frequently associated with a three-stage christology, although such an
interpretation of the historical meaning of the passage is also disputed.

---

22. Ibid., 183–89.
23. Wayne A. Meeks, *The Origins of Christian Morality: The First Two Centuries* (New Haven
and London: Yale University Press, 1993), 64. "Paul's most profound bequest to subsequent
Christian discourse was his transformation of the reported crucifixion and resurrection of Jesus
Christ into a multipurpose metaphor with vast generative and transformative power — not least
for moral perceptions." Ibid., 196.

In that interpretation, a preexistent Christ Jesus, who was in the form of God, negated himself in the incarnation, and even more in his crucifixion and death, so that God rewarded this faithful obedience by exaltation. In a christology from below, however, one takes the first meaning of scriptural interpretations of Jesus as referring to patterns that can be correlated with Jesus' life and death. In this context, the *kenosis* of self-gift or self-oblation would refer to Jesus' historical life completely dedicated to the kingdom of God. This dedication stayed the course to the end, through his passion and ultimately his death. On the basis of that dedication to God, God raised him from death and exalted him.

This historical reading of the roots of the meaning of this passage does not deny the possibility of metaphysical interpretations, but suggests that these begin with attention to what occurred in history. Jesus' *kenosis*, then, began with Jesus' life as a historical prophet. His dedication of himself and complete fidelity to God's cause, that is, the kingdom of God, led to his being raised from death by God. This observation, in turn, short-circuits a kind of kenotic christology from above that subtly begins to turn self-negation as such into a good and begins to inform Jesus' suffering and death with positive value. What is positive in Jesus' ministry is not self-negation but self-gift, dedication, self-transcending obedience, and commitment to the cause of God. This is not self-negation but self-disposition. The only thing it negates is selfishness, an egoism or false pride and autonomy that do not correspond with the reality of the human condition. The easy confusion of these concepts helps convert some theologies of the cross into morbid, self-demeaning spiritualities of asceticism for its own sake, or worse, for self-improvement and merit. The positive object of self-disposition or dedication to God's values and what Jesus called the reign of God are left far behind.[24]

Paul's Second Adam and pioneer christology-soteriology draws a theology of the cross into itself.

This christology of Paul lays out a fundamental floor plan for much of his thinking. Some exegetes believe that this paradigm lies behind Paul's use of the christological hymn just discussed. The basic idea is

---

24. It has to be clear here that this is no polemic against kenotic christology, for that designation alone does not say much. What is addressed here is a clear abuse, which all know can exist because it has existed and continues to have an influence on too many Christian lives.

structurally simple but breathtaking in its scope. The parallelism between Jesus Christ and Adam is stated directly in this text from Romans: "Then as one man's trespass led to condemnation for all men, so one man's act of righteousness leads to acquittal and life for all men. For as by one man's disobedience many were made sinners, so by one man's obedience many will be made righteous" (Rom 5:18–19). By putting Adam and Jesus Christ in parallel, Paul keeps his christology close to history: the second Adam, like the first, is a human being. But Jesus is placed within a vast horizon that includes all creation and all of human history: he is the turning point for the human species, the pioneer that will begin and lead a new humanity from this point onward and reaching into the absolute future. It thus holds out Jesus as the model for a new humanity and more narrowly a Christian way of life.

Two specific elements of this christology bear direct relevance to the way a theology of the cross in all its negativity may be integrated into a soteriology that has direct bearing on the Christian life and devotion. The first point is the reference of this christology to the human person Jesus and the way he lived his life; the second is the theme of "recapitulation" that so influenced Irenaeus and Christian language after him.

First, the imaginative referent of this christology and soteriology is Jesus of Nazareth. In a way that reinforces this focus, the soteriology highlights Jesus' activity as a human being as precisely that which contrasts with the way Adam behaved. Moreover, this soteriology even pinpoints the specific actions of Jesus which save: Jesus is savior because of his obedience, his act of righteousness. Against the temptation to limit the saving activity of Jesus to a single righteous act of obedience in accepting his death, an anthropology such as Rahner's which was discussed earlier gives a more adequate account of where, anthropologically speaking, such an act of obedience could have come from. It must be seen as an integral part of a whole life's self-disposition and attitude that were continually played out in history and that led up to what is taken as a decisive point. In other words, the righteous obedience of his commitment to the kingdom of God that characterized Jesus' whole life and person is what stands in contrast to Adam. This was not constituted by passive virtues, but active; Jesus was not savior and pioneer by his quietism but by his activism in the sphere of God's reign in history. In a second Adam christology Jesus was not savior by being beaten up and executed, but by his active ministry all the way to death, even a death on the cross.

The second theme that has bearing on salvation and a theology of the cross is the theme of recapitulation. James Dunn says that Paul seems to suggest "a recapitulation or rerunning of the divine program for man in which the first Adam's destructive error was both refused and made good by the last Adam, thus opening the way for the fulfillment of God's purpose for man (cf. Heb 2:6–15)."[25] Earlier I alluded in passing to the fact that Irenaeus spontaneously inferred from this idea of recapitulation that Jesus should have lived out the full life cycle in order fully to sum up in himself what it means to be human.[26] But if Jesus did not recapitulate and draw up into his life the experience of growing old, what he did recapitulate in facing his painful execution is something still "more" in need of salvation. For absolutely nothing calls out for salvation more than innocent suffering and a seeming propensity among humans for violently killing the innocent or letting them die. Nothing more deeply challenges the coherence of human existence itself. This is what is "assumed" or "taken up" by Jesus' commitment to the kingdom of God.[27] But to think that this "acceptance" or "embrace" of suffering is something that Jesus wanted, or that God wanted for him, or that his acceptance of it made it in any way good, is absolutely to betray what is going on here. Jesus' death can only be understood as salvific dialectically; he died in his mission to negate the negation that suffering and death are. That he was punished and executed for doing so is itself an evil. What was and is salvific is that God raises this kind of life into life everlasting.

CONCLUSION

To sum up, these notes point to a theology of the cross in which Jesus' death remains the evil thing that it was. But it, his death, was saved by his resurrection because he was saved by his resurrection. Both Jesus and his death are saved dialectically. The meaninglessness of innocent suffering, in Jesus' case or generally, is not rendered meaningful; returning to

---

25. James D. G. Dunn, *Romans 1–8* (Dallas: Word Books, 1988), 297.
26. Jaroslav Pelikan, *The Christian Tradition,* I *The Emergence of the Catholic Tradition (100–600)* (Chicago: University of Chicago Press, 1971), 144.
27. The implicit reference is to the soteriological maxim, "what is not assumed, is not redeemed."

the absolute premise of this construction, Jesus' torture and execution are evil, not good, and they cannot be made into a good or made meaningful in themselves even by salvation. This scandalous negativity remains and gives salvation its dialectical character. But, from the perspective of history, Jesus' resurrection saves these negativities by promising a possibility of their meaningfulness in a higher and infinitely expanded context that lies in an absolute future and for which Jesus' resurrection is the earnest of hope. The principle, that God and not Jesus' death saves, remains intact. But through a dialectical logic, Jesus' actual physical torture and death become the media or instruments for God's revelation, dialectically, through a negative experience of contrast. Jesus' positive dedication to the kingdom of God was intensified when confronted by the highest possible challenge, the voluntary surrender of one's life. This is something that would not be as clear if Jesus had died of old age: it would have left open as a possibility that the lives of millions who suffer innocently and without relief and never reach old age but die unjustly before their time would stand outside the logic of Jesus' own life. Jesus' kenotic self-emptying, in the sense of complete self-dedication to the kingdom, is climaxed by God's exaltation of him, and this resurrection transforms even such a death, which is in itself meaningless and evil, into something meaningful, not in itself, but in his being raised by God.

This is a constructive theology of the cross. It assigns no positive or redemptive value to Jesus' suffering and death in themselves. The basic and fundamental cause of salvation is God acting in human life the way God acted in Jesus. Luke's portrait of Jesus' ministry clearly underlines how God as Spirit impels Jesus' fidelity to his vocation, even to the end. And God, creator and author of life, saves Jesus by raising him from death. This was revealed in the protracted Easter experience. This resurrection constitutes the salvation of Jesus, and thus too the salvation of his death. This actual resurrection of Jesus also represents the ultimate salvation that awaits all human beings, because Jesus is the new Adam, the pioneer, and first-born of many. Moreover, the revelation of this resurrection of Jesus and of all human beings also constitutes salvation in this world for those who become caught up in this faith. It gives hope and thus potential meaning for innocent suffering to all those who internalize the pattern of Jesus' life of resisting and combating such suffering in this world.

Chapter Five

CATHOLIC PLURALISM ON RELIGIOUS PLURALISM: RAHNER AND SCHILLEBEECKX

☙

THE ISSUES connected with pluralism, like the issues connected with the development of doctrine during the past two centuries, are generating a great deal of theological energy. Many different theological positions on the status of Jesus Christ relative to other religions and religious mediations compete for common acceptance. Many theologians have built typologies to map the terrain, so many different typologies that now one finds a pluralism of maps. Presuppositions make a great deal of difference on this issue, and the relation of positions to each other can be schematized in a variety of ways. For example, when a typology is laid out and positions are lined up, one should note the point of departure: does the development begin from the right or from the left? On the one hand, a theologian may presuppose a single normative Catholic theology on this question, and from there seek to open this position further toward some accommodation to religious pluralism. On the other hand, another theologian may simply accept a situation of a pluralism of religions and of christologies in relation to it but, rejecting relativism, seek to establish features about Jesus that are universally relevant and normative.

I shall try to thread my way between these alternatives with my definition of pluralism and the goal and strategy of this chapter. As to pluralism, I mean unity amid difference, or differences within a common field of shared faith, beliefs, and commitment. In other words, I use the term "pluralism" not to refer to sheer multiplicity, but to differences held together within some common bond of unity. As to my goal in this presentation I want to illustrate nonpolemically two types of

103

thinking that are quite different and that may be considered on the right
and the left side of some mythical center on this question. Perhaps they
relate to each other as late modern and postmodern. In any case, rather
than build types, I have chosen Karl Rahner and Edward Schillebeeckx
to illustrate these two different theological positions, both of which I
consider viable today.[1]

My strategy in representing these two theologians consists in drawing
a broad, schematic outline of the position of each thinker with the intention of drawing out the contrast between them. I also want to represent
their way of approaching the question as typical of two different methods and styles of theological reflection that obtain in Catholic theology
today, and to further suggest that they represent two distinct "gener-
ations" of theologians. Unfortunately this strategy does not allow an
adequate reconstruction of their arguments. I hope that those familiar
with either or both of these major Catholic thinkers of our time will fill
in the blanks and supply the nuances. Of course one should not forget
the many elements that bind them together, not least of which is a faith
and commitment to Jesus Christ as savior from God. The representation of their positions will demonstrate the many things they share in
common, but the point is to contrast them and thus demonstrate pluralism. I am not attempting to break new ground in this discussion, but
to make plain the current situation of Catholic theology and open it up
for discussion. The contrasting methods, styles, and positions of Rahner and Schillebeeckx represent many of the differences among Catholic
theologians today, so that charting their development and the structure
of their reasoning helps to explain the situation of Catholic theology.
By drawing out the logic and contrasting these two quite different ways
of approaching Jesus Christ and religious pluralism in the theologies of
the two most eminent Catholic theologians of the twentieth century, I
hope to demonstrate a plausible and legitimate pluralism on this question
within Catholic theology.

I will proceed as follows. In a first area, referred to as "life situation
and context," I briefly contrast the formation of each theologian and

---

1. I do not suggest here that these two positions exhaust the field. The two theologians are
chosen because of their stature and the depth and range of their theological production. Each
has generated in his turn a large, coherent world of theological understanding within which his
response to this particularly crucial problem is situated.

particularly their difference in age at the time of the Second Vatican Council and how they reacted to that council. In part two I outline two significantly different methods of theology. The third part contrasts in parallel their stances on doctrines that have a direct bearing on christology and the evaluation of other religions. And in part four I contrast their understanding of Christ and other religions.

LIFE SITUATION AND CONTEXT

I begin with a consideration of the life situation of Rahner and Schillebeeckx because their relative ages and periods of formation have significant bearing on the difference between the positions they developed.

Rahner

Karl Rahner was born in 1904 and in the course of his Jesuit formation and university training was schooled in philosophy and theology during the 1930s.[2] I will say more about his method in theology further on, but one can characterize him as a theologian who mediates Christian doctrine through philosophy. Rahner accepted the turn to the subject in metaphysics, as in the Kantian influenced philosophical work of Joseph Maréchal and the existential ontology of Martin Heidegger. One of the major problems, if not the central theological issue, that Rahner addressed in his work was extrinsicism, the pervasive supposition that God's initiative in revelation and grace comes completely unexpected from outside the human sphere.[3] Rahner's early works included a transcendental philosophical interpretation of Aquinas's theory of knowledge, a philosophy of religion, and articles that reinterpreted the scholastic theology of grace. One of Rahner's best known theological constructions, the "supernatural existential," proposes that from the very beginning, always, and everywhere human existence unfolds within the gracious and personal offer of God's self as saving grace. This grace at the time was called

---

2. Biographical data on Karl Rahner can be found in Herbert Vorgrimler, *Understanding Karl Rahner: An Introduction to His Life and Thought* (New York: Crossroad, 1986).

3. Maurice Blondel defined the term "extrinsicism" and the extrinsicist imagination in his essay "History and Dogma" in *The Letter on Apologetics and History and Dogma*, ed., trans., and introduction Alexander Dru and Illtyd Trethowan (New York: Holt, Rinehart and Winston, 1964), 226–31.

supernatural to plainly distinguish it from the order of creation and the suggestion that it might be owed or necessarily given. His discussions in these areas provided him with a point of view and a set of categories that remained fairly constant throughout his career. He thus possessed a broad framework within which his christology would neatly fit.

No event influenced Roman Catholicism and its theology in the twentieth century more than the Second Vatican Council. In many ways it stands as a watershed in Catholic history and life. A definite "before" and "after" Vatican II marks Catholic theology. When the council closed in 1965 Rahner was 61. His writings up to the council provided major resources for it, and after it concluded he continued to interpret the council in an aggressive, forward-looking way. One can delineate distinctive new elements in Rahner's later theology, but on the whole the structure of his thinking, which I will describe further on, did not change radically. One reason for this lies in its open transcendental character: it is able to absorb new developments into itself.

Schillebeeckx

Edward Schillebeeckx was born ten years after Rahner in 1914 and as a Dominican began his theological formation in the late 30s, pursued his studies through World War II, and completed them with a year in Paris and continuing work on a dissertation as he began teaching in Louvain in 1947.[4] His neo-Thomism also included a turn to the subject as found in the phenomenology of Merleau-Ponty and French personalism. In 1958 he moved from a seminary situation to the University of Nijmegen. He too participated in Vatican Council II as a *peritus*. In 1965, Schillebeeckx was fifty-one, in almost exact mid-career. But the historical forces that generated the council and the council itself impelled him toward a thoroughgoing transition which can almost be described as a reinvention of himself as a theologian. Over a period of several years during the late 1960s he immersed himself in the study of secularization, the historicity of human consciousness, hermeneutics, and critical theory, all of which contributed to the construction of a new set of presuppositions and a

---

4. Biographical data on Edward Schillebeeckx may be found in John Bowden, *Edward Schillebeeckx: In Search of the Kingdom of God* (New York: Crossroad, 1983) and Philip Kennedy, *Schillebeeckx* (Collegeville, Minn.: Liturgical Press, 1993).

distinctly new method of theology relative to the first phase of his writing. In many ways Schillebeeckx mirrors in his own person the change that was occurring within a large segment of Catholic theology itself.

Let me draw the contrast between these two theologians in this first topic. Without having the space or resources to develop the point here, I believe that the ten year difference in age of these two theologians made a significant difference in their future work after the Second Vatican Council. Other factors also played a part. But the fact is that while Rahner did not substantially alter the structure of his theological method Schillebeeckx did. Rahner remained consistently modern in his universally relevant transcendental method. He is quintessentially modern in addressing the problem of extrinsicism and, in overcoming it, providing an understanding of divine grace as a divine appeal within the human itself that can be understood by all. Schillebeeckx too began as a modern, but was so deeply affected by the problems of the absence of God, negativity and suffering, social oppression, pluralism, and historical relativism that they elicited the creation of what was for him a distinctly new method in theology. In many respects Schillebeeckx internalized many of the concerns which would later be called "postmodern."

METHOD IN THEOLOGY

Nothing carries more weight as a prerequisite for understanding a theology than the method of the theologian. Given this crucial importance, let me try to capture the contrast in the methods of these two theologians in concise and terse formulas that add up to no more than caricatures, but very different ones. Here more than ever I am offering broad interpretations of these theologians which stand in great need of added nuance. But the point lies in underlining the difference between the two theologians and bears no polemical intent.

Rahner

Rahner's transcendental method in theology can be characterized as a correlation between an analysis of the self-transcending structure of the human person and the doctrines given by the Christian tradition. Rahner generates the meaning of these doctrines by an analysis of their saving significance as that is actually or implicitly experienced in the human subject. In this way Rahner's method combines dialectically a dynamism "from below," provided by a transcendental existential anthropology and epistemology, and what comes "from above," as given by revelation and supplied through the tradition.

Rahner's method in theology presupposes the unity of the human race, a universal human structure, and the participation of each person in this formal a priori structure of nature and existence. Rahner also posits the theological premise drawn from scripture that God communicates God's self as Spirit, or light, or love, or grace to all humankind, every single person, for his or her salvation. This forges an existential unity of nature and grace, while preserving their distinction, and provides the platform for Rahner's use of phenomenological analysis of the human subject to discover and draw out the existential meaning of the doctrines and thus overcome extrinsicism. For example, God's initiative in grace does not stand over against the human but completes it by drawing the human spirit in knowledge and freedom out of and beyond the self toward transcendent fulfillment. Also, Rahner finds that Jesus of Nazareth is the Christ not because the divine Word stands over against the human, but because Jesus is constituted as "hypostatic union," the unity of Jesus of Nazareth and the divine Word as one subject. This union represents the fulfillment of the human as such, the archetypal unity of the divine with the human, and the human fully realized. Methodologically, therefore, the Christian message does not announce something alien to the human but is transcendent ratification of what was created for this end in the first place.[5]

Schillebeeckx

I turn now to the method of theology that Schillebeeckx employed after 1970.[6] It may be characterized as a historical method of critical correlation by which the data of Christian doctrines are mediated through a concern for the social historical conditions of human existence. Schillebeeckx does not completely dismiss transcendental analysis as is shown in his characterization of basic human trust and negative experiences of

---

5. The method of Karl Rahner is represented in his *Foundations of Christian Faith: An Introduction to the Idea of Christianity* (New York: Crossroad, 1994). One can see the logic as I've described it here in most general terms exemplified in the table of contents of the work.

6. See Mary Catherine Hilkert, "Hermeneutics of History: The Theological Method of Edward Schillebeeckx," *The Thomist* 51 (1987): 97–145.

contrast.[7] But he distinctly moves through these formal analyses to fix on the concrete negativities of human suffering and the frustration of human existence in various historical forms. This historical consciousness drove him to take up history and exegesis in order to reconstruct Jesus' ministry and the origins of christology. Thus he too combines elements which come "from below" and "from above," but the consistent framework within which they mingle lies in historical existence. For example, he refers to formal anthropological constants, but he derives these empirically from historical description rather than from an appeal to the a priori conditions of personal existence.[8] Also Schillebeeckx begins christology with Jesus of Nazareth who, he concludes in the first moment of his christology, is the parable of God in the way his ministry unfolded. Then, with a historical imagination in place, he traces the biblical testimony to resurrection and christology.

The contrast between these two theologians on method roughly mirrors the contrast between early and late Schillebeeckx, and it can be sharply drawn. The framework of Rahner's theological thinking is universal or total; it encompasses all human existence, although he became increasingly concerned with historical applications. Schillebeeckx's later theology is confessionally based in Christian faith, focuses on human suffering in history, but it reaches out toward universally relevant significance. Rahner breaks out of the trap of extrinsicism, but remains concerned with making sense of Chalcedon, hypostatic union, the appearance of the Christ in an evolutionary world. By contrast, Schillebeeckx, against the backdrop of historical existence, its contingency, suffering, and seemingly ultimate annihilation, mounts an apology for Christian faith by telling the story of Jesus and interpreting his resurrection as grounds for hope in the future. Rahner tends to accept doctrines as a given and then goes to work reinterpreting them; Schillebeeckx tends to do a critical historical archeology of their genesis. Rahner's transcendental method is smooth and stresses the continuity of human existence and Christian doctrine; Schillebeeckx's historical method attends more to

---

7. These ideas are developed during what may be called the middle period of Schillebeeckx's theology. He writes of them in *God the Future of Man* (New York: Sheed & Ward, 1968) and *The Understanding of Faith: Interpretation and Criticism* (New York: Seabury Press, 1974). These are universal structures of experience in human existence.

8. Edward Schillebeeckx, *Christ: The Experience of Jesus as Lord* (New York: Seabury Press, 1980), 731–43.

negativity, inequality, and the jagged character of human development. These two methods are not contradictory; one might even make an argument for their complementarity. But in themselves they are significantly different, and they lead in different directions.

PREMISES TO THEIR POSITIONS

I move now to what I call premises to the positions of each theologian on Christ and other religions. These premises consist in various theological stances on doctrines which directly influence an appreciation of Jesus Christ and the status of other religions. To accentuate the differences here I will line up the doctrinal themes and contrast Rahner and Schillebeeckx on each one. I have, in fact, drawn these themes mainly from Rahner where they are related systematically, and I make the contrast by drawing Schillebeeckx into the framework of Rahner's thought.

Trinity

"Trinity" is the name of a doctrine about God and not a name for God.[9] Rahner carefully crafted a theology of the immanent trinity. Other trinitarian theologians frequently quote his use of the Barthian axiom that the economic trinity is the immanent trinity, an axiom which forbids disjunction between the two dimensions of this mystery. In the economy of salvation the Son and the Spirit are like the two arms of God in the one personal self-communication to and embrace of humankind: the Son or Logos having become flesh in Jesus of Nazareth, and the Spirit being the self-communication of God to all humankind in grace. The distinction of "persons" within the Godhead is real, just as the distinction of God's self-communication in Jesus, which can only be the incarnation of the Son, is really different from the general communication of God as Spirit. The former self-communication of God as Son involves

---

9. "Trinity" is the name of a doctrine about God that developed in the course of the fourth century. Nowhere in the Bible is God called "trinity" in the way God is called Yahweh or, by Jesus, Father. Rather, various metaphors in the Bible, such as "Spirit," "Word," "Wisdom," and others are used to express and characterize ways in which God is experienced in the world and in the life of the religious community. It is good to recognize that "trinity" is not a name of God but a theological interpretation and doctrine about God so that the doctrinal status of this language be clear: it is derived specifically from two symbols that record the way the Jewish and early Christian communities expressed their experience of God present and at work "economically" in their lives. See chapter 8 for more discussion of these symbols.

hypostatic union, the latter self-communication of God as Spirit is not hypostatic union but a presence of God to human beings by what Rahner calls quasi-formal causality. This represents God's real personal presence which, unlike a created form, does not constitute a being or quality as such but is a divine self-communication or offering.[10] Rahner postulates that there is no real distinction between God communicating God's self in this threefold pattern of creation, incarnation, and sanctifying self-gift as Spirit and the essential character of God's own reality.

Interestingly, Schillebeeckx has no developed theology of the trinity. Schillebeeckx confesses belief in the reality of the immanent trinity, but provides no indication whether his failure to develop a theology of the trinity is just something he never took up or a matter of principle. In other words, whereas one can say that Rahner's theology of the trinity is both a premise and a context as well as a conclusion to his christology, one cannot say whether a doctrine of the trinity is operative in Schillebeeckx's later christology at all, nor whether this is systematically deliberate or not. But it is consonant with his christology from below which, by beginning with a consideration of Jesus of Nazareth, does not begin with a doctrine of the trinity but regards this doctrine as something that developed out of christology.

Nature and Grace

I return again to the issue of the relationship between nature and grace because it provides a fundamental framework for understanding the economy of God's dealing with human beings and their response, and because of the contrast between the language of Rahner and Schillebeeckx on this topic. Rahner's major contribution to Catholic theology in this crucial area consisted in overcoming an extrinsicist understanding of a supernatural intervention of God, while at the same time preserving the transcendent and utterly gracious character of God's salvation. He did this with a simultaneous distinction between the natural and supernatural orders of creation and redemption and an affirmation of their intimate unity. Finite creation is created for salvation. Creation or nature or more simply human beings, while possessing a certain autonomy, have always existed within the actual offer of God's supernatural love

---

10. Rahner, *Foundations*, 116–22.

and self-gift, so that in fact nature and grace are inseparable orders and existentials. Rahner supported this vision of reality with a metaphysical distinction of a twofold "relation" of God to humankind by the efficient causality of creation and the quasi-formal causality of self-presence or gift of divine self. This distinction preserved both God's freedom and human freedom for a real dialogical relationship. But the contribution of Rahner lay equally in the inseparable and intrinsic unity of these two orders.

The contrast with Schillebeeckx at this point remains subtle, undeveloped, but in many ways crucial. In his later theology Schillebeeckx does not discuss the issue of nature and supernatural grace in the terms laid out by neo-scholasticism. By contrast he does discuss the theology of creation and the creator in terms that include within creation itself the saving love and intention of the creator. In other words, Schillebeeckx collapses the discussion of nature and grace into the theology of creation itself. But this does not amount to a reduction of God's grace or self-communication to necessity; he employs the terms of personalism and proposes a personal creator who creates out of love. Freedom, gratuity, and love are built into the creative act itself and do not have to be distinguished from it.

The prominence of Schillebeeckx's doctrine of creation allows him to make moves that avoid certain problems that in the past had encumbered Catholic theology. First, he bypasses completely the possible dualisms that the "natural/supernatural" distinction tends to foster. These were discussed earlier.[11] It was noted that Rahner too overcame this problem with a more complex construction of the "supernatural existential." Schillebeeckx encompasses Rahner's view in his notion of creation. Thus, second, Schillebeeckx conceptually simplifies the relationship between God as creator-savior and humankind. The creator God is savior; God as savior is creator. The very idea that these are two different kinds of actions of God is eliminated before it becomes a problem that has to be solved. Third, Schillebeeckx's turn to the doctrine of creation encourages a theocentric point of view for understanding the person and role of Jesus Christ.[12] I will draw this out further on in this essay.

---

11. See chapter 3, pp. 56–57.
12. Schillebeeckx's theology of creation and its bearing on salvation is concisely analyzed by Dorothy Jacko, *Salvation in the Context of Contemporary Secularized Historical Consciousness: The*

Universal Offer of Salvation

The idea that God offers salvation to all human beings is actually a major premise that Rahner supports with considerations of the Old and New Testaments.[13] Its importance appears negatively when contrasted with traditions maintaining a restricted order of salvation, and positively in the role it plays in explaining the salvation mediated by Jesus Christ. Schillebeeckx shares this conviction.

The Salvation Mediated by Jesus

This point and the next draw near to the heart of the matter, and one can begin to see method and premises coming together in a distinct systematic vision in each thinker. The issue here concerns the broad lines of each theologian's theory of redemption.

Rahner conceives of Jesus as the event in history that fulfills or brings to completion the history of God's self-communication for human salvation. It is not that grace or God's offer of saving love had been absent from the world prior to Jesus Christ. But the decisive, definitive, final, and as it were total self-communication to humankind occurred in the hypostatic union of the Son or divine Logos with human nature in Jesus of Nazareth and Jesus' human response. All of God's being-present to and with human beings finds its completion and fulfillment and archetypal goal in Jesus Christ whom God intended from the beginning. Jesus really is the center and keystone of Rahner's overarching and total vision of creation and the dialogue between God and human beings in history. For Rahner, the reality of the relationship between God and human beings was altered in the event of Jesus Christ. What began as promise and was offered provisionally in the course of history up to Jesus became definitively and publicly ratified or sealed in the Jesus event.

Schillebeeckx's redemption theory appears modest relative to the expansive cosmic vision of Rahner; he brings a reader down to earth. In fact, Schillebeeckx does not want to make a distinction between a theory of how Jesus saves and the actual salvation that he mediates in history. But forcing what he does say of how Jesus saves into these categories, it appears that Jesus saves by revealing and actualizing God at work for

---

Later Theology of Edward Schillebeeckx (Ph.D. Dissertation, Toronto: University of St. Michael's College, Toronto School of Theology, 1987), 83–136.

13. Rahner, *Foundations,* 142–52.

human salvation in history. The creator God has always been saving from the very beginning, so that what occurs in Jesus is a revelation of what has always been going on. He also proposes a traditional exemplarism through which Jesus provides a God-given model of who God is and what it means to be human. In other words, as in Rahner, salvation went on before Jesus and goes on outside his overt historical influence. But Schillebeeckx makes no appeal to a metahistorical role of Jesus as the final cause of God's universal and efficacious love of human beings; historically Jesus saves where he saves, where people actually come under his influence. Compared with Rahner, these theological conclusions also constitute serious religious claims, but they stay closer to the ground.

Jesus the Universal Cause of Salvation

Focusing even more pointedly on the role and place of Jesus Christ in the salvation that God offers to humankind, one should not forget three positions which Rahner defends and which are all of a piece. The first is the traditional claim that all grace is the grace of Christ. No grace or salvation comes from God that is not christic or mediated by Christ. The main logic for Rahner's understanding of this comes from its being integral to the whole vision that includes a trinitarian God. The creator is the triune God, who creates through the Son and in view of the incarnation. But, secondly, Rahner also holds that the facticity of the historical life of Jesus plays a role in the salvation of all, including especially the active surrender of Jesus on the cross. Jesus' historical acting out of the divine self-communication and his total positive response to it constitute the unity between God and human existence in himself that is the very goal toward which all saving grace was oriented as toward its fulfillment or climax. And, thirdly, since such a divine movement can have only one goal or climax, there can be only one incarnation of the Logos. The incarnation of the Son in Jesus could happen only once, and it is thus the absolute fulfillment of God's saving will toward which all other experiences of grace in history are oriented as to their climactic realization.

In contrast to Rahner's large and encompassing vision, Schillebeeckx begins with Jesus. His method leaves him dealing with Jesus as part of human history which is also a history of salvation. His historical focus in a christology from below leads him to consider Jesus, first, as the savior of Christians, and then to examine his universal relevance, without moving to the more abstract or general level of metaphysical characterization. I am not aware of Schillebeeckx denying that all grace is the grace of Christ or that the Logos could only become incarnate once. But his overall christology and view of other world religions do not fit with such claims.

In sum, this survey of certain key doctrinal areas enables one to see how logically the methods adopted by each thinker, and the way they construe certain basic issues surrounding christology proper, inevitably lead them in different directions. I referred earlier to Rahner's theology having a component that begins "from below" in an analysis of transcendental human existence. But it also derives from the acceptance of authoritative doctrines that constitute the pervasive context of his thinking. Trinity, the cosmic framework in which he understands what occurred in the event of Jesus, and the universal causal role that Jesus plays in salvation add up to a relatively tight metaphysical vision of all reality and the human phenomenon in it. By comparison, Schillebeeckx's thinking stays closer to historical data, from its starting point in Jesus to its claims regarding the impact of Jesus' saving action. Jesus mediates salvation, but the question of whether Jesus causes the salvation of all is almost precluded by the historical boundaries that contain Schillebeeckx's imagination. I now want to draw the conclusions of these two diverging ways of theological reflection on the case study in point, the relation between Jesus Christ and the mediations of salvation in other world religions.

CHRIST AND OTHER RELIGIONS

We arrive at the fourth and last point of this discussion of comparative constructive theology. How does each theologian understand Jesus Christ in his relation to other religions, and the status of other religions relative to him? I shall not deal with the christological problem in the terms of Chalcedon although both theologians have something to say on that. I restrict my remarks to more general issues by summarizing Rahner's view of Christ and the other religions in three points and considering Schillebeeckx in contrast with these.

Rahner[14]

The first feature defining Rahner's position on the relation of Christ to all other religions and media of God's salvation resides in his christocentric vision of the whole of reality. It is not simply that Rahner's faith finds its mediating focus in Jesus Christ; such is true of all Christians because it defines what a Christian is. It is rather that Rahner's objective conceptualization of the cosmos is trinitarian in a way that places Christ at the center. Christ provides the lens from which everything is understood because, in the metaphysical scheme of things, Christ is the keystone of overarching reality. Metaphysically, Christ the Son is the beginning of reality as the medium and goal of God creating, the middle or center of human history by his incarnation, and the end of human history as representing its final or eschatological goal in resurrection.

Second, within this grand metaphysical vision, other religions are truly valid and willed by God, but their liceity or continued being willed by God is conditional upon the nonexistence or nonpromulgation of the revelation of Jesus Christ. Relative to a full acceptance of religious pluralism this view may seem narrow, but Rahner proposed it first against Christian exclusivism, and in that context it is genuinely expansive; the religions play a real saving role in the lives of their constituents. Moreover, the condition that Rahner postulates for the liceity of other religions, namely, the lack of an objective promulgation of Christianity, could be broadly interpreted within Rahner's framework in terms of a real existential availability, that is, that Christianity be a concretely viable option, which for most non-Christians it is not. Therefore, relative to the availability of salvation and the possible mediation of salvific grace in other religions, Rahner's position is open to a fairly broad interpretation. But it remains the case that the religions themselves are interpreted intrinsically within an objective christological framework.

Third, therefore, the world's religions do not enjoy theological autonomy. When located within Rahner's conception of the role of Christ and the place of the Christian phylum in human history, the grace mediated by other religions is really the grace of Christ. Jesus Christ is thus actually constitutive of the salvation which, on a historical level, may concretely

---

14. One can find the essentials of Rahner's position on Christ and other world religions in Karl Rahner, "Christianity and Non-Christian Religions," *Theological Investigations* 5 (New York: Seabury, 1974), 115–34, and *Foundations,* 311–21.

be mediated by any given non-Christian religion. One can say that Jesus Christ is the cause of the salvation that occurs in the lives of people who live their religious lives within other religions.[15] Jesus of Nazareth is the incarnation of God in an absolutely unique way that is qualitatively different than the presence and effectiveness of God in other religious mediators. Such an incarnation could happen only once, and its occurrence makes Christianity God's own religion, so to speak, in an absolute way. Absoluteness here means that everything else is related to it, and it entails the logic that the religions are in themselves lacking and bear within themselves an orientation toward being completed by Christianity. All religions are related to Christianity as to their fulfillment. Thus Rahner recognizes a de facto pluralism of religions, but not pluralism in principle. Religious pluralism is something that is anomalous and in principle should be overcome.

Schillebeeckx[16]

Lining up the parallel but contrasting positions on Schillebeeckx's part, we can begin with his overall vision of reality as being theocentric. Schillebeeckx reappropriates the doctrine of creation, and he sets up the two doctrines of creation and eschatology to form the framework for a theology of history.[17] Consistent with this, his christology from below begins with the historical person of Jesus and not with trinity nor the metaphysics of nature and grace. Thus Christ is not portrayed as the center of Schillebeeckx's cosmology. That position belongs to God, creator

---

15. Rahner explains this causality not simply on the ground of finality and the orientation of the religions to the manifestation of what is going on in them in the Christ event, and not simply in the single incarnation and hypostatic union of the Son in Jesus of Nazareth, but also historically in the response of Jesus to God's self-communication as Word. In a sense the hypostatic union and the saving event are not finally complete until Jesus' complete yes to God in the acceptance of his death. See Karl Rahner, "The One Christ and the Universality of Salvation," *Theological Investigations* 16 (New York: Seabury, 1979), 199–224.

16. One can find the essentials of Schillebeeckx's position on Christ and other world religions in Edward Schillebeeckx, "The Religions and the Human Ecumene," in *The Future of Liberation Theology: Essays in Honor of Gustavo Gutiérrez,* ed. M. E. Ellis and O. Maduro (Maryknoll, N.Y.: Orbis Books, 1989), 177–88, and Schillebeeckx, *Church: The Human Story of God* (New York: Crossroad, 1990), 159–86. Schillebeeckx's position is concisely analyzed by Diane Steele, *Creation and Cross in the Later Soteriology of Edward Schillebeeckx* (Ph.D. Diss., Notre Dame, Ind.: University of Notre Dame Press, 2000), 252–294.

17. I draw this conclusion not only from Schillebeeckx's performance, but also from the section in the Christ book where he provides a schematic outline for his theological vision. See Schillebeeckx, *Christ,* 629–44.

of heaven and earth and the goal of the movement of history. Schille-beeckx's large vision of reality is theocentric. I should not, however, give the impression that Schillebeeckx has counter-assertions to each of the elements of Rahner's christocentrism; he does not emphasize that his vision is theocentric, for in other ways, as with all Christians, his *faith* in God and appropriation of God are mediated by Jesus of Nazareth and thus christocentric. It is important to keep this distinction already alluded to in mind: Christian faith in God is by definition christocentric because it is faith in God mediated by Jesus. But this does not neces-sarily translate into a christocentric vision of reality. For example, Jews and Christians relate to the same God and share elements of a common body of scriptures and revelation, but Jews are not christocentric in their worldview and many Christians are not as well.

Second, all religions are finite, none are absolute; even Christianity is mediated historically through the finite creature Jesus of Nazareth. Schillebeeckx works with the traditional principle that God is transcen-dent infinity, so that God's absoluteness cannot be contained without remainder in any finite piece of created reality nor the whole of it. Uniqueness does not mean absoluteness despite the fact that unique-ness and absoluteness tend to be confused. Thinking within the context of historicity, Schillebeeckx understands that all religions share a mea-sure of particularity, individuality, and autonomy. When they are taken together in a theocentric framework, on Christian principles of the uni-versality of grace and God's saving will, one must think that there is more revelation in many religions including Christianity than there could be in only one.[18] The uniqueness of religions refers to their historical individu-ality and particularity, a logic that also applies to the uniqueness of Jesus Christ. More practically, and referring to a growing general conscious-ness, Schillebeeckx makes a point of saying that in today's world one cannot affirm the superiority of one religion over another. Many factors converge to call the a priori superiority of one religion over another into question. Globalization, a sense of the radical character of historicity and pluralism, a sense of how religion defines a culture and a people, and life together on the planet, all make the doctrine of the superiority of one

---

18. "As a consequence of all this we can, may and must say that there is more religious truth in all the religions together than in one particular religion, and that this also applies to Christianity." Schillebeeckx, *Church*, 166.

religion over others the equivalent of a declaration of war.[19] One has to take account of the intrinsic ethical implications of doctrinal views.

Third, other religions according to Schillebeeckx are valid or legitimate in principle. I take the phrase "in principle" to mean that the fact of religious pluralism is a good. This view derives from a historical consciousness that recognizes the limited character of every religion relative to ultimate reality itself. All religions are particular, autonomous, and unique; and religions other than Christianity do not take their value from their anonymously mediating what has been effected by Jesus Christ and what is on that basis contained in Christianity. The fundamental issue that Christian theology should address in this matter relates primarily to its own self-understanding, that is, relative to Jesus Christ, in such a way that it protects the autonomy of the other religions rather than absorbing them into itself. In Schillebeeckx's theology this is achieved by interpreting Jesus Christ not as constitutive of the salvation that is mediated by other religions but as the mediator of specifically Christian salvation and more generally as revelatory of the character of salvation as such. On the one hand, Christian revelation and salvation are universally relevant because the God revealed in Jesus is the creating and redeeming God of all. On the other hand, that same God is present to the world religions independently of Jesus.[20] Religious pluralism in principle, in Schillebeeckx's view of human history, does not have a negative valence. He is quite explicit on the point that it cannot and should not be overcome. "From all this I learn that (even in the Christian self-understanding) the multiplicity of religions is not an evil which needs to be removed, but rather a wealth which is to be welcomed and enjoyed by all."[21]

Summing up this contrast between Rahner's and Schillebeeckx's appraisal of Christ and the religions, one could say that Rahner's is a totalizing view of Christianity. He gives less play to the concrete unfolding of history in its particularity.[22] His christocentrism relates all other religions to Christianity as their fulfillment. Schillebeeckx too has

19. Edward Schillebeeckx, "The Uniqueness of Christ and the Interreligious Dialogue," Address to the Catholic Academy in Munich (April 22, 1997), 4, 16–17, of a manuscript in English translation.

20. Schillebeeckx, "The Religions and the Human Ecumene," 183–84.

21. Schillebeeckx, *Church*, 167.

22. Johann Baptist Metz, *Faith in History and Society: Toward a Practical Fundamental Theology* (New York: Seabury Press, 1980), 163–65.

a totalized view of reality, but the worldview does not revolve exclusively around Jesus Christ. His is a Christian vision of God as creator of heaven and earth, and a theology of history leading to eschatological fulfillment. Jesus is universally relevant in revealing that eschatological fulfillment in the kingdom of God, but other religions are autonomous; they too contain revelation and do not necessarily relate to him as their fulfillment.

CONCLUSION

As a conclusion to this exercise in comparative theology I wish to submit the proposal that, as different as these two positions are from each other, they are both acceptable or valid, at least at this time. Let me first draw out how different these two christologies are and then take up the question of how they can live together in a pluralistic situation within one church.

The differences between Rahner and Schillebeeckx on the question of Christ and other religions are quite dramatic, and this can be illustrated by reviewing their contrasting stances on foundational conceptions. First, although Rahner proceeds methodologically from below in some respects, which were mentioned earlier, his theology on this issue is really controlled by an imagination that also works "from above," specifically by his reliance on the doctrine of the immanent trinity. By contrast, Schillebeeckx argues consistently from below and within a framework of history and historical consciousness. But his method is far from reductionistic, and he is not lacking in metaphysical and transcendental principles. Second, Rahner proposes a christocentric vision in which Jesus Christ is the absolute bringer of God's salvation. The descending incarnation of the Logos which occurred in Jesus can happen only once. By contrast Schillebeeckx works within a theocentric framework in which Jesus is the bringer of God's absolute salvation; he nowhere limits the decisive saving presence of God in history to a single event. Third, Rahner accepts religious pluralism in fact but not in principle. The religions actually mediate God's salvation, but in his metahistory, with the coming of Christ, they no longer should exist but should find their fulfillment in Jesus Christ. Schillebeeckx, by contrast, accepts religious pluralism in principle. His historical consciousness recognizes that the pluralism and fragmentation of history suggest that the same God's saving presence can be mediated differently and independently in different religions. These are two significantly different christological conceptions of the person of Jesus Christ in relation to other religions.

Without passing judgment on these theological stances of Rahner and Schillebeeckx, I can address the place where each will appear vulnerable to critiques from the other side. First, relative to Rahner: the weakness of his position when viewed from the pluralist quarter concerns its intelligibility. The pressure appears in his dogmatic insistence that Jesus is the absolute savior while all other religions are relative and inferior to Christianity. This looks like simple dogmatism and Christian imperialism or self-assertion in a de facto pluralistic world. In response, I believe that Rahner still expresses the faith of the majority of Christians on this point. Also, one can remain within his position and at the same time soften the absoluteness of Christ by raising up other religions toward a more autonomous status.[23]

Second, relative to Schillebeeckx: when people view his pluralist position from the perspective of theologies that have controlled the field since the period of the christological councils, they will likely question its fidelity to scripture and tradition; the tradition seems to affirm the absoluteness of Jesus Christ which Schillebeeckx questions. In response, it is crucial to recognize that his granting autonomous validity to other religions in no way undermines the high christology established at Nicaea and Chalcedon. This fallacy is actually quite common: theologians enter the list on the basis of an adversarial framework, as though what God does in one place competes with what God does in another. But affirming that God acts in other religions independently of Jesus in no way minimizes what God has done in Christ. Therefore, while Schillebeeckx expresses the faith of a minority of Christians today, they are a significant minority and on the increase both in Africa and Asia where there is greater familiarity and appreciation of other religions, as well as in the West as formerly Christian nations increasingly become religiously pluralistic.

---

23. This has been done by Jacques Dupuis in his *Toward a Christian Theology of Religious Pluralism* (Maryknoll, N.Y.: Orbis Books, 1979). I take Dupuis to be expressing an essentially Rahnerian position, but with new emphases, especially relative to the doctrine of the trinity, by drawing out in a more explicit way how God, as Christians speak about God, can be understood to be working in other religions and the whole world outside the Christian sphere.

Finally, what can be said about the validity and viability of both of these positions? Can they both coexist in one church? I am not sure whether one could find a knock-down proof of the viability of both of these positions, but I can suggest two arguments that explain why it may be possible to consider them as being able to coexist in one church.

The first argument rests on the distinction between theology and Christian faith. What holds the Christian community together is not a common theology but a common faith. Both of these theological positions are grounded in a common Christian faith which they try to render intelligible in the circumstances of the world today. That faith is faith in God as God has been revealed in the ministry and person of Jesus of Nazareth, understood to be the Christ. Jesus in Christian faith is sacrament or symbol of God, making God present and revealed for our salvation, and thus the object of worship. Both positions are based in this faith and bring it to expression in an uncompromising way.

The second argument appeals to the discipline of theology and its criteria: both theological positions possess a coherent, comprehensive, and integral character. By their coherence I mean that each theologian operates with a distinct method of theology and a broad range of intelligible and traditional premises, and each systematically generates a holistic view of things. By comprehensive I mean that each thinker has a broad sweeping view of reality in which his particular theological position on this matter is a part. Their positions on this issue are not erratic but are consistent with broader plausible interpretations of Christianity that in turn support their particular theses. And by integral I mean that each has conformed to the general formal rules of theological method for generating a valid conclusion: their theological conclusions are faithful to scripture, intelligible in our world today, and generative of Christian life. One can also add another dimension to these qualities: they are recognized as such by others. Each position has a constituency which more or less resonates with each construct.

In conclusion, then, a consideration of the two significantly different christologies of Rahner and Schillebeeckx seems to show that a real pluralism of such theologies of religion is possible and even desirable within a single Christian church.

Chapter Six

JESUS AND CHURCH MISSION

༑

S INCE THE 1960s the number of vocations to a permanent mission-ary life in other lands has steadily declined. There is no single reason to account for this change in Catholic missionary activity. Many factors both in North America and in the countries receiving missionaries feed into a changing situation. It is part of a larger pattern of decline in candidates for priesthood and religious life. We are witnessing a major shift in religious self-understanding and behavior that began after World War II and the Second Vatican Council. These changes should not be counted negative in all respects. For example, it does not necessarily im-ply a lack of religious fervor. There are other agencies, some of them secular, that mediate temporary and longer commitment to service in other lands. Many religious congregations have lay associate programs which attract a good number of volunteers. Catholic colleges and uni-versities also sponsor service programs abroad. Many formerly mission churches have assumed missionary responsibility for their own areas and beyond. But after acknowledging the complexity of the movement dur-ing the last half of the twentieth century, one must admit that something profound is influencing permanent religious vocations in North America to foreign missionary life.

In 1967, when I was a theology student at Woodstock College in Maryland, the school sponsored an ecumenical and interreligious conference on missions which was attended by some of the leading missi-ologists in the United States and from around the world. Jean Daniélou, S.J. gave the keynote address in which he outlined the missionary man-date, the nature of mission, and its goals.[1] Daniélou offered a purely dogmatic account of the grounds or foundations of the mission of the

---

1. Jean Daniélou, "The Missionary Nature of the Church," *The Word in the Third World,* ed. James P. Cotter (Washington: Corpus Books, 1967), 11–22.

church. The mission of the church is rooted in the mission of the Son and Spirit within the Godhead and the missionary mandate of the risen Jesus as depicted at the end of Matthew's gospel. The goal of mission is to establish the church in other lands and to convert all people to Jesus Christ. A further goal is the christianization of society and culture. The parousia waits upon the spread of the gospel to all nations. Presupposed in all of this is that the church is the ordinary means of salvation and that all people are called to be Christian.

This more or less standard view of the nature and goal of Christian mission in its church-centered and Catholic form of that time reflects some classical themes that will underlie any understanding of it. The Christian movement is expansive, reaching out to all, because Jesus and the God he reveals are universally relevant. The church should be a sign to all the nations and thus is called to be so set up as to be visibly recognized as a public institution in every land. But the grounds on which this missiology was laid out by Daniélou in 1967 have been thoroughly eroded; scarcely a single point in it has not been questioned or qualified today as it was beginning to be questioned even then. It is not that Daniélou got it all wrong. But in the years since the Second Vatican Council developments in North American society, in the world, in intellectual culture, and in theology have made his theology of mission incredible today.

It is not my intention to show that the erosion of the credibility of the theology of mission since the Second Vatican Council is the reason for the steady decline in missionary vocations. As was said above, social changes of this sort can rarely be explained by a single cause. But the two developments, the one behavioral and the other theoretical, are part of the same complex historical phenomenon. They are not unrelated. A theology of mission represents in theoretical terms the language and perceptions of a given community at a given time. I take it that Daniélou's theology was an expression of the broad common consciousness of the community at large just at the time when it was beginning to change. By contrast, what is the theological basis for mission in our time?

The aim of this essay is to discuss the problem of the foundations of mission from the point of view of theology.[2] The particular issue that

---

2. At this point I should express a number of reservations and qualifications about this project. There are others far more competent than myself in missiology and the theology of missions, not to mention missionaries themselves, who would shed a great deal more light on this whole

this essay addresses has two dimensions. First, the standard conception of the nature and goal of missionary activity, that which was partly responsible for generating missionary vocations prior to the 1960s, has gradually been undermined and is no longer viable. In the first part of this essay I outline some reasons for that development. The second part of the essay will be an attempt at a constructive reinterpretation of the grounds and goals for mission. But this must be done within the context of the very factors which have subverted the former theology. In other words, the same developments that have undone the earlier theology of mission provide resources for a new and revitalized notion of mission which is relevant to our situation today. Therefore an appreciation of the constructive theology is conditional upon a recognition of the elements of our situation today that have signaled and mediated the change.

DEVELOPMENTS SINCE VATICAN II

Much has happened in the world, in the church, and in the discipline of theology since the Second Vatican Council that has a bearing upon world mission. Rather than present a chronicle of that development, I have chosen five themes that have an immediate bearing upon how one understands the missionary activity of the church. Since most people are aware of these developments, my point is not to explain them but simply to raise them up as the premises for the constructive understanding presented in the second part of the essay. The five areas are globalization, postmodernity, christological developments, a new consciousness about religious pluralism, and the idea of dialogue. Many of these themes have been touched upon or developed in earlier chapters of this book; they intersect with each other and, from a certain perspective, constitute aspects of the new situation of the church in the world. Together they constitute a kairos, a critical situation ready for a new historical development that is actually underway.

---

problem. It will be apparent that I am carving out a very narrow segment of the discussion. My goal is to bring the resources of recent developments in theology, more specifically in christology, to bear on the question of the theological foundations of mission as that is expressed in the relation between Jesus and mission.

A New Global Situation

The peoples of the earth are becoming interdependent and united in a new and unprecedented way, especially since the breakdown of the Soviet block in 1989.[3] Many factors are contributing to this process of globalization: the triumph of liberal capitalism as the ruling economic ideology, the technologies of travel and communication, the migration of peoples. The ever increasing dynamism toward the unity of the world, or "one world," carries with it a number of polarities or tensions that unfold concretely in the lives of countless people in different ways, and yet they may be generalized.

One tension is between the local and the global. More and more the one world must be regarded as polycentric. Whereas the natural tendency of any region or culture is to draw the world-map around itself at the center and to regard the rest of the world through that lens, the reality is becoming more like a balance of powers and influences. The economic, technological, and popular cultural power of the Western nations and cultures must be careful not to alienate their clients. Less developed nations live in a tension between affection for Western goods and alienation by Western values and norms that can destroy local cultures. To the self-consciously globalized world, despite the fact that its numerical strength now lies outside the Western world, the Christian church still appears to be a Western religion. And it is tainted with an imperialist past.

The tension between the local and the global also appears within the church itself. The church has become in a new way a world-church which is trying to sink firm roots in African and Asian cultures. As a communion of local churches around the world, the church continually experiences various tensions between the center and the periphery, between what is common to the whole church and what is local and indigenous. A major problem in one part of the church may not exist in another, and the solution to it may cause a major problem in another part of the world if it were universalized. Because the authority, wealth, and cultural strength of the Catholic church still lies in the West, the tension between the center and the periphery will inevitably increase.

---

3. Robert J. Schreiter, *The New Catholicity: Theology between the Global and the Local* (Maryknoll, N.Y.: Orbis Books, 1997) describes the new situation of Christianity in the world in broad clear strokes.

Another tension that divides our contemporary world is rooted in the division between the rich and the poor. Whole groups of people appear to be trapped in destitution and injustice as national governments in underdeveloped areas become poorer and less able to cope, and the nations of the developed world grow richer. The Christian cannot look out on the world and accept a policy of survival of the fittest. The human race has begun a new existence in world-solidarity that demands a planetary conception of the common good. The themes of liberation theology are not passé but find a new relevance with an ever more massive urgency.

Yet another area of tension can be identified when one considers the church in relation to other religions on the world stage. When one attends to the whole church around the world, it cannot be viewed in itself, in isolation, so to speak. The church is no longer the exclusive religion in any particular region. The church now exists in an explicitly pluralistic worldwide context as one religion interacting with others. In other words, the regional isolation of all the religions is breaking down. This sets up a situation in which two forces pull against each other: maintenance of firm Christian identity as a distinctive religion over against being reduced to the status of one religion among the others. The tension is genuinely ambivalent. On the one hand the situation seems to undermine the identity of Christianity insofar as it has been conceived as the one true religion. On the other hand, the new situation opens the way for Christianity to become truly catholic in the sense of embracing all cultures as genuinely other and as such both distinctive and theoretically open to receive Christianity. Inculturation thus ironically entails striving to be a partner with other religions in the non-Western cultures which they dominate.

The new global situation could be described at greater length. However, one thing is clear: any description today will no longer exactly apply in twenty-five years. Christianity now exists in a world that is rapidly changing.

A New Postmodern Culture

A number of characteristics point to a new intellectual culture that has been developing alongside the forces that have increasingly unified the world. The referent of the term "postmodernity" is what might be called the "thought-world" that is in some measure shared in the intellectual capitals of the world. In calling this culture "postmodern," I am not claiming that Western or world culture has passed a threshold beyond modernity. Rather I use the term to call attention to aspects of our shared consciousness that appear new. Four characteristics of the way educated people view the world today seem to be typically, and in some respects distinctively, postmodern.[4]

Postmodernity entails, first, a radical *historical consciousness*. By this I mean a loss of a clear sense of a *telos* in history and of organic development, and a feeling that human existence is simply adrift, in an utterly contingent or arbitrary way, subject only to the inner forces of nature and history itself. By comparison modernity seemed much more confident that it could remain within the framework of the universally human in its exercise of critical thinking. Evolution seemed to entail progressive development. It had a better hold of the universal aspects of the human as such. Postmodernity is suspicious of universal premises or suppositions as foundations for criticism. The individuality, particularity, and differences of the historical moment have grabbed the attention of postmodern consciousness.[5]

Second, postmodernity involves a critical *social consciousness*. The human subject of the Enlightenment, the autonomous rationality which was the source of universal truth, has yielded to notions of truth and value that do not easily transcend a particular social arrangement. It was not that modernity was uncritical: it questioned everything deeply, but it did so precisely on the basis of autonomous reason and the transcendental subject. It possessed a transcultural subjectivity and rationality as a common basis for all thinking. Historicity, the sociology of knowledge, and a recognition of the social or collective relativity of the linguistic bases of thought have made rationalist criticism more modest by altering the framework of judgment.

Third, postmodernity involves a *pluralist consciousness*. Globalization has provided a vehicle for this collective insight. Differences that are now directly encountered cannot be minimized as superficial, because they too often engender conflict. In a pluralist consciousness, Western

---

4. Among many works on postmodernity I have found these two most helpful: Paul Lakeland, *Postmodernity: Christian Identity in a Fragmented Age* (Minneapolis: Fortress Press, 1997); David Tracy, *On Naming the Present: God, Hermeneutics, and Church* (Maryknoll, N.Y.: Orbis Books, 1994).

5. See chapter 2, pp. 34–37.

culture no longer commands the center, for there is no one center but only a variety of local centers of thought. Applied to religious mediation, no religion can claim to be the one true religion, nor one people to be a chosen people. No individual or individual group or culture can design or possess a metanarrative that encompasses the whole; that perspective is simply not available. Truth is only attainable in fragments. But those fragments can be true and important. We have to begin working with them collectively, together, not to overcome pluralism but to benefit from it.

And, fourth, postmodernity involves a *cosmic consciousness*. Science is gradually mediating to our minds a cosmos that can no longer be imagined, because of its size, its age, and its macro and micro complexity. It is becoming increasingly difficult to conceive that earthly *homo sapiens* is the center of reality and not an epiphenomenon. This cosmic consciousness has a source that is eclectic and cumulative in science; because it grows out of an international community of scientists, it shares an awesome authority. Religion is being forced to make its way within this new view of the cosmos and the world. Popular religion will of course always remain, and we will never be without fundamentalisms. But theology has to attend to the requirements of a scientific view of reality.

These four characteristics help to describe what cannot be defined and what has been called here an "intellectual culture." This means, negatively, that the four interlaced aspects of this consciousness are not doctrines or truths, but biases, feelings, intuitions, and suspicions. These ideas operate as implicit premises and heuristic filters for appreciating what qualifies as claims to truth. More positively, a culture may be regarded as a unity of ideas, values, and behaviors which define a certain form of life. As such, like the peculiarities of a language, the distinctiveness of a culture remains invisible at its territorial center and more visible at its boundaries. Since postmodernity points to an intellectual culture that spans specific linguistic cultures, its influence is still broader, vaguer, and more diffuse. But it is nonetheless real and conditions the understanding of educated people throughout the world. This culture of postmodernity, as I have depicted it, appears threatening to Christian faith in its catechetical form. But it is no more challenging than Hellenistic culture appeared to the Christian movement at the dawn of the second century. This culture should not be viewed only as a threat, but also as a lure to create new construals of Jesus Christ and the church that meet the temper of our time.

A Historically Conscious Christology

Since the nineteenth century one can chart a gradual growth in the intensity of a sense of human historicity. During the last two centuries it has grown ever more intense and has come to bear on theology across the board. In the nineteenth century the question was whether and how doctrines could develop; since the late twentieth century the question has been whether and how doctrines could remain the same. The first chapter of this book described how historical consciousness has worked its way into the discipline of christology. In the course of the nineteenth and twentieth centuries the quest for the historical Jesus developed through phases until its impact was fully felt in the last half of the twentieth century. Study of the New Testament interpretations of Jesus Christ shows the pluralism of christologies in the church's normative witness. In chapter 2 I outlined a method by which historical consciousness can be integrated into a theological method for understanding Jesus Christ. Here I want to describe the affects of having integrated a historical consciousness into one's Christian faith.

The historically conscious person wants to know who Jesus was historically. This does not mean that this knowledge forms a logical basis for christology, because history as a discipline cannot generate faith in Jesus as the Christ of God. But it forms the point of departure and material content for Christian faith in God, for Jesus is the historical medium and focus of the Christian's encounter with God. Thus Jesus and his teaching informs that encounter and provides its specific, historically mediated content. Jesus, in his first-century Jewish particularity, is the constant imaginative referent that accompanies christological affirmations and doctrines.

Christology from below means keeping a historical perspective as one tries to understand more about Jesus theologically. Christology that is historically conscious is consistently linked with the person of Jesus; it does not drift away from its source and ground. All human understanding, as chapter 1 explains, is always accompanied by explicit or implicit imaginative forms, so that even in abstract theoretical matters where images do not predominate, they are always at work. In dogmas about Jesus the imagination is subtly drawn away from concrete history. A historically conscious faith in Jesus Christ "from below" intentionally relates what is said dogmatically about Jesus as the Christ back to Jesus of Nazareth. The imaginative portrait of Jesus thus acts as a norm and corrective of extravagant and docetic christologies.

A historically conscious christology will have among others the following characteristics: it will be attentive to Jesus' humanity, for this is its point of departure. A historical imagination will not find overt manifestations of Jesus' divinity during his lifetime. This christology will give specific attention to the historical ministry of Jesus. The historical quest for Jesus is a search for his particularity and his individuality. To achieve this it must reckon with the great variety of interpretations of him in the New Testament and across history. It does this partly by comparing them with historical data about him. A historical imagination makes one more aware of the speculative and time-conditioned character of many of the abstract doctrines about Jesus. A historical approach looks beneath the dogmatic portrayals of Jesus for people's existential experience of him, that which underlies all the interpretations and doctrines and which must be tapped anew in every historical period. Christology in the final analysis always emerges out of the faith encounter of Christians with Jesus as the mediation of God's salvation in their lives.

Religious Pluralism

The question of religious pluralism discussed in the last chapter has direct bearing on mission. Whether it is a cause or a symptom of historical consciousness, the attitude of educated Christians toward other religions today is considerably more open than in the past. People expect a pluralism of religions; other religions seem suited to the other cultures in which they emerged; the mystery of God cannot be exhausted from a single revelation or a single tradition or a single historical perspective. These are the attitudes of common sense, but they have come to expression in the technical arguments that make up the discussions of one of the most vital questions in Christian theology today: How are we to assess and judge Jesus relative to other mediations of God in other religions?

The comparative analysis of the positions of Karl Rahner and Edward Schillebeeckx in chapter 5 shows that the question of the place of Christ in the economy of God's dealing with humanity is an open question. Beyond the options represented there, a good number of coherent and mutually exclusive views on this subject, all argued on solid theological principles, dot the theological landscape. The literature dealing with the issue keeps expanding yearly. What are some of the theological positions that characterize the Christian attitude toward Jesus against the background of the fact of other religions? And how do they explain the role or function of Jesus in God's dialogue with the world?[6]

Moving from the left to the right, a thoroughgoing historically conscious position would hold for a pluralism of religions in such a way that there could be other savior figures on a par with Jesus. Another position would hold that amidst this pluralism of religions and religious mediations Jesus is a normative figure. At some point in a comparison with other religions the principle of contradiction kicks in; at a foundational level Jesus is perceived as the norm and criterion of the truth about ultimate reality. But in a pluralist context other religions with their own revelations would also be considered as normative precisely insofar as the truth which they contain is universally relevant.[7] A third position, again moving toward the right, would add to the preceding normativity that Jesus is the cause of the salvation of every human being that is saved. This reflects the traditional doctrine that all grace is *gratia Christi,* so that the appearance of Jesus constitutes the salvation of all, however this is explained speculatively.[8] And, finally, moving all the way to the right one finds the doctrine that conscious and historical contact with Jesus Christ is the only and exclusive medium of salvation. This means that there is no salvation outside of the church. This position is more common among evangelical fundamentalists and pentecostals than among mainline churches and theologians.

Discounting the position on the extreme right of the spectrum as theologically hard to reconcile with a loving and saving God, and without

---

6. J. Peter Schineller sets forth a typology of four positions on Jesus against the background of other religions and with respect to salvation in "Christ and Church: A Spectrum of Views," *Theological Studies* 37 (1976), 545–66. This typology, with some adjustments, still remains useful. The best introductory overview to a wide variety of positions on the Christian theology of religions is Paul Knitter, *Introducing Theologies of Religion* (Maryknoll, N.Y.: Orbis Books, 2002).

7. The position of Edward Schillebeeckx, reviewed in chapter 5, would fit here, but it also shares elements of the first, pluralist position with which I began.

8. The position of Karl Rahner, also reviewed in chapter 5, would correlate with this third position.

assuming the stance of any one of the other three, one can make some generalizations about their significance. Together they show the extent to which historical consciousness has opened up the Christian imagination in this area. First, all three exclude the exclusivism which provided the strongest motives for missionary activity. All three have abandoned the naively understood doctrine that there is no salvation outside of historical contact with Jesus. Second, all admit value in other religions and implicitly in other mediations of God in history, even though there are great differences in how this is understood. Third, all three recommendations favor a dialogue with other religions; they hold that Christians can learn from other religious traditions. This assumes that there is some form of revelation in the other religions. Because revelation and salvation are closely aligned realities, the notion of revelation may be understood to imply and include some form of salvation. And, finally, these three positions either implicitly or explicitly give some status to the medium or media that constitute the foundations of other religions. Again, this is said in principle as a possibility prior to any real existential contact with other religions and critical reflection upon them.

One can see in these developments how a postmodern consciousness is at work. The attitudes beneath these positions attribute a good deal of importance to the historical particularities of cultures. At the same time all the positions see God, as God is revealed in Jesus, at work universally in the world. This universal presence and activity of God is what ultimately injects value into other religions, as it does in Christianity.

Dialogue and the Demand for a New Concept of Mission

I now move to some of the consequences of these shifts in theology and the attitudes represented by them. What bearing does this have on the way the church addresses other religions and, more concretely, the people whose cultures are structured by other religious traditions? I cannot offer concrete or specific answers to these questions, because every actual situation of the church will call forth a differently nuanced response. What the church should actually be doing in the exercise of its mission is determined by the particular context. What I outline here are shifts that have a bearing on understanding the church's mission itself and only in that light actual missionary activity.

To begin, the word dialogue has assumed a central significance in defining the stance of the church vis-à-vis other world religions. The term itself suggests various nuances in the approach of the church to other religions.[9] Dialogue involves a give and take, a communication that requires not just testifying, announcing, and teaching but also listening, hearing, and learning. It presumes mutual recognition and at some level a sense of equality among the participants as a characteristic of the conversation. Dialogue is much more than actual exchange. It also defines a climate, a fundamental institutional attitude, and a strategy toward the other institution.

Dialogue also rules out any proselytism or aggressive, conquering evangelization. Evangelization must respect the freedom of the dialogue partner. Christianity should honor the right of people to hold the faith they do; the sanctity of a religious commitment is close to the integrity of people themselves. A militant or simply an objective, long-term strategy of overrunning or absorbing another belief system without taking account of its inner logic would so abuse the freedom of the people involved that such missionary behavior would contradict in turn the very essence of what Christianity stands for as a sign in history. I will expand on this in part two with reference to the doctrine of religious liberty.

The dialogical structure of missionary activity involves a shift in the motivation of the church and of the individual missionary relative to immediate goals, at least when compared with the view that no salvation is available outside of the institutional church. Individual Christian missionaries or ministers will not be driven by the same necessity to convert people of other faiths with whom they come into contact, or with whom they work. They may seek other common secular goals; they may work together in nurturing humanistic values or common religious values; they may seek simple mutual understanding. When and if they address each other, they may be satisfied to share the views of reality that come from their faith and which sustain them. This does not rule out altogether a concern for conversions, however, and I will say more about the symbolic amplitude of the idea of dialogue further on.

---

9. David Lochhead, in *The Dialogical Imperative: A Christian Reflection on Interfaith Encounter* (Maryknoll, N.Y.: Orbis Books, 1988), parses the variety of logics and goals of dialogue and thus helps clarify what can be going on in any given case.

Let me sum up here. How have the effects of globalization, a new sense of the postmodern conditions of self-understanding, historical consciousness in christology, a new appreciation of religious pluralism, and the new imperative for dialogue come to bear on the notion of mission that was presented by Daniélou after the Second Vatican Council? What is gone, or at least slipping away, in our situation today?

The first thing that has been qualified is the idea that God has acted exclusively in Jesus for human salvation. Since Jewish scriptures are part of the Christian Bible, God's action outside of Jesus has always been recognized. But we have a more expansive sense of this today. Second, a static and once for all given creation and cosmos is gone. Historicity is part of a broad evolutionary conception of the whole of reality that is in process and actually recognized as changing. Third, the dogmatic claims about Jesus Christ are not the point of departure for the understanding or practice of church mission. This does not mean that doctrines should be neglected or no longer have a role in religious understanding, but that theological imagination has shifted to give the particular, concrete, historical Jesus his due. In interreligious dialogue dogmatic claims are not the first word. Fourth, the concrete grounding of mission in explicit words from Jesus historically spoken has been undermined by historical critical study of the New Testament. We need another way of understanding this linkage of the mission to Jesus. Fifth, it is hard to believe that history is all worked out or predetermined, or that in the history we know the whole human race will become Christian. This latter belief, which formerly influenced the idea of the goal of missionary activity and provided a condition for "the end of the world," appears naive today when taken in an objective straightforward way. It is not that the conversion of the world is historically impossible; no one knows the future. It just does not seem realistic or concretely imaginable today. Consequently, sixth, the idea that the mission of the church is to baptize everyone and so to Christianize the world quantitatively, that is, through all individual human beings becoming Christian, also seems unrealistic. It is not apathy that prevents the Christian family from urging Christianity on the new Hindu or Muslim family that lives next door. It is a sense of respect for religious freedom, of appreciation of an appropriateness of Hindu faith for people of Indian culture, and a conviction that the same God whom Christians know by another name is at work in Hinduism.

But where does this leave Jesus and mission? What has taken the place of what is gone? The second half of this essay attempts to outline a way in which one can think constructively about the meaning of mission within the framework of a new world situation and postmodern consciousness.

JESUS AND MISSION

The missionary character of the church, the church's actual mission in history, and the mandate for the church's missionaries must be understood and formulated in a way attuned to the developments that have occurred during the second half of the twentieth century and the beginning of the twenty-first. Only then will such an understanding reflect the general consciousness of North Americans and engage their freedom with a credible challenge. Such a constructive account of the church's mission, therefore, will be based on the same principles that served to undercut the theology of mission that was in place up to and immediately following Vatican II. In what follows, I present an outline for such a constructive reappropriation of the church as mission around four basic ideas or themes: the idea of mission as a religious symbol derived from Jesus, the openness of history as the field of mission, the church's missionary character as mediated and shaped by Jesus, and, finally, dialogue as defining a framework for the unfolding of the church's mission.

Mission as a Religious Symbol

The idea of mission is a religious symbol.[10] That is, it is a concept that mediates and opens up to the imagination the perception and conviction that Jesus is from God, that he was sent, and that his life was commissioned by God. Given our sense of historicity, the meaning of this symbol is drawn less from a doctrinal conception of God sending and more from what is communicated by Jesus' public ministry. This is the historical source for the later doctrinal conceptions. The primary datum

---

10. By the term "symbol" I mean a thing through which something else is known; a symbol reveals something other than itself. Symbols may be concrete things or ideas and words. For example, sacraments are symbols and so are the words of scripture that refer to God. It is necessary to use this language of symbol to indicate that our knowledge of God is historical even though God transcends history absolutely; we do not know God immediately, but only through the symbols of history. See chapter 2, pp. 41, 46–47.

for a theology of mission is not the missions within the Godhead as this was depicted by medieval theology of the trinity, although this is not without its symbolic value. Rather one must begin with the fact that Jesus lived his life for a cause and with the character of that cause. The primary meaning of the symbol of mission must be read as a continuation of the narrative of the life and teaching of Jesus.

Jesus' mission was the kingdom of God. In the synoptic gospels, God's mission, as that is revealed in Jesus, is God's reign, God's rule, the implementation of God's values as opposed to selfish human desires: in sum, God's will. The reign of God is God's will being done. Christians read this will of God in the teaching and action of Jesus. It manifests itself in his call for repentance and conversion, in his parables of a reversal of selfish human values, in his healing of the sick, in his association with the poor, in his concern for the dignity, personhood, participation, and human flourishing of the marginated, in his instinctive siding with the oppressed and the underdog. These things which seem so earthly in the telling are of God; they are God's reign; they are God's and Jesus' mission.

The first point, then, is to read the meaning of mission both historically and symbolically from Jesus. The symbolic theological meaning of mission is drawn out of the historical activity of Jesus of Nazareth which reveals God's desires for human fulness.

Open History, Human Creativity, God's Cause

The mission of Jesus which was to be taken up in his time by his disciples is to be internalized by disciples in the world of today. The language of our theology and the logic of our action have to engage the contours of reality that have been established by the interchange between science and common sense. The mission has to be appropriated, first of all, in a history which is open. Educated people are getting a better picture all the time of the natural process through which the human race was created. These same people have a better understanding of the indeterminate character of human history and the arbitrary turns taken by corporate human freedom. Although human beings know more about their past, they know less about their future and have grounds for feeling insecure. The future of human history is open, and corporate human behavior is unpredictable.

The sense of historicity gives more weight to human freedom. Since human beings have a better sense of the measure in which the future is in human hands, freedom has new seriousness and more importance. The future is a human responsibility and a challenge. The character of human freedom in this situation takes on new overtones of creativity; to be human is to be free, and to be free is to do new things and create new reality. Along with this sense of historicity is a lack of an expectation that God will intervene in this world in place of human freedom. God does not do what God expects human beings to do with the freedom God gave them. A deep seated historical consciousness can be burdensome.

But the burden of human freedom is not borne alone. This is the testimony of the public ministry of Jesus. If God was active in Jesus, and Jesus is the new Adam, then one can read in Jesus God's being at work analogously in human beings, most explicitly in true disciples, but potentially in any person or group. Jesus is a revelation of the nearness and active presence of God, and God as Spirit is a source of energy and courage. This is not in its first instance a proscription for specific action. It is most profoundly a pervasive a priori that helps one to understand human history, to determine one's place in it, and to look for actual signs of God's presence within the activity of human beings. A frank appraisal of the world today would judge it an unfriendly environment for a large percentage of the human race. We need not dwell on the theme of evil and sin; they press in too closely to be ignored. But it is precisely against such a background that, when one encounters genuine self-transcending love, such love can be construed as a medium of God's presence and power. God is active in history through human agents, and from a historical perspective God's mission needs these human agents.

The Church as Mission

Calling the church a mission, a "being sent," is a symbolic statement that partially identifies the church's relation to God.[11] The meaning of the assertion is drawn from Jesus' embodiment and revelation of the effective will of God. The church was formed of disciples in order to

---

11. I address the pervasive character of the symbol "mission" as applied to the church in "Mission: The Symbol for Understanding the Church Today," *Theological Studies* 37 (1976): 620–49; "The 'Established' Church as Mission: The Relation of the Church to the Modern World," *The Jurist* 39 (1979): 4–39.

continue in history the mission of Jesus on earth. When the church is called the Body of Christ, this means that it is intended, or one could say "sent," to body forth the will of God, the values of God, the cause of God that Jesus represented to the world.

Now the church has always been seen to be or have a mission and to be missionary. But in the light of a new sense of the historical context in which we live, one gets a new perspective on the meaning of this mission by focusing the imagination on the Jesus of history. Jesus defines the mission of the church. Given the openness of history, and the radical pluralism of vision and behavior that human freedom spawns, the church is called to represent in a public way the values of God, God's will. These values and this will of God cannot be deduced from the nature of God, for the nature of God is not available to human reason. All contact with God comes about through the events of history, so that the only will of God the Christian knows positively must be related to the God who has been revealed in Jesus.[12] The historical mission of the church, its function in the history of the world, is to bear witness to this God and this God's rule. Surely the church has other tasks. As an institution it is called to care for its members, to nurture their faith, to be the support of their freedom as individuals. But if one is looking for the foundational rationale for the church's existence in the large scheme of things, this has to be construed as a continuation of what Jesus did in history.

This task is not an easy one and there can be no doubt that the church has and will always fall short in executing its mission. For this is not merely a question of a mystical or sacramental making of Jesus present to the world, although my point is not to minimize this but precisely to broaden its meaning. The idea of a mystical task, of which formal liturgy is an explicit part, actually describes the larger historical mandate to be the sign to the contemporary world that Jesus was to his by his preaching and healing, his liberating associations with sinners, prostitutes, and tax collectors, his prophetic reversals of commonly accepted human values. The point is to witness to the religious depth of the *missio Dei.*

---

12. There is much more to be said on this point that cannot be developed here. For example, the formula does not imply exclusivism, as though there were no other sources from which Christians might learn the ways of God. The only point being made here is the reminder that Christians like all others view things from their particular perspective. This is the reason why dialogue is so necessary.

The mission of the church calls for an engagement with society and culture. The church's mission demands that it be inculturated in whatever culture it subsists in and addresses. In this sense the church is missionary wherever it exists; the church in North America, or in any particular local region, is called to become inculturated in that region. Such an inculturation is the condition for its ability to bear witness to God as revealed in Jesus. But this inculturation does not mean being coopted by a culture, for the mission of the church is to render visible and audible God's values as manifested by Jesus. Jesus' own ministry shows that inculturation need not negate the prophetic edge. But one can say more: authentic mission demands a prophetic edge. Inculturation of Jesus' mission means confronting those areas in culture and society where human ways contemn the values of the kingdom of God.

This raises the question of whether one can find general norms for the authenticity of the church's mission that transcend particular cultures. Are there ways of judging the integrity of the church's mission in any particular culture? One can find such norms in the gospels where Jesus himself is portrayed as applying criteria of authenticity to his own ministry. When John sent his disciples to Jesus with the question of whether Jesus really was the one who was to come, he responded: " 'Go and tell John what you have seen and heard: the blind receive their sight, the lame walk, the lepers are cleansed, the deaf hear, the dead are raised, the poor have good news brought to them. And blessed is anyone who takes no offense at me" (Lk 7:22–23). Active concern for those who suffer that addresses the causes of their suffering is the historical measure of the authenticity of the mission of Jesus Christ.

The mission of discipleship, of standing for what Jesus stood for, belongs to the church on the level of institution and the level of community. When the church is looked upon as an institution, the public character of the mission is emphasized, for the various offices and officials in the church make up its public face. These offices are charged with the responsibility to animate the mission internally and externally: they exercise oversight and a nurturing ministry to foster the mission from within; they represent the church *ad extra* as spokespersons, leaders, and official representatives. When the church is looked upon as a community, all members who make up the church participate in this mission. To be a member is to internalize and assume responsibility for the intentionality of the community. Vatican II underscored the teaching that all people in the church share responsibility for the church's mission and participate in it.[13]

From this characterization of mission one can see that the term really describes a spirituality. Spirituality here means a deep conception of the rationale of Christian life, of the direction of life and the responsibility that go with being a Christian. This spirituality is an ecclesial spirituality, for its logic is that of being a member of a church which is a mission after the pattern of Jesus. It is also, therefore, a spirituality of disciple-ship, of *imitatio Christi*, but one that is read within the context of an open historicity and a focus on Jesus of Nazareth as the clue to deci-phering the meaning of historical existence in every new and particular moment.

Dialogue as a Framework for Mission

Another element needs to be drawn out in this characterization of Jesus and mission in the framework of the relatively new world of today, namely, the fuller significance of the idea of dialogue. The notion of dialogue draws its significance from more than one area of theological reflection: the intra-Christian dialogue of ecumenism, the dialogue of Christianity with the world, with culture or cultures, and most relevantly here with other world religions. But the term contains resonances beyond these explicit references. Dialogue points to a relatively new fundamental strategy of the church in the performance of its mission, and thus a major shift in the very conception of that mission.

I have noted the basic lines of the shift in the earlier brief consid-eration of dialogue with other religions. From a historicist perspective, Christians have come to expect other religions and also to value them. If God is the way Jesus reveals God to be, the lover of all human be-ings as God's own, one should not be surprised to find God intersecting with people at a variety of junctures and through various media of their history and culture; God meets people where they are in history. Vati-can II has taught the universal availability of God's saving grace, and

---

13. "Decree on the Church's Missionary Activity," *Vatican Council II*, ed. Austin Flannery (Northport, N.Y.: Costello Publishing, 1996), nos. 7, 23.

various theological rationales "explain" how God becomes present to all peoples.[14] These foundations lie beneath the call for dialogue.

Dialogue can be seen as a metaphor for a distinctive change in the conception of the church's mission and the way it is carried out. This change should be characterized cautiously because it is only now in the process of coming about. It may be conceived as a shift from a competitive mission to a cooperative mission.

At Vatican II the Catholic Church taught in its "Declaration on Religious Liberty" that each human being, and whole groups of people collectively, enjoy freedom with regard to their religious beliefs and practices. These should not and ultimately cannot be coerced in any way, because human relationships with God, although they come from God, originate and are deployed from within the depths of human freedom. God works in and through that freedom. This doctrine, which developed in the political dialectic between church and state in the West, also has direct bearing on Christian missions; it is a question of a fundamental and inherent human right.[15] This statement of principle, moreover, should be considered alongside of the realistic geopolitical estimate that the Christian church will not prevail over other religions in history. It is no longer imaginable that the whole world will become Christian in the foreseeable future. Mission theory has to unfold within a different vision than the one behind the missiology of Daniélou.

The relation of Christianity to the other religions can be seen as broadly analogous to the context in which the doctrine of religious liberty was generated. The separation of church and state means that the church is not a rival with other secular institutions in the various spheres of life; both enjoy autonomous spheres of authority, even though they overlap in certain areas, particularly with respect to ethics. So too, Christianity does not exist in a competitive relationship with other world religions, so that it does not compete with them for members. Quite on the contrary, the church holds that God's grace for salvation is operative in all people of good will, and hence in these religions, even though it does not explain

---

14. One of the arguments of chapter 3 is that the doctrine of creation by a personal and loving God has not been explored the way it should be relative to God's presence to and contact with all human beings. The categories of "natural" and "supernatural" have prevented the resources of that doctrine from being fully developed.

15. "Declaration on Religious Liberty," *Vatican Council II*, nos. 1–3.

how.[16] Therefore the stance of the church toward the world and other religions can be reckoned as dialogical. This implies openness toward the world, an entering into cooperation with other secular and religious institutions, a learning from the other human agencies of history. Only in the face of sin, or what Jon Sobrino has called the "anti-kingdom," does the church pronounce the prophetic judgment of God's values, and more frequently than not those values will be supported by other religions.[17] The forces of corruption and dehumanization are prevalent enough and should not be minimized. The church in representing the values manifest in the ministry of Jesus is hostile to all forms of oppression and suppression of human dignity. But enough of the ethical teaching of the church is shared by other religions, or there exists enough common ground, to provide a basis for dialogue. Dialogue with other religions will not mute but strengthen the prophetic voice. Thus the church may take its place in the world as a leaven of society and culture. But in a religiously pluralistic world this universal mission of the church does not necessarily entail constructing a Christian society in an explicit and formal way. It does not imply overcoming other religious communities.

The most important task and short-term goal of the church is not to seek conversions to itself, even though Jesus is universally relevant and the church invites all people to appropriate his message. It is not that a concern for conversions should be lacking: Who does not want to share the truth of his or her deepest convictions? But other religions think the same thing, and real conversion must be a function of freedom and spontaneous attraction. At no time in history have peoples been more sensitive to an imperialism of outside forces. Rather than seeking converts, the overarching mission of the church is to be a public witness to the mission of God manifested in Jesus. This is a universal mission because the kingdom of God as revealed in Jesus' ministry is relevant everywhere, to all people, in every situation. That God is personal, loving, and saving; that God is the creator of human life and the guarantor of human freedom and dignity; that God condemns all oppression and is against human suffering; that God enters into dialogue with human existence and will draw all reality back into the sphere of God's own life;

16. "Pastoral Constitution on the Church in the Modern World," *Vatican Council II*, no. 22.
17. Jon Sobrino, *Jesus the Liberator: A Historical-Theological Reading of Jesus of Nazareth* (Maryknoll, N.Y.: Orbis, 1993).

all this is potentially meaningful to every human being. Therefore the message should be carried everywhere; the mission is to bear witness to this message to all places and in every sphere of human life; there is no sphere where it has no religious, ethical, or humane bearing.

The new focus on the historical Jesus in christology that was described in chapter 1 has a direct bearing on mission theology. The missionary activity of the church in its narrow sense suggests a context of the church at its boundaries, where it is introducing Christianity for the first time. Mission in this limited sense is where the church is addressing people who have never heard of Jesus Christ in any serious or meaningful way. At such a juncture, the single most effective way of initiating the dialogue consists in a representation of the historical Jesus. Because this is the human Jesus "as he appeared" historically, this Jesus is able to be understood and appreciated in more or less direct terms. This appeal stands in marked contrast to a first introduction to Jesus in dogmatic terms. The stories about Jesus told with some degree of historical realism are what Christians and those who are not Christians have in common and can talk about. The leading edge of Christian mission in terms of dialogue, then, is the historical figure of Jesus himself. Introduction to him does not aim at conversation but at appreciation of his message and the mission of God's rule.

The point of this, of course, is not to dismiss the possibility of conversions. It is rather that the issue of conversions must be viewed and evaluated in relation to the overall historical mission of the church. Without some conversions this mission would not be carried forward in a particular place. The church is also interested in converts because of the truth of its message, which is relevant for all human beings.[18] But this mission is carried forward in and through dialogue with absolute respect for human freedom, without coercion, with full encouragement of the historical and cultural identity of all other ways of life that are not themselves hostile to the values of the kingdom of God. In sum, and this is the point, the mission of God mediated by Jesus and continued by the church is a noncompetitive mission to human freedom in history. When someone converts to Christianity, it does not necessarily mean

---

18. The issue of the aim at conversions in the Christian mission is discussed by Cardinal Jozef Tomko, Paul Knitter, Samuel Rayan, Kenneth Cragg, et al. in Paul Mojzes and Leonard Swidler, eds., *Christian Mission and Interreligious Dialogue* (Lewiston, N.Y.: Edwin Mellen, 1990).

that such a person believes that Christianity is a superior religion, but that the mission of Jesus is truly alive in this place and one desires to participate in it. The mission of the church is to be an active and clear sign of God's values as these are revealed in Jesus and to be resolutely nonaggressive and noncompetitive in seeking conversions, but active in supporting dialogue with other religions. This is a tensive relationship, and that tension can only be resolved in each local or particular situation. No set of generalized rules can be given for how this tension is handled in all situations.

CONCLUSION

Let me conclude by briefly summarizing the thesis of this essay. I have tried to uncover some of the characteristics of our distinctive situation today that have a bearing on an understanding of the church's mission. One aspect of that situation is the degree to which the politics of the world have been altered, creating new divisions between the rich and the poor, and how this globalization has affected the church itself. Our new situation is increasingly postmodern in its consciousness and this has affected how we understand Jesus Christ theologically. The new dimensions of religious pluralism, its direct proximity, and the imperative for dialogue have virtually transformed the context in which Christian mission is to be understood, and they issue a demand for its reconceptualization.

Three distinct developments in particular have a direct bearing on how one understands the mission of the church. Jesus research, the renewed critical historical investigation into what can be said about Jesus of Nazareth, has accented the way in which the Christian imagination should be focused on Jesus in the construction of its christology. In this framework the mission of the church is not conceived and formulated abstractly on the basis of dogmatic developments; it is conceived on the basis of a theological reflection that sees the church as a continuation of the earthly ministry of Jesus. The mission of the church today is determined by an analogous interpretation of Jesus' mission and ministry in correlation with the concrete situation in which the particular local church finds itself.

Another new development in a newly globalized world lies in the potential for division, war, and increasing suffering for the poor as cultures and nations press in on one another. Religion in general, and Christianity in particular, has to assume a global voice transcending an instrumental reason enticed by mercantile values. The Christian mission has to be prophetic, especially since the developed nations carry a Christian heritage. World poverty, hunger, and disease call out for a response from the Christian churches that is intrinsic to their reason for being.

The third area of church life and theological discussion that deeply affects how church mission is to be understood is the encounter with other religions. With a new sense of the historical necessity of pluralism, of the value of this pluralism, and of a conviction that God is at work within this diversity, the paradigm of dialogue takes on a new significance. Dialogue defines a fundamental posture of the church vis-à-vis the world, human cultures, and other religions. This new posture may be called cooperative in contrast to competitive. It looks for signs of God's grace everywhere and is supportive of initiatives wherever they are found; it cooperates with others in militantly resisting the forces of the anti-kingdom.

The final question is one of spirituality. Can such a conception of the mission of the church provide the motivation for a life-commitment to carry forward the Christian mission? Does "noncompetitive dialogue" have the power of the fundamentalist vision of saving non-Christian souls from hell? Is this a vision on which one could stake one's life and to which one could commit one's freedom "full time," as in a vocation? These are questions that will only be answered practically over time. But given the social oppression and suffering in the world today, given the discrimination and inequality, given the withdrawal of God and God's values from everyday secular life, and given the idolatry of dehumanizing values and the institutions dedicated to nurturing it, one has a clear negative horizon within which to discern the positive meaning of the kingdom of God and Jesus' mission. Moreover, when it is so situated, this is a mission that can be shared by many of the world's religions. The mission of God's kingdom that heals suffering, resists systemic oppression, respects and builds up the freedom and dignity of others, seems to provide as solid a basis for deep, lifelong spiritual commitment as it did in the time of Jesus. It may be that the decline in missionary vocations in North America is not at all due to a failure of the inner Christian mission, but to the sociological division of labor, especially the clerical and religious monopolization of missionary roles in the Roman Catholic Church. That this mission must be carried forward in a noncompetitive and dialogical way does not seem to endanger its attraction but to enhance it. And if this is truly the mission of God, if God, ultimately, is the object of this commitment, it will fill with infinite value the human freedom of anyone who takes it up.

Chapter Seven

OUTLINE FOR AN ORTHODOX
PLURALIST CHRISTOLOGY

⟜⟞

MANY CHRISTIANS TODAY, even those whose sympathies may lie
with a pluralist conception of Jesus Christ, do not understand
how a pluralist christology can be considered orthodox. This chapter
primarily addresses these Christians and aims at explaining, at least in
the form of an extended outline or map, the reasons why a pluralist
christology is orthodox. It does not attempt to prove the point, for such
a task would require a full-length study. It is written for a group of
people other than those who deny the possibility of an orthodox pluralist
christology, namely, those who are open to the possibility and are looking
for a rationale by which they can understand how it can be the case. It
is possible that the logic deployed here may find analogies within other
religious traditions. In other words, this essay, written in a religiously
pluralistic context, tries to show how people can be absolutely committed
to a religious tradition without competing with other religious traditions.

I begin by simply defining the terms as they are used in this discussion.
By christology I mean a Christian theological understanding of Jesus
of Nazareth with special attention to his status relative to God and to
other human beings. A pluralist christology affirms Jesus as the Christ
in a way that does not construe Christianity as the one and only true
faith and way of salvation uniquely superior to all others. An orthodox
christology meets the criteria of being faithful to the normative teaching
of the New Testament and the classical christological councils of Nicaea
and Chalcedon. It thus conforms to traditional doctrine and respects an
intrinsically conservative impulse of Christians.

With these definitions in place I develop the thesis in four parts. The
first offers some premises gathered from the domain of the philosophy of religion. In part two I outline schematically key elements of

148

the logical structure of christology. Part three then argues within that structure to conclusions about the way Christians can and should regard other religions. This will set up the conclusion in part four regarding the orthodoxy of this understanding of a pluralist christology.

This essay is not meant to break new ground in Christian theology. Everything that is said here is well known among Christian theologians and has been introduced to others in the earlier chapters of this book. It repeats several ideas developed earlier and brings them to bear on this issue. This allows me to state things succinctly, as though merely pointing to ideas, rather than developing them. The intent of this discussion is to bring together many of the insights that have been generated in christology into a clear unified statement of how a pluralist christology, understood along the lines that are drawn here, is orthodox.

BASIC CONSIDERATIONS IN THE MODE OF A PHILOSOPHY OF RELIGION

Often positions taken regarding fundamental questions in theology depend on premises that are tacit in the understanding and arguments of those who hold them. In this first part of the discussion I want to lay out a number of theses or propositions that set the context of the argument which follows. The Christian theologians who do not accept the conclusions arrived at in this chapter quite possibly disregard or dissent from the context defined by these principles.

Globalization

We have entered a new phase of interdependence and commerce among peoples that is having a major influence upon the existence of the human species. Globalization is opening up new ways of thinking that are relevant to all religions. Some of the features of this new world context that have a bearing on religious consciousness are these: a new vision of the universe and story of the world; an interdependence of all peoples so that each is affected by the other in a new way; new perceptions of the degrees of differences among us and the bonds that unite us; the possible values of pluralism understood as unity in difference; a new awareness of the fragility of human life on the planet and of corporate human responsibility for massive social oppression and suffering; a new humility in religious claims. When these factors are taken together they add up to a relatively new situation for Christian theology.

The Unity of Reality

The vision behind this proposal depicts reality as unified or held together in an integrated way: being is one. It proposes that the human species today is single and unified, although it was formed through various evolutionary biological trajectories and is shaped differently by cultural forms. Postmodernity attends to the differences, real differences, among human beings. But these are not such as to destroy a fundamental unity of the human species. In Christianity monotheism and the doctrine of creation, which has little to do with "creationism," correlate with a belief concerning the unity of the human race and a moral conviction about the equality and absolute value of human beings. Whether or not the basic unity of reality can be proved, it operates as a premise in these reflections.

Qualities of Religious Knowledge

Knowledge of ultimate reality is mysterious, mediated, and dialectical. First, religious knowledge has as its object transcendent reality which, insofar as it is transcendent, is not available for immediate perception and thus not able to be compared with our conceptions of it. This ultimate reality is often characterized as infinite or without any limits. It thus presents itself to us as unfathomable and incomprehensible mystery. Second, because ultimate reality is transcendent, human beings can only perceive and appreciate it through finite this-worldly symbols. Religious symbols are media by which transcendent reality is represented, embodied, made available to human consciousness. Religious symbols are mystagogical: they draw the human spirit through the capacity of the imagination into the realm of absolute and infinite transcendence. Third, the perception and knowledge mediated by religious symbols end up as inherently dialectical in the sense that they both represent and do not represent that which they mediate. Christian affirmations about God are simultaneously denied in their very affirmation in light of the transcendence of that to which they point and which they mediate.

Soteriological Character of Religion

The three qualities of religious knowledge just indicated can be developed more fully in a philosophy of religion by phenomenologies and epistemologies of religious consciousness. In such an effort, the three qualities together depict the human subject as *capax infiniti*, a transcendent openness able to discern and receive from, to learn about, and even to encounter an infinite horizon or realm. This fundamentally religious anthropology, especially when analyzed further by thinkers such as Augustine, suggests that the human subject is marked by an intrinsic desire to be, to resist nonbeing, and to act out a consistent impulse to continue to be absolutely. In a world where time leads inexorably toward death and nonexistence, such a permanence in being appears as salvation.

Whether or not any particular religious conviction is founded on a conception of eternal life, religions as such respond to the question of ultimate meaning and destiny of the human. They engage the self and the group whose lives they structure, and they define them in the broadest contexts of existence itself. In this sense, then, all religions are soteriological because they respond to the religious question which engages the fundamental rationale of human existence itself. I understand the "salvation" at the basis of all religious knowledge and conviction, therefore, in abstract and formal terms as part of an a priori and unprogramed desire within the human as such; this broadly and generically defined "salvation" takes on different forms in different religions. But salvation always correlates with the fact that religious knowledge responds to those human issues which affect individuals and cultures at a level that has a direct bearing on their ultimate destiny.

These four themes do not exhaust the tacit background of the proposal offered here, but they help define the field on which it is played out.

THE LOGIC OF CHRISTOLOGY

The significance of the title of this section, "the logic of christology," lies in its abstractness. One can represent the structure and dynamics of the study of Jesus Christ in Christian theology in such a short space only in the most general of terms. Christological discussion within Christian theology is so extensive and complicated that it constitutes a subdiscipline.

Although the particular option in christology represented here should be defended at greater length, it is stated here in the schematic form of five theses in order further to define the context for the discussion which follows.[1]

Jesus is the historical medium of Christian encounter with God, so that christology is interpretation of Jesus of Nazareth.

On one level this thesis consists in a straightforward descriptive statement of what goes on in christology. But at another theological level it implicitly contains the premises of a christology from below that some Christian theologians would contest. For example, some Christian theologians take the Christian scriptures as a self-contained or closed system of revelation and understanding which draws consideration of Jesus' historical life up into itself. This form of Christian theology and christology frequently takes an absolutist form. By contrast, christology "from below" is taken here to mean that, as in the case of any other historical set of convictions, to understand christology one must trace its historical genesis. That historical genesis began with the appearance of Jesus of Nazareth, although one should not forget that Jesus was born into a Jewish tradition.

The New Testament of the Christian Bible contains a pluralism of christologies, all of which share a soteriological structure.

The New Testament as a whole consists in a collection of interpretations of Jesus as the Christ and of his impact on the Christian community. That the New Testament does not contain one common christology but a variety of different christologies has been demonstrated by the exegetes of scripture and is commonly accepted. But some Christian theologians hold that some christologies have more authority than others, and they interpret these "higher" christologies which accent various conceptions of the divinity of Jesus Christ as normative relative to others which, in their turn, are viewed as stages in the development of a fully authoritative view. Still, many other theologians would support the proposition offered here that all of the christologies of the New Testament should

---

1. These theses are drawn from the christological development employed in Roger Haight, *Jesus Symbol of God* (Maryknoll, N.Y.: Orbis Books, 1999) and summarized in the argument of chapter 2.

be considered as having a certain validity and that none should rule out the others, even when they cannot be made to coincide logically. The phenomenon of the pluralism of conceptions or interpretations of such a basic element of Christian faith, namely, the understanding of Jesus Christ, should loom large in the Christian theological imagination. It provides a way of confirming through the internal dynamics of Christian revelation itself that pluralism is a positive and not a negative condition. In other words, the New Testament models and thereby authorizes for the believer a pluralism of beliefs regarding a single object of faith. In a situation in which uniformity in various forms or degrees constitutes the very problem to be overcome, this forceful demonstration of pluralism within the canonical literature of Christianity should not be overlooked.

The thesis also finds the unity of the various christologies of the New Testament to lie in their common soteriological structure. All have Jesus of Nazareth as their implicit referent or object of interpretation. Because Jesus is the event or historical medium through which Christians encounter salvation from God, all implicitly give expression in various different ways to that experience of salvation. This soteriological principle will play an important role in the interpretation of pluralist christology that is offered here.

The person of Jesus embodies a divine quality or character.

All of the christologies of the New Testament portray Jesus mediating salvation from God. The christologies of the New Testament, in various and diverse ways according to the different metaphors that make up particular christologies and the distinct historical traditions that lie behind each one, point to the presence, power, and quality of the divine in Jesus or at work through him. One way of explaining this is to appeal to a more general principle that the historical symbol which mediates salvation from God (Jesus) tends to share in the quality (divinity) of that which is mediated (salvation by divine power) because the symbol renders it present and effective. According to this principle one would expect Jesus to share in some way in the divine saving power and reality of God. This became a forceful argument in the development of the understanding of Jesus' divinity in the course of the formation of the doctrinal tradition.

*The point of the metaphor of incarnation and the doctrine of Nicaea
is that Jesus makes true God, and nothing less than God, present and
effective in history for human salvation.*

This thesis makes more explicit the principles and reasoning found in
the last thesis. But it can also be verified or at least corroborated by
historical-exegetical analysis of the metaphor of incarnation as that is
found in the Prologue of John's gospel, its most explicit instance in the
New Testament. It also correlates with an analytical account of the development of christology from the second century through the early fourth
century, which came to a term in the doctrine of Nicaea. That doctrine
says that the Logos or Word that was incarnate in Jesus is of the same
nature as God. This was officially declared as a response directly contra-
dicting the teaching of Arius who affirmed that what was present and
active in Jesus was a Logos who was less than God. This response has
turned out to be a classical Christian doctrine. The theological principle
that confirmed it was soteriological: if what was present and active in
Jesus was less than God, Jesus could not in the end be a bearer of God's
salvation.

If I may turn my attention for a moment to the dynamics of Christian theology as a corporate discipline, it may be useful to point out
that a good deal of confusion marks the various understandings of this
fundamental Christian conception and doctrine. Much of this confusion
is due to the diversity of presuppositions and methods in the discipline
of Christian theology itself. For example, one can point to widely different interpretations of the Prologue of John's gospel which contains
the clearest New Testament witness to a doctrine of incarnation. Some
theologians read the meaning of this witness right off the surface of the
text with little concern for the genre of literature they are interpreting
and the kind of faith-knowledge it represents. Regarding the doctrine
of Nicaea itself, this classic didactic statement of faith is often invoked
without attention to the assumptions and logic of the debates that pro-
duced it, as though it were a timeless and context-free statement. Some
interpreters deal with the doctrine as though its subject or referent were
Jesus of Nazareth, as if *Jesus* were preexistent, rather than God as Logos
who was represented as being present and at work in him. The doctrinal

formula sometimes functions in an argument as though it represented information about the internal life of God rather than what it is, a symbol of faith expressing its content. One reason why interreligious dialogue and the theology of religions promote better mutual understanding and self-understanding is that they impose an inner exigency to transcend merely kerygmatic language, which has a place within a community, and to engage beliefs with a more critical analysis measured by objective or at least public standards.

The point of the doctrine of Chalcedon is to confirm the human, creaturely status of Jesus and to underline the intrinsically dialectical character of orthodox christology.

The doctrine of Chalcedon is also a Christian classic. It says that the one individual, Jesus Christ, possessed or possesses within himself two distinct and different kinds of being: a human nature and a divine nature. These two natures are at the same time both inseparable and unmixed, distinct but joined to form one "person," a technical term roughly meaning a distinct, subsisting individual. This doctrine too has a history apart from which it cannot be adequately understood. Part of that history included a christological pattern of thinking that undermined what today is usually taken for granted by theologians, namely, that Jesus was a human being equal to other human beings in all things essentially human. To retrieve the figure of Jesus from an exaggerated emphasis on his divinity, Chalcedon proposed the formula of one person with two natures. The most adequate way to understand this classic doctrine is to construe it as intrinsically dialectical, that is, by not attempting to resolve the tension between these two natures, but to affirm both as, according to Chalcedon, distinct and inseparable, unmixed and undivided. This corresponds to the historical function of the doctrine which was to compromise between two competing theologies, the one emphasizing the divinity of Jesus the other his humanity, without sacrificing either.

This dense summary of the development of christology provides a platform to support further reflection on how christology may affect views of other religions.

OTHER RELIGIONS FROM
A CHRISTIAN STANDPOINT

The next discussion unfolds within the context of the classical doctrine of Jesus being a genuine human being but also embodying no less than God for our salvation. While remaining in that context what can a Christian say about other religions that both remains faithful to the classical doctrine and accommodates the new sensitivity to the value and vitality of other religious traditions? The extensive argument which follows is controversial within Christian theology, but it remains within the boundaries of accepted doctrine. I shall not present the reasoning in the form of theses, because such a strong assertion would betray its tentative nature with respect to general Christian sensibility, but I will advance the argument through distinct steps.

In Jesus the Christian encounters a God who as creator is immanent and active in all of creation. The idea of creation developed after the period of the New Testament into the doctrine of creation out of nothing. That formula implies a direct or immediate presence and activity of God to all finite reality. No form of presence and activity can be closer, for the being itself of the creature depends on God sustaining it in being. Christian belief in God entails a God who is so immanent in and present to all reality that all things, even though they are other than God, may be said to exist in God because God exists within them. This presence takes the form of personal love in those creatures able to respond to it. This God is transcendent but not distant.

Jesus reveals the very nature of this creating God to be loving and bent on the salvation of all. This has already been affirmed as part of the logic of christology. The usual way this teaching from the New Testament is stated is that God wills the salvation of all human beings. But I also want to underline that, when Christians affirm the revelation of God's universal will and character as benevolent and saving, this is applicable to all human beings. In the measure that such a proposition on the very character of God is true, it is relevant for all.[2] In other words, the subject matter aimed at here transcends the sphere of the socially and culturally relative. This is rather a matter that has bearing on the human as such. One can see the

---

2. Often the term "normative" is used for the word "relevant." But normativity has become an ambiguous and perhaps dysfunctional category at this point, and I use it sparingly.

significance of the conception of the unity of the human race at this point. A true characterization of the nature and character of ultimate reality is valuable for all human beings. In short, truth and what is often referred to as normativity in substantive religious matters are synonymous.

To be effective in history, God's active saving presence to all requires mediation through historical symbols and religious institutions. Historical effectiveness in this statement really refers to the revelation of God's saving presence and "action" relative to human consciousness. One can of course creatively imagine God at work within human beings apart from all human consciousness of it. But this would come very close to sheer projection. The issue in this discussion precisely revolves around human religious consciousness of the effectiveness of transcendent power immanent to the human condition. The discussion itself rests on the implicit premise that religious consciousness responds to and correlates with God's presence and power in history. Nothing less than this can explain the longevity and power of antique religious traditions.

From a Christian standpoint, therefore, a pluralism of religions is to be expected. That is to say, if one is convinced that God wills the salvation of all people, and that that salvation is not a sheerly eschatological reality but a presence and power in human life that is accompanied by some form of human consciousness of it, then it follows that the same consciousness will take the social form of a religion. This means that the multiplicity of religions from a Christian standpoint is not surprising, but entirely coherent with the Christian conception of God as transcendent but immanently present and operative in the lives of all human beings. Not to affirm an expectation of religious pluralism, or to be embarrassed by it, runs counter to the basic Christian conception of God. It would entail a view of God's saving will as not being universally effective in history. Positively, precisely because God as creator and savior relates to all of history, the articulation and experience of God's presence takes on multiple different forms.

The other side of the historicity of the experience of God's engagement with human beings is the limitation of any particular experience and expression of it. Given the limitation of all historical mediation, and given the transcendent character of ultimate reality, no single salvific mediation can encompass God's reality or human understanding of it. This represents the standard Christian view that God as transcendent should be characterized as infinite and incomprehensible. Ultimate reality, which in the Christian view is God, so transcends every and all finite mediations of it, that no single mediation of God can be said adequately to encompass or be equal to the infinite reality itself of God.

From the transcendence of ultimate reality, or God, it follows that no religion in the sense of a set of religious truths can adequately portray its object. Nor of course can multiple finite mediations. But from a Christian standpoint, the plurality of religions, with their symbolic variety and richness, mediate "more" revelation of God than any single religion including Christianity itself. To view one religion as the fullness of revelation in any historical or categorical sense does not cohere with the object revealed: there can be no such thing as a historical representation of infinite reality that is adequate or comprehensive. The frequently cited Christian idea that Jesus Christ is the fullness of God's revelation has a bearing on the ontological reality of God that is truly revealed because present and at work in him, but this cannot be understood in concrete quantitative or qualitative terms.

In the measure in which other religions are historically distinct from Christianity, autonomous in their mediation of revelation of ultimate reality, and true, they are relevant for all human beings. This idea applies the principle considered earlier, namely, the universal relevance of Christian truth, insofar as it is really true, to all religions. Likewise, if the beliefs of other religions are true in matters concerning the stance of humanity itself before reality and the character of ultimate reality in relation to the human, they are in that measure universally relevant. This correlation of fundamental religious truth and the universally human provides the very ground for interreligious dialogue. To subvert this universal relevance or "normativity" directly undermines the deep anthropological conviction that supports interreligious dialogue itself and the common interest in it.

But this means that Christianity should not be understood as absolute in the sense that it relates to no other religion while other religions are dependent upon it or relate to it as their fulfillment. The revelation of God found in any given religion possesses a historical autonomy that enters into a dialogical relationship with Christianity and other religions and not one of dependence. In the measure that the conceptions about ultimate reality are true, they are relevant to all and bear a normativity that makes a universal claim. This does not mean that all religions are equally revelatory of transcendent reality or the human; some may be more adequate and thus more universally applicable than others. But this is something that can only become apparent within a dialogical situation.

Thus the conviction that Christianity is not exhaustive, but that other religions contain salvific truth not formally contained in Christianity, can through inference be regarded as entailed in the teaching of Jesus. This formulation expresses the point of the argument that has been schematically outlined thus far. That point places the source and quality of the positive conviction about religious pluralism within the core of Christian faith and revelation. The positive view of other religions possesses its value in being drawn out of Christian revelation itself. That core consists in the nature of God revealed in Jesus as a savior God who wills the salvation of all whom God created, and the historical efficacy of that divine and salvific initiative. The conclusion, therefore, does not consist in a proposal that comes from outside Christian faith and threatens it, but lies implicit in the revealing message of Jesus himself. Surely the depths of Christian revelation are inexhaustible and always yield new convictions in new situations. Globalization and current religious dialogue and conflict have thus yielded new awareness of the implications of what has been revealed in Jesus Christ.

AN ORTHODOX PLURALIST CHRISTOLOGY

In this concluding section I will outline theological reasons that explain why the pluralist christology described thus far is orthodox. In this question we get closer to the narrow christological issue and the place it holds within Christian theology. The issue deals with the estimate Christians have of Jesus Christ in relation to God, and how this relationship of identity with God is explained. This is a complex discussion within a tradition which I hope will not be compromised by the following brief treatment in nontechnical terms. I will again resort to theses to ensure clarity and to measure the elements of the argument.

A christology is orthodox when it meets the three criteria of intelligibility, faithfulness to tradition, and empowerment of the Christian life.

An orthodox statement must first of all be intelligible within the context of the contemporary world. It would make little sense to proclaim a doctrine which people generally could not understand because it was alien to the worldview of a people. Transcendent mystery should not be confused with what is unintelligible. One must be more careful in stating this than the brief space allows, for Christianity stands against the sin of the world (in which it also participates) and contains what is in many respects a prophetic and countercultural message. But even prophecy has to be understood to be effective. Unintelligible orthodoxy gives no glory to God.

Second, orthodox doctrine and theology conform to the data of Christian tradition. Here tradition is taken broadly to include Christian scriptures and classical doctrines. "Conforming" in the context of historical interpretation does not mean literal repetition in new contexts, which inevitably betrays the very message that is repeated, but consists in an essential fidelity of interpretation in the present to the object of interpretation as that is given in and through the traditional witness. I have to assume here a sensitivity to the dialectical character of Christian theological interpretation: the community always lives in a tension, which often breaks out in dispute, between fidelity to the past and a contemporary possibility of relevance and meaning. All movement into the future along this line of loyalty to the past entails contention, because orthodoxy demands interpretation, and all interpretation is contextual.

The third vital criterion for the adequacy of orthodox interpretation consists in the preservation of the soteriological character and empowerment of the traditional teachings. The soteriological structure of religious faith becomes practically real in the spiritual life it simultaneously reflects and generates. An orthodoxy irrelevant to the spiritual life becomes empty and therefore nonexistent. Let me now measure the pluralist christology presented here by each of these criteria.

A pluralist christology is surely intelligible in today's globalized world.

It is precisely the current world that has raised the question to which pluralist christology is the answer. The more common problem for Christian consciousness consists not in the applicability of pluralist christology to our current situation but in whether such an understanding conforms with scripture and classical doctrine and the manner in which it empowers.

A pluralist christology conforms to the data of Christian tradition insofar as it "explains" how no less than true God is present and active in the life of Jesus.

Often the idea of orthodoxy has been reduced to whether or not a christology adequately portrays the agency of God at work in Jesus. Although orthodoxy entails more than that, the divinity of Jesus is a central issue. In the New Testament this agency of God is primarily expressed through the symbol of God's Spirit. Less frequently but dramatically it is also represented as an incarnation of the Word or Wisdom of God in the human individual Jesus. Other christologies imply or connote the presence and agency of God in less forceful metaphors. None of these images confuse Jesus with Yahweh or identify him with the one Jesus addressed as Father.[3]

Christology today also employs the symbols of God's Word and God's Spirit to formulate or express God's agency in Jesus. A pluralist christology can be formulated in a language that privileges either one of these symbols. A particular pluralist christology would have to be worked out in considerably more detail before a judgment could be made on its orthodoxy. The goal of such a christology is to preserve the idea of God acting in Jesus in a language of today's culture that is proportionate to the way the christologies of the tradition represented God acting in Jesus in the language of the cultures in which they were proposed. It is worth noting in passing that no christology is ever without critics within Christian theology.

Regarding the construction of an orthodox christology, it is crucial that Christians understand that the issue a pluralist christology has to contend with is not how "high" the christology is or how "distinctly divine" it portrays Jesus. The issue rather is whether what is predicated of Jesus is so unique to him that it cannot be shared by others. If God's being present and active in him bears no parallel with our own relationship to God, then the whole topic of his relevance for us and our

---

3. It is often said today that Jesus did not preach his own person, but was theocentric in focusing his message on the reign of God. This contextual reflection is important and significant. This whole discussion aims at negotiating a shift from christocentrism to theocentrism. Christian faith is necessarily christomorphic because Jesus Christ is the central symbol focusing Christian faith on God. But Christian faith is not necessarily christocentric, but can be theocentric, in the way it construes all objective reality.

salvation is undermined. The point of incarnation language is that Jesus is one of us, that what occurred in Jesus is the destiny of human existence itself: *et homo factus est*. Jesus is a statement, God's statement, about humanity as such. To encourage discontinuity between Jesus and other human beings is to miss the basic point of incarnation and Jesus' being the Second Adam. The projecting upon Jesus of a divinity that radically sets him apart from other human beings does not correspond to the New Testament and undermines the very logic of Christian faith.

Analogously, if God's being present and active in Jesus has no comparable manifestation in other religions that mediate consciousness of God or ultimate reality at work for human salvation, then once again the content of the revelation of Jesus about God is undermined. The identification of Jesus with God's Word means that what Jesus says about God is true. God, and not less than God, is truly at work within humankind as such and thus within various religions. Therefore one must expect incarnations of God in other religious mediations analogous to what occurred in Jesus. This entails no diminishment of what occurred in Jesus, but a new recognition in the light of Jesus' revelation of what God does outside the Christian sphere.

A pluralist christology empowers the Christian life insofar as it proposes Jesus as representing a meaning and direction of human existence that leads to final salvation in the reality of God.

The New Testament contains a pluralism of understandings of how Jesus Christ is savior. There is no single answer to the question "what did Jesus do for human salvation?" The many soteriological formulas all reach out toward the mystery of God's saving approach to human beings in Jesus without being able to encompass it. That salvation appeared in his public ministry. It is read in a crucial way in a life dedicated to the reign of God that leads through death to God's raising of Jesus into divine glory. Many other images and symbols across the New Testament characterize the way God acted in Jesus for human salvation. But all of these metaphors and conceptions are not equal; many depend upon the particular culture and tradition in which they were constructed. For example, a pluralist soteriology rules out conceptions of the salvation mediated by Jesus as limited and confined in principle to Christians. The teaching of the New Testament that God wills the salvation of all human beings has been brought into new focus in today's context as an essential element of the meaning of Jesus. This renewed emphasis has so relativized the exclusivist themes that are also found in the New Testament that, when they stand alone, they seem like cultural myopia.

Orthodoxy is not measured by any one of its three criteria, but in the balance of all three.

There are multiple ways of expressing a response to the narrow christological question of the status of Jesus Christ in relation to God and other human beings. This is true especially of the New Testament, before christological discussion became narrowed down to the terms of an incarnation of the Word of God. But in all the christologies of the New Testament, that which binds them together is the soteriological conviction that God has worked human salvation through the mediation of Jesus of Nazareth. That mediation of salvation is the point of christology in this sense: the experience of salvation is that out of which christological reasoning is generated, and that which it attempts to explain and express. In the New Testament and patristic periods that experience took the form of the culture, language, and problems that were raised at that time. The tradition was intelligible to those who formulated it in the terms of the historical moment.

That logic is not different today. A pluralist christology conforms to the data of the past in the measure that it preserves the existential point of the many christologies of the New Testament and the classical doctrines: namely that it is truly God who is operative in Jesus Christ for human salvation. In other words, the measure of orthodoxy cannot be reduced to the comparison of words today with words of the past as though the words had no historical basis and communitarian life. A pluralist christology conforms to tradition when it preserves the existential, soteriological, and spiritual point of past teachings. Therefore a christology is meaningful and orthodox in the measure in which it intelligibly expresses and "explains" the salvation from God that Christians experience in and through Jesus of Nazareth. But to be intelligible today that explanation must include within God's reign the possibility of the effective salvation of all in history. And the concrete efficacy of that entails in its turn recognition and functional validation of the religions that make the religious question and the experience of ultimate reality available to people.

The new and distinctive character of pluralist christology lies in its noncompetitive premise and context.

I conclude this schematic map of a christology that is pluralist and orthodox with a statement of where its specific difference from earlier christologies lies. This does not consist in lowering a Christian estimate of Jesus, but in expanding its relevance. The difference lies in recognizing that what God has done in Jesus, God does generally. Pluralist christology does not differ from christologies of the past in what it affirms about Jesus Christ, but in the context in which christological doctrine is formulated and in the noncompetitive way in which Jesus Christ is understood. Pluralist christology recognizes that other religions and other religious symbols mediate the "same" transcendent source and power of salvation. Put simply, pluralist christology is orthodox in affirming the basic experience and conviction of Christians regarding the true divinity of Jesus, but it does so in a noncompetitive way. It simply recognizes that what God has done in Jesus, God can do in other religious mediations and does.

Chapter Eight

TWO TYPES OF CHRISTOLOGY

ﮞﮯ

A FEW DECADES AGO Karl Rahner wrote an important essay on two basic kinds or types of christology, one from below and one from above.[1] This distinction of Rahner does not correspond with another similar sounding contrast between a so-called "high" christology and a "low" christology. A high christology generally refers to an understanding of Jesus Christ that highlights his divinity, whereas a low christology would so stress Jesus' humanity that his divinity appears to be compromised. Rahner's point is really quite different from the high-low contrast referring to the content of an understanding of Jesus Christ. He sought to clarify something prior to content, namely, a major difference in the possible method or approach that one followed in order to form such an understanding. In a method *from* below, one begins one's reflection with the testimony of scripture to Jesus of Nazareth and experience of him today, and one as it were "ascends" to an understanding of Jesus' saving work and divinity. A method from below could also be called an ascending christology. In a method *from* above, one begins with the authoritative teaching about Christ's divine status, and from this dogmatic and metaphysical platform one interprets the issues connected with christologically understanding Jesus of Nazareth. Both methods of christology can yield a "high" christology. In what follows I work within the logic of a christology from below.

Since Rahner wrote that essay various shifts in the culture of theology have called into question the variety of methods in christology that proceed from above. These have been highlighted in earlier chapters. Generally speaking, a historical consciousness demands that an understanding of any historical phenomenon be negotiated through a study

---

1. Karl Rahner, "The Two Basic Types of Christology," *Theological Investigations* 13 (New York: Seabury Press, 1975), 213–23.

of its origin and genesis. This exigency is matched by the actual explosion of research that has been devoted to the effort of grasping the way Jesus appeared to his contemporaries during his earthly ministry. Again, speaking generally, the intellectual climate of Europe and North America militates against readily accepting things on the basis of sheer authority. Running parallel to this critical dimension of postmodern culture, one finds in christology an apologetic dimension that seeks to show the credibility of Jesus Christ in terms that appeal to the historical Jesus and the ways in which he responds to present-day existential questions. These developments help to explain why most of the christology being written today has abandoned a point of departure and method "from above."

The two kinds of christology that I wish to develop here are a Logos and a Spirit christology. And these are both to be understood within the framework of christology from below. Ordinarily one tends to think of a Logos christology as precisely a descending christology, for it has usually entailed a three-stage narrative of the preexistent Logos, who was incarnated in time, and then exalted. But I shall try to represent a Logos christology within the same ascending logic as a Spirit christology in order to represent it as responding to the exigencies of our culture.

It must be understood that this laying out of these two types of christology is reportorial. I shall be doing little more than pointing to and stating what theologians are developing in detailed constructive arguments. The goal here is not to justify or even explain the inner logic of these two types of christology, but to offer an appreciation of the shape and direction of these developments. I hope that I can accomplish this in five points. The first consists in a general commentary on the multiple christologies that are found in the New Testament. The second supplies some religious and cultural background from the Jewish scriptures that provides a context for understanding the historical faith witness to Jesus as the Christ. The third proposes a way of understanding New Testament christologies as interpretations of Jesus with the use of the two most significant symbols drawn from the Hebrew scriptures. This provides a general understanding of the provenance of Spirit and Logos christologies respectively. In the fourth point I will underline the distinctive character of Spirit and Word christologies and the strengths of each. And the fifth will respond to the viability of these christologies as the church encounters the third millennium.

THE WITNESS OF THE NEW TESTAMENT TO MULTIPLE CHRISTOLOGIES

The New Testament witness to Jesus Christ presents itself in many different genres of literature, and it contains a large variety of different interpretations of Jesus. Whether it be the four gospels, each of which is distinctive, or the letters of Paul, or the other treatises that make up this book, the same person Jesus is understood in quite different ways. In the past, these differences were not emphasized, but seem to have been considered accidental to the overwhelmingly central point that Jesus was the Messiah, the Christ of God, who eventually came to be recognized as the Logos and Son incarnate. It is characteristic of our historically conscious culture to recognize the real differences in the various appreciations of Jesus that were generated in different communities, by different authors, writing in different situations, with a different set of interpretive categories, to address different questions or problems. The differences among New Testament christologies are such that these many christologies cannot be reduced to one overarching paradigm; to do so would be precisely to negate the distinctiveness of each one.

But at the same time, without disturbing or neglecting the differences, one can still recognize within the intentionality of each that its point is to assert that Jesus bears salvation from God. This common denominator does not remove the different ways of understanding how this is the case. But it does serve to show how different christologies can to tolerated, or better, welcomed in a single large community. The multiple christologies can be understood to constitute a pluralism, where pluralism means not sheer diversity, but difference within a larger unity. That unity is the fixation of faith on Jesus as the one who mediates and represents the initiative of God for human well-being. But that common response to Jesus is actualized in different ways in the community. For one who recognizes the historical limitations of every interpretation, these differences are far from being unfortunate. The New Testament canonizes such pluralism by binding together these various interpretations of Jesus within its own covers, thus giving us a fuller witness to his identity.

One can draw from this fact of the pluralism of New Testament christologies the principle that pluralism in christology may be positively valued. The reasons for the pluralism of New Testament christology also govern the church in the present situation and at any given time. As the interpretations of Jesus in the New Testament were different because they were historical, so too should different communities that make up the great church today appreciate Jesus somewhat differently according to their situation, culture, languages, problems, and so on. It would not be too strong to say that the New Testament actually prescribes pluralism in christology.

It is not the case, however, that all the christologies of the New Testament are equally valid, compelling, or prevalent in their own time, nor that they are equally able to be appreciated in other cultures. Some New Testament christologies that were common in early Palestinian communities found little purchase on Greek sensibilities and, for lack of relevance, fell away or were never taken up.

I want to focus attention on two major types of christology in the New Testament, namely, a Spirit christology and a Word christology. These two christologies are important in the New Testament because they provide patterns for understanding Jesus Christ into the future. Much of present-day christology can be divided between Word or Logos christologies and Spirit christologies. But before turning to these two types of christology, it is essential to discuss however briefly the thought-world or religious culture from which these christologies came. I thus turn immediately to the Jewish background of the New Testament.

THE OLD TESTAMENT PERSPECTIVE FOR UNDERSTANDING THE NEW TESTAMENT WITNESS

Christians have been accustomed to interpreting the Jewish scriptures from the perspective of Jesus Christ and the New Testament. But with the rise of historical consciousness it has become increasingly clear that the Old Testament bears an autonomous, self-contained meaning within itself and prior to construals from a Christian perspective. The interpretative significance of the relationship between the Old and the New Testaments in the other direction is much clearer. One simply cannot understand Jesus Christ outside of the context of Israel, the history that led up to his appearance, and the Jewish scriptures which early Christians used to explain him.

This relationship has to be sharply defined when the question concerns trying to understand the meaning of how God acted in Jesus in such a way that Jesus may be understood to be divine. Christians are constantly tempted to read back into the language of the New Testament the doctrinal meanings or understandings it possesses by virtue of the theological and conciliar tradition. Why not, since these doctrines are true and characterize Jesus as he really was? The response to this question is theoretically unambiguous: because these understandings are the product of later development, whereas the New Testament language, insofar as it is taken as historical witness, has to be understood in its own autonomous context. To read later doctrine into the New Testament is anachronistic, even though later doctrine may legitimately have developed from this earlier canonical writing. Assumed in this position is a distinction, but not a separation, between the "original meaning" of the scriptural witness and the legitimate meanings it releases into the future. Rather than interpret the historical meaning of the New Testament witness from the perspective of its future, one must as a first step return to the relationship between the Jewish scriptures and the New Testament to establish the context and trajectory within which these texts were written. Only then may the more explicitly hermeneutical reading of the text from a present-day standpoint and horizon legitimately release new meaning that is truly within the text and has bearing on our time. To indicate how such a strategy helps to illuminate the christological symbols of the New Testament I will present how one biblical scholar makes this case.[2]

The thesis proposed by Terence Fretheim is straightforward: we have to rely on the Old Testament to understand the New Testament witness to how God acted in Jesus. One finds no radical discontinuity here, because the way Jews thought about God in the Old Testament provides the source and the matrix within which reflection about God's action in Jesus took place (202, 205–6). This can be shown by tracing this continuity across five axes: God in the Old Testament (1) enters into relationship with creatures; (2) is present to creatures and immanent in the world; (3) takes human form and appears; (4) became an enfleshed word; and (5) suffered. All these topics throw light on how God acted in Jesus.

---

2. Terence E. Fretheim, "Christology and the Old Testament," in Mark A. Powell and David R. Bauer, eds., *Who Do You Say That I Am? Essays on Christology* (Louisville: Westminster John Knox, 1999), 201–15. References within the text are to the pages of this essay.

First, God in the Jewish scriptures is close to creation, not radically transcendent and distant but always in relation to human beings and history: "the God of the Old Testament has less 'emptying' to do in the incarnation than does a God who is conceived in such 'wholly other' terms" (203). God is constantly present to and negotiating with human beings. Thus God said to Abraham: "I am God almighty; walk before me, and be blameless. And I will make my covenant between me and you, and will make you exceedingly numerous" (Gen 17:2). In such a context the incarnation would appear as "the supreme exemplification of this kind of divine relatedness and its irrevocability" (208).

Second, in the Jewish scriptures God dwells in the world God created and thus is immanent to or within the world: "the heavens become a shorthand way of referring to the abode of God *within* the world. God's movement from heaven to earth is a movement within the creation. God — who is other than world — works from within the world, and not on the world from without" (208–9). "The Lord, God of hosts, he who touches the earth and it melts, ... who calls for the waters of the sea, and pours them out upon the surface of the earth — the Lord is his name" (Amos 9:5–6). "To suggest that God first entered into time and history in the Christ event is to ignore this wide swath of Old Testament material. God's act in Jesus is an *intensification* of this already-existing trajectory of God's way of being present in and relating to the structures of the world" (209). God cannot be thought to be absent from the world; rather God's continuous presence manifests itself as by degrees more intense at certain times and places and perhaps supremely intense in the incarnation in Jesus.

Third, the form of theophany in the Jewish scriptures throws light on the idea of God taking human form. "Throughout the Old Testament, God takes on human form and appears. God does not become human for the first time in Jesus" (210). In several instances of theophany where God appears in human form, "the human form does not compromise divine transcendence. The finite is capable of the infinite. The empirical world can serve the task of 'clothing' God" (210). The symbol for God becoming "incarnate" in the world in human form is the angel. "Now the angel of the Lord came and sat under the oak at Ophrah" (Judg 6:11). "And the angel of the Lord appeared to the woman..." (Judg 13:3). These instances of theophany provide a perspective on how belief in the incarnation in Jesus was generated and understood. "The incarnation would not be a radical move for those steeped in Old Testament texts. To use an earlier formulation of mine, 'there is no such thing for Israel as a nonincarnate God.' The Old Testament God is a God who is prone to incarnation, and once again, the interpreter can discern a divine trajectory of which *the* incarnation is climactic" (211).

Fourth, prophecy provides a perspective for understanding what is meant by the enfleshed word. Jeremiah and Ezekiel provide examples of the word of God becoming embodied in the person of the prophet (211–12). "Then the Lord put out his hand and touched my mouth; and the Lord said to me, 'Now I have put my words in your mouth'" (Jer 1:9; also Ezek 3:1–3). These examples do not correspond exactly to the word becoming flesh in the fourth gospel, but they provide a context and a trajectory of thought for understanding what is going on imaginatively in the use of the symbol.

Fifth, and finally, the Old Testament bears witness to a suffering God. God says: "You have burdened me with your sins; you have wearied me with your iniquities" (Isa 43:24). Thus if one were to so conceive the crucifixion, "God did not suffer for the sins of the world for the first time on the cross" (212).

This analysis of the thought-world that lies behind the New Testament's christological interpretation of Jesus of Nazareth forms part of the historical critical study of the Bible that must be integrated into christological interpretation today. A couple of principles can summarize how it fits into present-day thinking. A first principle may be stated in terms of guarding against the natural tendency of reading back into the New Testament witness understandings which are familiar because of the doctrinal tradition of the church. We will indeed have to draw the meaning of the New Testament forward into our time for it to be relevant for human existence in our world. But that methodical and interpretative move should not be confused with what the canonical representation of the community's faith in the early church was saying. The Prologue of John's gospel was rightly drawn forward into the debate at Nicaea, but its use in that debate is quite other than the presuppositions and type of thinking that generated the original meaning of the text. One cannot use Nicaea as an exegetical premise for understanding the historical meaning of the Prologue.

172 Two Types of Christology

A second principle would state the need to represent the religious cultural world of beliefs in which Jesus of Nazareth appeared and the kind of thinking and language that ultimately gave voice to the faith in his messiahship. On that premise, the foregoing analysis shows the considerable continuity between the New Testament language and the understanding of God that went before. The context and the subject matter did not yield the radical antitheses or alternatives of later christological thinking: Jesus is or is not divine; God is or is not present to Jesus; Jesus is or is not qualitatively different from other presences of God to the world. This does not make these new distinctions, when they occurred, illegitimate. But the symbols and metaphors for thinking about God in the scriptural context were both more nuanced and less rigid than in later debates. The later debates, by so narrowing the context, risked losing a broader religious perspective. Indeed, the New Testament has ways of "explaining" what is meant by incarnation in symbols that are much more fluid and open, quite different from each other, and yet point in the same direction. The two principal symbols are "Spirit" and "Word."

THE SCRIPTURAL MEANING OF
SPIRIT AND WORD APPLIED TO JESUS

One way of establishing the meaning of the biblical symbols "Spirit" and "Word" as these are used in the Hebrew scriptures and in the New Testament would be to establish the distinctive traits of each metaphor on the basis of its usage. This historical critical method is essential and crucial; without it one would not be speaking about these particular symbols in this particular case. But at the same time, after that investigation has been completed, one still must respond to the question of how these terms have a bearing upon the way we understand ourselves in a postmodern society at the beginning of the third millennium. In order to satisfy the apologetic character of christology, one must have a way of interpreting these symbols in such a way that they make sense in our current world. I shall do this by, first, treating these categories as religious symbols; second, finding their meaning in the experience they imply; and, third, pointing to the experience and logic that lie behind the predication of these terms to Jesus.

First, then, the categories from the Hebrew scriptures that were used to interpret Jesus in the New Testament are mental or conceptual symbols, as distinct from concrete symbols.[3] Because God is not available to us in an immediate way for direct apprehension, God must be conceived, thought about, and spoken of in symbolic terms. A symbol in this case means a concept, metaphor, or analogy that opens up the mind and heart to God as transcendent reality, and thus gives expression to religious consciousness. In classical scholastic theology language and thought about God was analogous. This meant that it never reached its transcendent object directly, but only through the similarity and dissimilarity of finite things. To call language about God symbolic accomplishes much the same thing. The tension in analogical language about God is one of negation and affirmation. The dynamic tension in symbolic language consists in the mind reaching toward the transcendent reality which the symbols points to and makes present, while at the same time recognizing that the finite symbol itself falls far short of this transcendent object.

Second, symbols express and mediate an experience of God. Therefore, one must find the meaning of symbols in the experience that they codify. That experience has both a particular and a generalized meaning. Such symbols as God's "Word," or the "Spirit" of God, or God's "Presence," or God's "Wisdom" all relate to particular experiences of God in this world. The kind or mode of experience reflected in each symbol is somewhat distinctive insofar as it is specified or named by a different metaphor. Word and Spirit are not the same ideas. But at the same time, as in the different New Testament christologies, one can find common denominators in the experiences that are symbolized in these various symbols. For example, all of these symbols refer indirectly or mediately to God. It is God's presence, or wisdom, or power that is being experienced and that gives rise to the symbol. This is proven by the fact that, while they are discrete and distinct symbols, they are sometimes used interchangeably. In various usages in the scriptures one finds a practical equivalence between these symbols: Word = Wisdom = Spirit.

Third, when these symbols are used with reference to Jesus, they signify that God is encountered in Jesus. The common dimension of the

---

3. I use the term "concrete symbol" to refer to things, events, places, or persons which as objects (or subjects) point to something other than themselves and make that reality present and available within themselves.

various experiences that come to expression in the metaphor that Jesus is Son of God, or the Word of God, or the Wisdom of God, is that the transcendent God has been manifested or disclosed in the person of Jesus. The Spirit of God is God immanent and at work in the world. God as Spirit is God's power and energy by which prophets and leaders do great deeds. To say that the Spirit was at work in Jesus' life reflects the experience of the disciples that God is encountered in Jesus' person and ministry. The primary historical basis for the idea that Jesus is the Wisdom and Word of God was the quality of Jesus' teaching and pro-phetic portrayal of the truth of God reigning. Jesus' teaching and life were experienced by the disciples as actualizing the presence and values of God in history. These symbols took on more meaning in the light of the experience that Jesus was raised and exalted with God and in the expectation that he would come again. But the primary historical event that bestows meaning on these symbols is the salvific encounter of God in the person of Jesus. The symbols of "Spirit" and "Word" have to be understood historically as having their basis in the historical ministry of Jesus and the reaction of the disciples to it.

THE STRENGTHS OF
A SPIRIT AND A WORD CHRISTOLOGY

Spirit and Word christologies share much in common; both are confes-sional or faith statements that express a religious encounter with God in and through the ministry of Jesus. The person of Jesus himself medi-ates the saving presence and power of God. At the same time, however, the two ways of expressing this meeting of God in Jesus are different. These differences encourage a closer look at Spirit christology and Word christology in order to bring out what is distinctive about each. I will do this first with reference to scripture. In the next section I will consider their relation to classical doctrine and their potential for empowering Christian life today.

Spirit christology offers the most prevalent direct answer given by the New Testament to the question of how God was present to and at work in Jesus. Most typical in this regard are the synoptic gospels which all depict God as Spirit at work in Jesus' ministry. "God's 'Spirit' is virtually always synecdoche for God himself, and is usually a way of speaking of God's *presence* while preserving his transcendence."[4] Luke especially represents a consistent Spirit christology. God as Spirit is the power overshadowing Mary and enabling her to conceive Jesus, her son. The Spirit empowers Jesus for his ministry at his baptism and is the witness to his authority when he inaugurates his ministry in Nazareth. God as Spirit is the power by which Jesus is able to exorcize and heal. And after his exaltation, the risen Jesus sends the Spirit to animate the community of his followers. There are of course many other titles, and hence christologies, at work in Luke, the other synoptics, and the rest of the New Testament. But this Spirit christology responds to the broad general question of how early Christians, and perhaps people during his lifetime, expressed their recognition of the presence and power of God in Jesus' life or person. The foundational metaphor of this christology is empowerment: God as Spirit, the principle of life and dynamic energy, is present and active in Jesus in a special way.

Although Word or Logos christology is less prominent in the New Testament, it became the all-embracing framework for understanding Jesus Christ after the first century. Other christologies were neglected, or minimized, or absorbed into the commanding paradigm of the incarnation of God as Word or Logos. Many reasons account for this, not the least of which was the affinity of Logos language to the dominant Greek intellectual culture of the Roman empire. But the origins of this christology are not Greek; they lie in Jesus himself, in the tradition of Jewish wisdom, and in the cult of Jesus that began shortly after his death. People had experienced the presence of God in Jesus' teaching and life, and they continued to relate to the risen Jesus in the assemblies of the Jesus movement and in prayer. The purest form of a Word or Logos christology is found in the Prologue of John's gospel. But this Logos christology may be understood as a development that runs parallel to other Wisdom christologies. Personified Wisdom, that is, the Wisdom of God, is conceived as being represented in Jesus and his teaching. The fact that several expressions of this Wisdom christology are hymns suggests that they originated in a liturgical setting. The basic metaphor underlying this christology is incarnation: God as Word or God as Wisdom "comes down" and is embodied

---

4. M. Turner, cited by Robert F. O'Toole, *Luke's Presentation of Jesus: A Christology* (Rome: Editrice Pontificio Istituto Biblico, 2004), 221.

in the person and ministry of Jesus. But the novelty of this descent has to be softened in light of the Old Testament perspective presented earlier.

The relative merits of these two christologies are usually characterized in oppositional terms relative to the christological norm of the Council of Chalcedon which affirmed that the constitution of Jesus Christ was such that he was truly human and truly divine. Measured by this template, Spirit christology leans toward, protects, and even emphasizes Jesus' humanity, because the metaphor of empowering seems to presuppose an integral human being in whom the Spirit dwells and acts. This allows the life and ministry of Jesus to appear more credible in a modern and postmodern culture. With this christology one can imagine a continuity between Jesus and ourselves, although the Christian's relationship to Jesus entails the idea that Jesus must have been empowered by God as Spirit in a way that amounted to a qualitatively superior kind of union. But the continuity between Jesus and human beings generally, in turn, confirms the relevancy of Jesus' life and teaching for human existence as we know it and makes the imitation or following of Jesus imaginable.

By contrast, Logos christology emphasizes Jesus' divinity, because the personification of the Word of God is often read as a distinct or hypostatized form of being that "in the beginning" was "with God" (John 1:1). When this three-stage christology is read as literal report, it yields an understanding in which the preexistent divine Logos assumes a human nature and becomes an actor in history, and then is raised or ascends to the divine realm. There is but one divine subject through the three stages. In this christology what one encounters in Jesus is truly other, truly divine: Jesus is a presence and manifestation of the divine in history. The divinity of Jesus becomes magnified when the descent-ascent scheme is isolated from its Jewish context. If the world is conceived as alien territory for God, incarnation appears radical. In a secular world Jesus becomes an aperture in history which Logos has entered to be a "visible" representation of God: in him we have seen God's glory (John 1:14, 18).

THE VIABILITY OF A SPIRIT AND A WORD CHRISTOLOGY IN THE FUTURE

These are stereotypical readings of Spirit and Word christologies, which do not take into account all the resources in the tradition itself that allow a more balanced reading of each. By "the tradition" I mean the continuous, existential history of a real encounter of true God in Jesus to which the New Testament and the patristic doctrines give witness. The viability of these christologies lies in how well a certain reading continues to open up or "explain" the Christian encounter of God in Jesus. Such a reading must be dialectical in the sense that it allows the tension contained in the classical Chalcedonian formula its full play: Jesus is both fully human and fully divine. In other words, both of these christologies have to be understood or interpreted within the context of these parameters.

What are some elements of the tradition that allow a Spirit christology, which tends to reenforce Jesus' humanity, to also adequately express Jesus' divinity? Three reflections on the tradition help to explain why this christology can maintain the balance of Chalcedon.

A first reflection is aimed at clearing away the objection that Logos language is the only way of expressing Jesus' divinity. This common misapprehension is supported by the hegemony of this language throughout the patristic period, and by the fact that the definition of the divinity of Jesus used Logos language. But an analysis of the problem addressed at Nicaea and the solution offered in the Nicene Creed show that the precise issue raised by Arius did not concern the term "Logos" which all accepted. The problematic assertion of Arius was that what was present and active in Jesus was less than divine, indeed, a creature. In response to Arius, Nicaea's Logos language was the vehicle for affirming Jesus' divinity, and the term "Logos," which was never in question, was thus not set up as an exclusive christological language.[5] To have done so would have contradicted the pluralistic witness of the New Testament.

The second reflection follows the first in pointing out that the canonical status of a Spirit christology was guaranteed when, like the symbol Logos, Spirit too was affirmed to represent true God. In principle, then, Spirit is not less divine than Logos, and whatever can be said of Jesus' divinity by using Logos language can also be expressed in terms of Spirit.

The third reflection is the principle from the theology of Karl Rahner affirming that the more God is personally present and at work in

---

5. The patristic conciliar context that provides the background and reference points for several of these reflections cannot be developed here. A brief account of the development of patristic christology and the doctrines of Nicaea and Chalcedon can be found in Haight, *Jesus Symbol of God* (Maryknoll, N.Y.: Orbis Books, 1999), 244–98.

human freedom, the more human freedom comes into its own and is autonomous.[6] This dialectical principle does not fully *explain* the divine presence to Jesus Christ. But it helps to understand how Spirit christology, precisely in preserving Jesus' humanity, also affirms his divinity. The self-communication of God as Spirit to Jesus' spiritual person, in a supremely intimate way, is not a possession that takes over Jesus' free spirit, but releases it to be most fully human. It is, in the tradition of the Jewish scriptures, an intensification of God's presence in the person of Jesus. The divinity of Jesus has to be understood precisely in the dynamic conjunction and interaction within a personal relationship between Jesus and God as this relationship is enabled and animated by God's self-presence and power.

Logos christology too, if it is to meet the exigencies of today, must incorporate the correctives from the tradition that protect it from compromising Jesus' humanity. Two elements of the tradition are particularly relevant here. The first consists in a literary and epistemological reflection on the symbolism of "wisdom" and "logos" when they are applied to Jesus. Already mentioned is the tendency to read back into the New Testament the developed metaphysical presuppositions of patristic theology and even the doctrine of the trinity. The primary witness to Jesus is expressed in metaphorical and symbolic language; it does not provide us with direct objective knowledge about the inner life of God and God's outreach to history. Rather this language is the expression of religious experience and an encounter of Jesus in faith.

Second, in the resistance of Antiochene to Alexandrian christology in the fifth century one sees a reaction against a three-stage Logos christology that is monophysite, that is, a christology that so reduces Jesus' humanity to an instrument of the Logos that, in effect, Jesus is constituted as singly one divine being or "nature." In contrast to this, the Antiochenes affirmed that Jesus was an integral human being in whom God as Logos dwelt from the very beginning. However inadequate the

---

6. Rahner states it this way: "the axiom for understanding every relationship between God and creatures... [is] that closeness and distance, or being at God's disposal and being autonomous, do not vary for creatures in inverse, but rather in direct proportion. Christ is therefore man in the most radical way, and his humanity is the most autonomous and the most free not in spite of, but because it has been assumed, because it has been created as God's self-expression." Karl Rahner, *Foundations of Christian Faith: An Introduction to the Idea of Christianity* (New York: Crossroad, 1994), 226.

Antiochenes may have been in affirming the unity of the person of Jesus, they maintained a Logos christology that fully affirmed both the humanity and divinity of Jesus. An analogous accommodation is required today by those Logos christologies that do not represent Jesus as fully human and consubstantial with us. It is difficult to see how the classical three-stage christology that began "from above" can be anything but misleading in a historically conscious culture. But an Antiochene accommodation will overcome the problem.

To conclude, these two types of christology will continue to be the subject of discussion and debate as the church gradually encounters a postmodern world. Both of these christologies have the potential to open up religious experience to an encounter of God in Jesus. In different ways they mediate a response to the person who is looking for a transcendent meaning of human life in history. Logos christology regards Jesus as one who reveals God's wisdom; as such he is God's Word of revelation. To a faith searching for reason and coherence in the world and in the universe, Jesus can disclose the ultimate intentionality and destiny of creation in a personal, loving God. Spirit christology regards Jesus as one who was empowered with the very power of God; God as Spirit was at work in him. To a faith searching for a path in an arbitrary and chaotic history, Jesus discloses a way of life empowered by God and directed toward realizing God's values and aims in history. Both present Jesus as God's standard in history without removing Jesus from history but by seeing God at work in him in a way that reveals God and God's will.

Which is the more adequate christology? This cannot be decided on the level of types. Much will depend upon how a particular formulation of either of these christologies meets the criteria of the tradition, the requirement of intelligibility or credibility in our current world, and the existential demand for relevance to life in history. But this is a matter of discussion. The pluralism prescribed by the New Testament will not be superseded in a church that spans the cultures. Passive agreement on matters that deeply engage the human is impossible in a postmodern context. As long as there is pluralism and discussion in christology, one will know that Jesus Christ is still alive and relevant in the community.

Chapter Nine

THE FUTURE
OF CHRISTOLOGY

E VERY ESSAY that deals with the future begins with an apology which essentially says that, when people talk of the future, they do not really know what they are talking about. The future does not exist and, when it becomes the present, always turns out differently than was imagined. But since everyone knows this, they can relax and not be concerned about the quality of this speculative discourse. In effect we may say that, because none of us knows the future, we are all free to talk about it.

But some disciplines can do better than others in extrapolating from the present into the future. Statistical sciences can come rather close to determining some things: for example, meteorologists do fairly well in predicting the weather. For my part, I want to enter this discussion with a method or at least a strategy that is considerably less than scientific. It consists of extrapolating or projecting the future on the basis of present experience together with certain familiar patterns that measure or channel changes in human thinking and valuing. I do not draw these models from academic theory, but from common experience and common sense.[1] I remain on this common sense level in order to highlight where the development I am referring to is occurring. My attention focuses upon development in the ideas and attitudes of educated, middle-class Christians in the mainline churches who are being drawn along with the times and culture in which we live. In other words, development here is being carried by the Christian faithful at large insofar as they reflect on the matters under discussion.

---

1. Although drawn from common experience and common sense, these constructs may either reflect methodically developed theories or be raised by disciplined reflection to such a state. But I prescind from those issues here.

It will become evident that this effort has at best a tentative character. This projection into the future is not controlled by statistical data, or necessary axioms, or the laws of logic. So let me state my method and procedure in the pointed way in which I understand them. This is an essay at reading the signs of the times in the American churches, and my evidence rarely transcends an appeal to common experience today. I make this appeal in two stages. I first point to three general patterns which help illumine what goes on in the process of how people's thinking develops or changes. If such patterns obtain generally, they should also apply in religious matters. These descriptions of how development occurs will thus serve as devices for peering into the future. Thus, in the second step, on the basis of these three ways of understanding how development unfolds, I speculate as to how christology might develop. What the reader will have to judge is whether these descriptions of development have any merit, and whether the data I feed into them yield the projections that I foresee.

To summarize the structure of the argument, the development has two parts: Part one contains three homely descriptions of the dynamics of how people change their views. Part two applies these patterns to the development of christology in two areas. The first is the area of comparative theology, which may be considered as a discipline closely related to the practice of interreligious dialogue, but which I treat on the level of becoming aware of the other religions and the impact this makes. The second is the question of the divinity of Jesus and how this is to be experienced and understood in the future.

THREE PATTERNS OF
HOW DEVELOPMENT OCCURS

Development in people's thinking occurs in three different ways: spacial contexts change, temporal contexts also change, and experiential or mental horizons expand. Although these descriptions do not constitute theories of development but are meant as phenomenological descriptions that appeal to experience, I will also refer to sources that could be mined in an effort to build these descriptions into theories. It will also become evident in the descriptions that these three are not completely distinct, but overlap. I do not propose these patterns as being in any way exhaustive;

one can find other logics of the development of understanding.[2] I set up these particular descriptions simply because I find them commonplace and useful.

Appearance within a New Spacial frame of Reference

The first pattern of development that I wish to highlight may occur when something appears within in a new spacial context. The metaphor of putting an old picture in a new frame is particularly simple and instructive. As the picture takes on all sorts of new perspectives in the various new frames into which it may be inserted, so too traditional understandings or propositions may take on new meaning when located in a new "spacial" context.[3] I remember visiting a small church in northern Spain: the former church had been razed to be replaced by a new brick and glass structure that was light and modern. But the architect had preserved the baroque altar piece and inserted it into the bright sanctuary where it filled the space behind the altar and rose, with all its wooden nooks and crannies, high above it. The clash and the fit of the modern and baroque welded into one unified construction could stimulate a debate as to whether the altar piece was preserved in the new mid-twentieth-century modern church, or whether the architect had created something utterly new by situating the old piece in a new place.

Applying this metaphor of spatial change, of putting a picture in a new context, may appear to be something of a reach in the case of theology. But what if we speak in terms of an imaginative framework for understanding? By this I mean a set of assumptions or presuppositions about reality that provides the context of meaning, or one's image or picture of the world. Most of our classical doctrines were formulated within the imaginative framework of a pre-Copernican universe, a relatively small earth and cosmos created all at once by God. Our language of redemption usually presumes that the first human beings were created in a whole and integral way, in a state of perfection, from which they fell, setting up a situation of sin, which in one way or another caused a break

---

2. For example, reactionary developments may recoil from the incursions of new data and impel a reappropriation of the past in much more traditional but still transformed terms.

3. In the comparison, the sense of the term "spacial" is analogous: the literal sense of space is broadened to include the imaginative framework for cognitive apprehension.

or alienation from God and which required a redeemer. The new picture of the universe that has evolved in the course of the nineteenth and twentieth centuries is quite different: an unimaginably long period of creation of the cosmos, a stunningly long and intricate period of the formation of the planet earth, the gradual evolution of life, and finally the human species. Although these imaginative frameworks have not been completely determined, still the overall picture provides little space for an original pair, created in wholeness, or a fall, or an original sin in the Augustinian sense that we have inherited in the West. The whole background picture and story of the rise of humanity has provided a new imaginative context within which Jesus Christ and christology must be set, and this new setting will provide new meanings and understandings.[4]

A variety of current areas of study might provide theoretical resources to move beyond this loose, impressionistic allusion to this form of development. The topic of inculturation has become a major area of discussion since the Second Vatican Council. What happens when doctrines transmigrate into new cultures, worldviews, and language systems? For example, if one depicted postmodernity as an intellectual culture, as distinct from a set of doctrines, and if christology were to be inculturated into this new cultural framework, Jesus Christ would be understood differently simply by being inculturated into a new imaginative framework.

Appearance within a New Temporal Frame of Reference

Development also occurs as people's objective ideas, convictions, and commitments move through time. Many theories of development through time mark the theological landscape. Here I want to appeal more loosely to the basic metaphor of the narrative which always moves forward into new contexts. Nothing human — no idea, value, theology, or doctrine — nothing human can be understood outside of a narrative context because human existence is historical existence. Existence always moves in time; nothing is stable in time; nothing is unchanging in time; to be a human being is to move irreversibly through time. And this narrative always involves continuity and change, some dimension of sameness and always change. Meanings are not and cannot be stable, but

---

4. This theme provides the leading edge of the discussion of christology by Michael Morwood, *Is Jesus God? Finding Our Faith* (New York: Crossroad, 2001).

one can find something within them that remains constant over history, at least insofar as the human subject that is changing retains a basic identity and entertains the same object.

Consider this example of radical change and continuity proposed by Sandra Schneiders:

> [L]et us imagine a six-year-old child whose distant and financially irresponsible father dies. For the child and her mother the event is an unmitigated tragedy. They have lost the only support they know, however minimal it might have been. A couple of years later the widow meets and marries a man who loves her and the child and fills their lives with an affection and material security they have never known. The death of the natural father which produced the possibility of this new set of relationships is no longer a tragedy in their lives but a liberating grace. The effective history generated by the originating event, namely the death of the natural father, makes the event itself of the death, now experienced as integral to a new life and interpreted within a new horizon, a genuinely different reality. In a very real sense the event, although unchanged in its material facticity . . . , is completely different in significance, that is, in its historical reality and meaning because of its integration into the history that it effected.[5]

Besides the standard modern theories of the development of doctrine, hermeneutical theory also provides resources for giving this kind of development a solid theoretical grounding. The interpretation theories of Hans-Georg Gadamer and Paul Ricoeur both take historical consciousness seriously, and they formulate ways in which continuity, sameness, and relevance to the present can be retrieved from past classics precisely in the face of recognition that history can mediate radical change that threatens the past with irrelevance. More important for our day, John Thiel offers a postmodern theory of development which fully acknowledges the discontinuity of the present from the past and yet finds a way in which the past is drawn up into a new present-day narrative framework.[6]

---

5. Sandra M. Schneiders, "Living Word or Dead(ly) Letter: The Encounter between the New Testament and Contemporary Experience," *Proceedings of the Catholic Theological Society of America*, 47 (1992), 51.

6. John E. Thiel, in his *Senses of Tradition: Continuity and Development in Catholic Faith* (Oxford: University Press, 2000), 56–95, develops a "retrospective," as distinct from a "prospective,"

Understanding in a New Expanded Horizon of Experience

One's understanding of reality also develops through an expanding horizon of experience and knowledge that all knowing subjects spontaneously undergo. This would apply as well to theological matters. Developmental psychology provides a wealth of categories and theories that illumine how persons, and perhaps also groups, develop through the broadening of horizon of experience within which they situate that which is understood.

We all have recourse to our own experience of this pattern of a developing understanding: we simply understand things in new and different ways as we move through the life cycle and as we collect and process new experiences which shape the way we understand reality. The metaphor of an expanding horizon suggests visually how new understanding occurs. The physical horizon is the line where earth and sky appear to meet; the psychological horizon is the visual space or scope within which we perceive objects. As a horizon broadens, more objects are included within the picture, their positions and values change in relation to each other, and they take on new dimensions and significance. As one's existential horizon becomes broadened and opened up, one's own identity develops, mediating changes in insight and judgment that may be quite radical. But at the same time the knowing subject remains continuous despite change, and the elements and causes of change can be analyzed and justified. One thus possesses in this phenomenon of human development an excellent example of how sameness and difference, continuity and change, congeal in the process of change.

The common experience of human development has been studied extensively, and one need only mention the names of such thinkers as Erikson, Kohlberg, Gilligan, Fowler, and Kegan who represent various theories of human development. These theorists provide the categories and distinctions that enable one to analyze the development of doctrine from the perspective of the psychology of the knowing subject.

---

theory of tradition and development of doctrine. Theories of development that employ an "organic" root metaphor conceive of development moving forward into the future from the perspective of a seed-like given that contains virtualities that open up in the course of the dialectics of history. A retrospective theory of development admits more discontinuity: the standpoint is a present time that constantly changes as it moves forward, but which consistently looks back to the past to discover relevant truth. The community continues to create new bridges across which it draws the past forward into ever new contexts.

Fowler's analyses, because they focus specifically on faith development, are particularly apropos here.[7]

What I have presented in this section are not theories of development, but three descriptions of and appeals to common experiences of how development occurs. These experiences could be more adequately accounted for by theories of development that are already in place, or they could be enhanced by more rigorous application of one or another of the resources that I have noted. I shall use them as lenses or heuristics for reflecting on how christology might develop, or has already begun to develop, into the future.

TWO AREAS OF CHRISTOLOGICAL DEVELOPMENT: OTHER RELIGIONS AND JESUS' DIVINITY

More specifically I want to apply these rough descriptions of development to two areas of christology: the status of Jesus Christ in relation to other religious mediations, and the question of the divinity of Jesus. In our situation today the two areas are mutually intertwined. The issues are sensitive, and yet the questions raised are open questions. Both areas have generated some intense discussion, but the discussions themselves promise no simple or easy answers. Insofar as these issues will continue to come under intense discussion, it would be hard to imagine that there would be no development in the Christian community's appreciation of them. Perhaps the deployment of the three formal or structural models of development might help forecast the way in which the development will unfold. But I am predicting less the content of the development of christology in the future and more the direction it might take. In fact I assume that the development will leave the intention of the traditional doctrines intact, while the way they are understood and explained may change considerably.

Attitudes toward Jesus in Relation to Other Religions

In mainline Christian theology, if one could determine a point of departure for development within the topic of the relation of Jesus Christ to

---

7. See James W. Fowler, *Stages of Faith: The Psychology of Human Development and the Quest for Meaning* (San Francisco: Harper & Row, 1981).

other religious mediations, it would probably best be described as inclusivism. By inclusivism I mean the belief that readily grants that God saves
people of other religions, and uses their religious to do so; but in the
fundamental scheme of things Jesus Christ remains the ultimate cause of
their salvation. Karl Rahner's explanation of what he called "anonymous
Christianity" provides a clear example of this position. Generally speaking it represents the current position of the Roman Catholic Church,
probably most people in the mainline churches, and a majority of Christian theologians. The question I ask, then, is whether the three ways in
which development transpires that I have outlined can shed light on how
development beyond this position might unfold.

In the new spacial frame of the cosmos. I drew the first metaphor describing development in spacial lines, as when a picture is placed in a
new frame. Analogously, what happens when one transfers the story
of redemption by Jesus Christ into the imaginative framework of the
evolving universe, planet, and species, which affords little or no place
for the creation, fall, and rescue that has been the traditional Christian story? It seems clear that all educated people will gradually come
to internalize this new picture of the origins of our cosmos, world, and
selves. In the same measure the traditional story of origins, even when
recognized as a religious symbol, will appear archaic, a puzzle whose language blocks or intervenes into Christian faith rather than mediates and
expresses it.

By contrast, one way the new picture of the world might provide
a positive impulse toward a new constructive understanding revolves
around the themes of creation and the immanence of God to all reality. The scientific story of creation redirects attention to the Christian
doctrine of creation. In itself, the scientific conception of the origin of
the universe, the earth, and the human species appears awesome and religiously charged: potentially it bears religious power. One can read in
this picture the ongoing creation of God or God as Spirit as an internal
divine presence and creative force in the process itself. The sheer size of
this imaginative vision expands beyond the traditional creation myth; it
dwarfs and compacts the human race and thus takes on a more explicitly
universal character. Gradually one begins to think in a theocentric frame
of reference as distinct from a christocentric framework. This refocusing

of attention on God as creator, allowing God to be operative in all people and in all world religions, may well be accompanied by and perhaps will require an adjustment of our understanding of Jesus Christ within this larger frame of reference.

In the new story of the human race. The second context for projecting development is narrative, the one-way passage through time in which old meanings take on new valences and enhanced significance. In the "process" understanding of reality which history and the hard sciences have forced on our imaginations, we now have to understand the human phenomenon in narrative terms. Moreover, in that open-ended story, I think most would agree that we are entering a new stage of the history of the human race, where more and more we are becoming one world. In a way that has never happened before, all the "others" have now become members of my human community in a new concrete and practical way; the alien "enemy" has become a neighbor and a possible "friend." In this situation we cannot in principle provide a metaphysical grounding for competition and imperialism by defining Christianity as the only true religion, thereby relegating other religions as inferior to Christianity.[8] More and more thoughtful Christians are seeing the deep problems, both intellectual and moral, in their current self-understanding. The new stage of the human story, which in various settings and places involves the intermingling of religious people from different faiths, is gradually forbidding an a priori stance of superiority.

In place of regarding the other as inferior, one might envisage another possible although somewhat idealistic scenario of how peoples of different faith might gradually begin to interact. The attitude of the dialogue partners progresses from a relationship that might be characterized as an objective "us and them," to a more personal encounter described as an "I-Thou" relationship. But this is not the final goal. The movement into closer relationships in the human community and the broader context of an ongoing creation-centered picture of the world encourage us to hope that our relationship to other religions will develop into a

---

8. To understand Christianity as the only true religion would be "a virtual declaration of war on all other religions." Edward Schillebeeckx, "The Uniqueness of Christ and the Interreligious Dialogue," a paper delivered to the Catholic Academy in Munich, Bavaria (April 22, 1997), manuscript, p. 5.

"We" relationship in which, as we face our common world, we share our distinctive religious experiences in a noncompetitive way.[9]

In comparison with the former isolation of the religions from each other, the new stage in the human story will not allow a priori self-definitions of superiority. The new situation will gradually engender new attitudes of a priori acceptance of what God is doing in other religions as, in their contexts, roughly on a par with what God has done in and through Jesus.

In a new expanded horizon of experience. The spontaneous development of personal human existence and consciousness provides the third dynamic for understanding development in christology. All people continually revise their positions on everything as they constantly draw in new experiences and expand the horizons within which they situate the object under consideration. One of the catalysts expanding Christian horizons correlates with the shrinking of our globe. The media of communication bind people more closely together and at the same time expand human consciousness. This can lead to gradual acceptance of pluralism, including religious pluralism, a positive evaluation of it, and finally a positive view of other religions. On the one hand, God as Spirit is working in their constituents; on the other hand, a plurality of religions provides "more" revelation of God than a single religion in its particularity could. Let me be clear about the object of understanding in this expanding consciousness: it is Jesus Christ as the mediator of God's salvation to me and all those who share in the Christian faith and thus confess the same thing. That remains constant. What shifts, therefore, is not the object of christology, but assessment of how, as a mediator of God, Jesus stands in relation to other religious mediators that bind the constituents of the various religions to what they understand to be absolute or ultimate. The direction of this shift will be away from an a priori taking for granted that Jesus alone causes the salvation of all, including those who are not consciously related to him, in the direction of a perception of other religions also as vehicles for, in Christian terms, God's immanent presence to the human and a human encounter with

9. I borrow this scheme from Wilfred Cantwell Smith's sketch of stages in the progress of interreligious dialogue in *Towards a World Theology: Faith and the Comparative History of Religion* (Philadelphia: Westminster Press, 1981), 101, 193.

God. This will lead to various theories in which people view the religions in a less competitive way. Relative to christology, the development
will be toward a view of Jesus as God's real and efficacious bringer of
salvation but not necessarily in a superior and competitive way.

To conclude this part, we can say that these three prognosticators all
point in the same direction with slightly different logic. Let me now turn
to development around the topic of the divinity of Jesus.

The Divinity of Jesus

How would one describe the conception of Jesus' divinity currently in
place in the mainline churches? I do not intend to set up an easy caricature
as a target on which one can train his or her guns. Nevertheless certain
features of the common understanding of the divinity of Jesus Christ
flow from basic doctrine and catechetics. Most people and a majority of
theologians presuppose the doctrine of the trinity as a metaphysical background for the incarnation of the Son or Logos. Jesus is divine because
the historical figure Jesus of Nazareth is the incarnation of the second
person of the trinity. For a number of decades it has been commonly ad-
mitted by theologians that this language of traditional christology tends
to undercut the integrity of Jesus' humanity. This I believe will change as
Jesus Christ is more and more understood "from below," that is, in terms
of a christology that begins with and focuses on Jesus as a person in history.[10] In the following discussion of how this might occur I presuppose
that the formal divinity of Jesus Christ is a constant, the object of the
development, but that this divinity will be understood and affirmed in
new ways. How do the three ways in which development transpires help
to illumine how that development might go forward?

In the new spacial frame of the cosmos. When we situate the Christian
story of incarnation into the new picture of the world as provided by science, it occasions some shifts in understanding. One possible shift may be
a new recognition of the power of the doctrine of creation. I am inspired
at this point by Edward Schillebeeckx's theology of creation, and I can
reduce the logic of this possible development to three insights.[11] The first

10. If one is in an interreligious context and called upon to explain who Jesus Christ is, one
will almost automatically begin the explanation with an account of Jesus of Nazareth. If one
began with a doctrine and theology of the trinity, the interlocutor would be lost rather early in
the exchange.
11. See chapter 3, pp. 63–66.

is that creation is an ongoing process and reality; God is always creating. Second, highlighting the doctrine of creation allows one to conflate the natural and supernatural spheres. God creates out of self-giving love and God's gratuitous love never withdraws from God's creation, even when it appears to be absent, as in the story of Job. Third, since God is never distant from God's creating, neither is God distant from God's creation, but always directly and personally present to all creatures, especially those who can personally respond, such as human beings.[12]

How does this affect a conception of Jesus' divinity? One would have to say greatly, if the tacit supposition in understanding Jesus' divinity lay in a view that God is absent or withdrawn from the world. The doctrine of creation allows for no distance between the creator and the creature that needs to be overcome.[13] Are there degrees of God's being present? Or should we imagine differences in God's presence from the side of creation? Answers to these questions and an understanding of incarnation can be construed as occurring through the dynamics of God's creative activity itself and within the new conception of our cosmos. The premise is not that God is distant, but that God is within and personally present to every human being. But, to use an expression of Edward Schillebeeckx, Jesus appears as a proleptic concentration of God's creating presence and activity that mirrors the intention and goal of creation itself.[14] What makes Jesus divine? Nothing on the side of Jesus as creature can make Jesus divine. Jesus is divine because of God's presence and action in him in a supereminent way.[15]

---

12. See Edward Schillebeeckx, "God the Living One," *New Blackfriars* 62 (1981): 357–70, and "I Believe in God, Creator of Heaven and Earth," *God Among Us: The Gospel Proclaimed* (New York: Crossroad, 1983), 91–102. For interpretation of Schillebeeckx on this issue, see Dorothy Jacko, "Salvation in the Context of Contemporary Secularized Historical Consciousness: The Later Theology of Edward Schillebeeckx" (Ph.D. Dissertation, Toronto: University of St. Michael's College, Toronto School of Theology, 1987), 83–136.

13. Jacko, "Salvation in the Context of Contemporary Secularized Historical Consciousness," 94–99.

14. "Therefore 'christology' is *concentrated* creation: belief in creation as God wills it to be." Edward Schillebeeckx, *Interim Report on the Books Jesus and Christ* (New York: Crossroad, 1981), 128.

15. Schillebeeckx describes Jesus as a concentrated and concealing mediation of God's nearness to human existence. Jesus' story is a parable of God "because the mediated nearness of God's offer of mercy to man is conveyed in a more concentrated form than elsewhere in the revealing and the concealing mediation of Jesus. Nowhere else has there ever been such a concentration of concealing mediation — Jesus was even sent to his death in the name of orthodox religion. Nowhere else too is God's direct and gratuitous nearness in him so tangibly present for the one who, in *metanoia* (self-criticism), goes forward openly to meet him — in the tradition of the

In the new story of the human race. The second axis of how development might occur revolves around the idea of the passage of time and narrative. In the discussion of the question of the relation between Jesus Christ and other religious I proposed that the human race is entering a new temporal context of global solidarity in which the religions of the world are rubbing shoulders with one another. Add to this the conviction just outlined, that God self-communicates to all people and thus becomes operative in their religious lives, and the idea of the uniqueness of Jesus Christ as it is currently understood will be challenged. In classical christology the uniqueness and the divinity of Jesus were correlative terms; divinity understood in terms of an incarnation of God as Logos explained an absolute and qualitatively different uniqueness of Jesus. In the physical and historical world as it is currently understood, it becomes more and more difficult to affirm the uniqueness of Jesus in such absolute and divisive terms. Jesus' divinity will be understood as correlative with the genuine divine revelation and mediation found in other religions.

Now I take it that such a development is underway at the present time and will continue as a matter of fact. But how is it to be reckoned theologically? Some theologians view such a development negatively. Critics often use such terms as "flattening out" or "reduction" to describe the development that is going on. One reason for this sometimes lies in the fact that the critics themselves do not develop. They do not make the shift from a literal, pictorial sense of incarnation to a broader framework for understanding the presence of God at work in Jesus and a comparison of this with God at work in other religions. But from the perspective of christology from below, one can and must still claim the uniqueness of Jesus in the different but real sense of a historically distinctive presence of God to the world through Jesus. One may also insist that Jesus is truly divine, even though he is not the only divine mediation.[16] As long as Christians remain Christian, they will be attached to God through Jesus in such a way that they find God's salvation in and through him.

Church, he is even called the 'true God.'" Edward Schillebeeckx, "The 'God of Jesus' and the 'Jesus of God,'" *The Language of Faith: Essays on Jesus, Theology, and the Church,* ed. Robert J. Schreiter (Maryknoll, N.Y.: Orbis Books, 1995), 106.

16. Knitter succinctly sums up his position that Jesus is "God's truly but not only saving word" in his essay, "Five Theses on the Uniqueness of Jesus," *The Uniqueness of Jesus: A Dialogue with Paul Knitter,* ed. Leonard Swidler and Paul Mojzes (Maryknoll, N.Y.: Orbis Books, 1997), 3–16, at 14.

Thus one may understand the development as an extension of the divine reality that Christians encounter in Jesus, to an affirmation that God also addresses other people in analogous ways in other religious mediations. The new conception, should it arise, would not subtract from Jesus, but would allow Christians to imagine other religious mediations as potentially on the level of Jesus. In effect, this new understanding would be saying that we Christians, through Jesus, have learned about what God is doing in the whole world through various religions.

In a new expanded horizon of experience. I turn now to the third path of development mediated through an expanded horizon of the perceiving and believing subject. Analysis of development from this perspective corresponds to and confirms the former scenarios. Once again, the constant in the development lies in the foundational experience of Christian faith: the Christian is one who encounters God in Jesus. On the one hand, this existential encounter of the revealing presence of God in Jesus for our salvation provides the basis for affirming Jesus' divinity. On the other hand, this consistent encounter occurs within an expanded horizon which includes several new factors: a revised recognition of God's closeness and immanence to all of creation, a conviction that God works for salvation in the whole of creation, and an inquiring human spirit that expects to find other true manifestations ("incarnations") of God in history. The result is an affirmation of Jesus' divinity which is realistic but not exclusive. The affirmation of Jesus' divinity says both that God is at work in Jesus in a distinctive and historically unique way, and that God can also be present and at work in other historical symbols of God that are also unique.

How will theology judge a development that says that Jesus is divine in a way that allows for the divinity of other religious mediators? The response to this question, I believe, reveals how our horizon has changed. In a situation of relative isolation in which one religion correlates with one culture, pluralism appears as a threat. Within a narrow horizon of consciousness, to recognize the possibility of other "incarnations" of God is to relativize and so neutralize the incarnation in Jesus. But the situation of religious pluralism mediates another broader horizon of consciousness: all mediations of God are themselves by definition finite; one finite religious mediation or one single historical religion cannot fully reveal the mystery of God; no human argument or conviction can limit or contain the possibilities of the transcendent God; so that, finally, no reason requires that the possible existence of other divine mediations necessarily undermines in any way the true presence of God actualized in Jesus. Even more strongly, a consciousness of pluralism in the future may judge that restricting divinity to Jesus would be unfaithful to the revelation of God mediated by him.

CONCLUSION

How will christology develop in the future? Let me conclude this reach into the future with a few brief summarizing propositions.

The first thing that is sure is that christology will develop; theology never remains the same. People in developed industrial cultures sense this movement in history as never before. The problem of development today lies not in explaining how change can legitimately occur, but in trying to find some continuity and stability amid the rush into an open future.

Second, relative to how it will develop, I have suggested some mechanisms which are meant to help understand how change is occurring. What I have done with this construction of types of development merely sets forth frameworks which help to take notice of and describe what is actually going forward. These imaginative structures also help facilitate the appreciation of how these developments follow a coherent human trajectory. They can be expected. But these types are not technical or explanatory theories.[17] They serve only in helping common sense to situate what is going forward.

Third, however, we do not really know what the content of christology in the future will be, or even where the mainline center of gravity will be located. No one can know the future. In reality, anyone who speaks of the future does so by projecting certain aspects of the present ahead. The developments I have described have already been set in motion. This whole essay simply uses these frameworks to imagine and project the direction of what is already happening among many Christians and what will continue to work its way. But these developments may not command the field; other aspects of our situation may elicit developments that coexist with or even supercede the tendencies I've selected. But whatever

---

17. The discussion of Thiel in *Senses of Tradition* contains a technical analysis of development, and the retrospective, postmodern theory is the most adequate among those he considers.

the predominant tendencies may be, it is hard to imagine a future that will not be pluralistic.

Thus, fourth, it follows that we can be absolutely certain of one thing, namely, that what I have suggested as the future of christology will neither ring true for nor be accepted by all. Therefore we may hope that the conversation dealing with these issues will continue, and that the pluralism among Christians that is already in place and pertains to the understanding of our most central doctrine will become more explicit and refined.

Epilogue

JESUS SYMBOL OF GOD:
CRITICISM AND RESPONSE

꒜

J ESUS SYMBOL OF GOD was published in 1999 and was reviewed fairly widely.[1] It seems like a good time to open up a broad dialogue on the methods and issues involved in christology by responding to these reviews with special attention to the negative critiques.[2] Responses to these critics may also serve the purpose of responding to questions that may have arisen relative to this work. In any case this whole book may be taken as a response that enters into dialogue about the issues.

I have organized this response by following the trajectory of ten major topics that constitute the essential line of the argument. I will divide each topic in its turn into three parts: the first introduces the central point that I strove to make relative to each topic. Together, these first points serve cumulatively as a review of the logic of the whole work. In the second part I report the criticisms that have been made with respect to the topic under consideration. This will be less than satisfying, of course, because I can do little more than report the objection and not develop it the way it could be unfolded. But it should be recalled that the length of book reviews did not allow the reviewers to develop these critiques at length. Finally, I conclude each section or topic with a response to the critique that is likewise schematic. The goal here is not to bring the conversation to a conclusion, nor to convince my critics, nor to prove my point. None of these goals could be realized in a brief essay. My hope extends no further than that the whole essay will add up to some kind

---

1. Roger Haight, *Jesus Symbol of God* (Maryknoll, N.Y.: Orbis Books, 1999). Cited in the text as JSG. A bibliography of the reviews cited here is found on page 215. References in the text are to pages in these reviews.

2. I have written another response to the questions asked by Edward Jeremy Miller in "Traditional Christology for Our Time: A Response to Edward Jeremy Miller," *Horizons* 27 (2000): 179–84.

of representation of the critical conversation in christology which our situation today demands.

A GENETIC METHOD

In developing the christology of *Jesus Symbol of God* I employ a method which is generically referred to as a christology from below. The employment of such a method represents a major shift in the imaginative framework within which christological discussion unfolds. By an "imaginative framework" I mean the encompassing set of presuppositions and assumptions that define the point of departure and the method that guides the reasoning of a work. I call this a genetic method because it attempts to lead one through the process and logic of the original construction of the classical doctrines about Jesus.

Criticism

Oakes rejects most of modern theology generally (*JR,* 305) and JSG appears as another instance in which modern theology has capitulated to culture. Buckley and Sykes dismiss a christology from below in principle, but for different reasons: for Buckley it involves a mediation that risks compromise of Christian truth; for Sykes the method as it is used generally by theologians is confused and unstable in its various applications. Kilby is suspicious of the vagueness of the category of experience and the abuse it has engendered. For Buggert, the method is radical and functions reductively, restrictively, and ultimately negatively by making Jesus or Jesus research a single absolute norm. Nicholson leans in this direction. McFarland portrays the work as polemical and criticizes its hermeneutical method because of its supposition of a common Christian experience (250).

Response

I find that many have their own construal of a christology from below. As a generic term, it takes on different meanings in the work of various theologians. As an analogous term, then, it may for some prove to be confusing. That puts the burden on theologians to define or explain what they mean by such a method and to display it consistently in their arguments. But in the end, I fail to see why one cannot chart the historical genesis of christology which is itself a historical phenomenon. As in the case of other historical phenomena, an account of that protracted historical genesis will illumine the elements that feed into its character.

The critique of reductionism in principle is false since the work asserts explicitly that there would be no christology without an Easter experience. "Though he asserts that Christology's moorings must be based in the 'historical' Jesus, christology is not merely a historical encounter: rather, it is 'existential-theological'" (Berkey, 346; also Mallon, 239 and Smith, 281). I will say more about this under the topic of the resurrection.

I admit that the category of experience can be abused: What qualifies as experience? Whose experience? And so on. I use the appeal to experience in almost tautological terms to indicate that meaning has its final basis in some form of engaged, referential consciousness. This stands in contrast to the tendency in theology for words and language to assume an uncritical and "purely" notional meaning that has floated away from concrete self-conscious reflection. Given the amount of christology that fails to awaken experiential correlates, a reference to experience does not seem inappropriate. Kohler recalls Jung's prescription that only an appeal to experience can rekindle the meaningfulness of Christian symbols in our time (Kohler, 51).

Close attention to experience reveals it to be a very personal and even individual category, even after recognition that it is always mediated by a community and its language. The very idea of a "common" experience thus appears problematic if "common" were interpreted to mean "same." Even the shared and mutually agreed upon experience of two friends is not so identically the same experience that it undermines their individuality. Common experience is always analogously common, partly or in some respects the "same" and partly different. Without some common dimension of Christian experience (salvation through Jesus) the formal normativity of scripture would lack material content. I read McFarland's criticism as itself analogous to what one might find in Lindbeck's postliberal critique of theology that appeals to experience. For myself, I find that what Lindbeck proposes as a cultural-linguistic approach to doctrine and theology is extremely useful, but that as a method it need not be proposed polemically. Transcendent reality and the religious faith of a community directed toward it can bear many different approaches.[3] JSG is not intended as a polemical theological work.

REPRESENTATION OF THE JESUS MATERIAL

Carrying out a genetic method entails beginning with the historical person Jesus; a christology from below has its point of departure, but hardly its end-point or conclusion, with Jesus of Nazareth. But consideration of the abundant literature of the historians concerning Jesus in turn binds the imagination to the this-worldly Jesus and thus convinces us that Jesus was a human being. The word "binds" should not be understood in some excluding and restricting sense. But it reminds us that the subject matter of christology is none other than Jesus of Nazareth, since Jesus risen is Jesus of Nazareth, and one can have no purchase on the risen Jesus apart from the historical figure. Such is the logic of proper names.

I invite people into the literature on Jesus of Nazareth because it can mediate a major shift in one's thinking in contrast to the image of Jesus created by the tradition of doctrine, catechism, and liturgy.[4] Christian imagination has largely been schooled into a docetic type of image of Jesus that spontaneously regards Jesus of Nazareth as God, the Nicene preexistent Son who took on or clothed himself in or "added on" to himself a human nature. Once again, depending on the situation of the reader, this attention to Jesus of Nazareth can possibly revolutionize the christological problem: the question is not how Jesus as God can possibly be really human, but how this man Jesus of Nazareth can be truly divine.

Criticism

I said that there was a consensus that Jesus did not preach himself, but the kingdom of God. A critic cites E. P. Sanders to the effect that Jesus presented himself as viceroy of God (Baxter 402). Another feels

---

3. See George Lindbeck, *The Nature of Doctrine: Religion and Theology in a Postliberal Age* (Philadelphia: Westminster Press, 1984). In writing *Jesus Symbol of God* I was faced with a dilemma: Its theological suppositions and method were developed in the work *Dynamics of Theology* (New York: Paulist Press, 1990, and presently Maryknoll, N.Y.: Orbis Books, 2001). But one cannot publish a book that presupposes the reading of another. Thus I tried to represent some of the major methodological suppositions presented in the early work in the first chapter of JSG, but this could only be done schematically. A good portion of the negative critique of JSG arises out of disagreement on issues relative to fundamental theology.

4. This theme is pursued in chapter 1 of this work.

that JSG does not pay enough attention to Jesus crucified and risen (Lane). Hamilton says that I "separate" what we can know of Jesus and how we respond to him. Moloney (149) and McFarland (251) criticize my critique of the hypostatization of the Logos as epistemologically questionable. Weinandy criticizes the whole work in every respect.

Response

Whether or not there is a consensus on the assertion, I would hold along with many others that Jesus subordinated himself to the Father and the kingdom of God. I should underline here what everyone who has read this literature knows: there is no consensus on the details of Jesus' ministry. In fact the discussion shows a great diversity of interpretation. In the face of this I believe that the christological significance of Jesus research does not lie in the details, but in the historical and truly or integrally human character of the referent of the various portraits, and the many aspects of the strictly existential religious encounter with God that Jesus mediates.[5] These two dimensions must be held together at all times in the discipline of christology as distinct from the discipline of history.

It is correct that I could have said more about Christ's passion and would if I were writing the book now. Chapter 4 of this work should remedy that situation. But in JSG as here I wanted to dissociate my interpretation from various excesses in soteriology that sometimes portray Jesus' suffering as something positive or communicate the idea that God positively willed or "sent" Jesus in order that he might suffer. Jesus' suffering was evil, not willed by God, but caused by human beings, and in itself Jesus' physical pain is not redemptive but, as an example of the good or innocent person suffering, a possible scandal. One needs a negative experience of contrast to recognize how Jesus' suffering can be revelatory.[6]

Relative to the discipline of christology, I do not separate historical knowledge of Jesus from the way we respond to him, but I distinguish

---

5. The existential character of this appeal and response does not run counter to the social aim of Jesus to prepare Israel for the coming kingdom of God.

6. Borrowed from Edward Schillebeeckx, the phrase "negative experience of contrast" refers to the dimension of positivity that serves as the background or horizon for an appreciation of a truly negative experience as precisely negative and to be resisted. See chapter 3, pp. 67–68, and chapter 4, pp. 94–96.

these two elements and for good reasons. In fact historians make such a separation, and it is important to recognize the specific limitations of the canons of critical history. But as the title of the work indicates, a constructive christology cannot separate encounter of the object of religious mediation (God) from the religious mediator (Jesus).

A number of exegetes, especially those dealing with the Logos christology of John's gospel, recognize a shift from personification, where the idea of the Glory, or Word, or Wisdom, or Breath of God is the figure of speech in which the term is spoken of "as" or "as if it were" a person, to hypostatization, where the same idea is conceived as corresponding or referring to a discrete entity or objective being, or is reified into a free-standing "something." But I know of no firm consensus on when this hypostatization occurred relative to Logos and its being predicated of Jesus. The problem is intrinsically delicate: How does one determine clearly how or when such a shift occurred, when a good metaphor appears *as* and, according to some theories, sometimes *is* "literal" predication? The issues relative to the christology of John's gospel are truly complex: is this predominantly Jewish literature? Is the Jewish word for God Yahweh? Does the cultural context of the work assume a whole world of gods that fill the ether much like the electronic communicators that fill our earthly air? One cannot proof-text the divinity of Jesus from John's gospel.

The genetic method of this christology from below constitutes the most fundamental definition of its imaginative framework. Weinandy, best among others, exemplifies criticism of the work on the basis of presuppositions other than those from which it was written. Practically speaking everything said about JSG in his review is either understood or evaluated within or from another imaginative framework, even when he tries to represent my argument. The change of meaning entailed makes it impossible to respond without going through his critique sentence by sentence to show the difference between his portrayal and my intention.

THE EASTER EXPERIENCE

Early in the chapter on Jesus' resurrection I lay down some clear statements that define the premises of the discussion. One of these is the straightforward statement that Jesus was really raised out of death:

"[T]he resurrection was the exaltation and glorification of the whole individual person, Jesus of Nazareth. The one who was resurrected is no one else than Jesus, so that there is continuity and personal identity between Jesus during his lifetime and his being with God" (JSG, 124). Jesus' real and paradigmatic resurrection was into God's sphere and thus a matter of faith; it was not historical in the sense of an empirical event. The continuation of a historical, genetic approach thus shifts to a consideration of the Easter experience of the disciples, for which a broadly historical structure is provided symbolically in the Emmaus story. I generalize this story in turn into a four-point theory: its elements are a memory of Jesus, a strong faith/hope, an impulse of grace or illumination, and the view that stories of the empty tomb and appearances are expressions of the new Easter faith/hope.

Criticism

My treatment of the resurrection generated a good bit of criticism. For example, what exactly this Easter experience was is not clearly delineated (Baxter 403). Others insist that the resurrection was a historical event that afterward involved some kind of appearance. Lane thinks that the chapter entails some confusion between the terms resurrection and Easter experience (380). Doubling back on the Jesus of history, in saying that Jesus is the subject matter of christology I seem to slight Jesus risen. More than one author believes that I make Jesus' person and message the "basis" of belief in the resurrection. Hamilton says that I hesitate "to describe the Resurrection as God's action in raising Jesus." And Oakes claims that I hold that Jesus' resurrection was into the memory and life of the community, thus vindicating his critique of the method of the work (*JR* 305–6).

Response

All of the many portrayals of the Easter experience that one finds across the discipline of christology are hypothetical constructions, and mine is offered in only the most general terms. For my part I have never read a plausible representation of the resurrection as a historical event; many assert it as such, but how should this historical event be imagined? It certainly is not necessary to conceive of the resurrection as "historical" in order to affirm it as real any more than the resurrection of others, for whom Jesus is the "first-born," must entail a "historical" resuscitation of their bodies. The same reasoning applies to the appearances: I do not see what ultimate difference it would make relative to the reality of the resurrection whether or not Jesus appeared to the disciples historically in the sense of physically or empirically.[7] Relative to practical spirituality, the postulate of "physical" experiences of Jesus risen tends to undermine the faith required for recognition of the resurrection and thus creates a gap between the first disciples and ourselves.

I do not harbor any confusion between an Easter experience, whose subject was the disciples and is ourselves, and the resurrection, whose subject was Jesus and, we hope, will be ourselves, although my text may have betrayed me in places. And surely I do not underestimate the importance of the resurrection because I hold that the emergence of christology depended upon *Jesus* (emphasis) being *risen* (equal emphasis). The experience of Jesus being really raised by God is the connecting link between Jesus in his ministry and the emergent Christian faith.

The idea of Jesus' message being the basis of the resurrection makes no sense; and while some have held it was the basis of the Easter experience, I do not. But I place Jesus as one of the four elements of the theory stated above and illustrated in the Emmaus story. Jesus crucified and risen is the subject matter of christology; no separation is intended here; but we know nothing about Jesus risen apart from Jesus the historical person. Hamilton is mistaken in saying that I do not say that God raised Jesus: perhaps I do not say it often enough, but then who else would have raised Jesus? Oakes is simply wrong in his interpretation of my position on the resurrection for I hold and explicitly state in more than one place that Jesus the person is really risen and lives within the sphere of God.

PLURALISM OF
NEW TESTAMENT CHRISTOLOGIES

The New Testament contains a pluralism of christologies. I take this to be a fact established by exegesis. The relevance of this fact lies in the

---

7. There is a difference between an experience which enabled the disciples to say that Jesus was alive and one that encountered Jesus alive, but neither requires the physicality or empirical character of the appearances of Jesus.

normativity of the New Testament for Christian theology: pluralism in christology should be considered normative for the church. There have been no criticisms in principle of the idea of christological pluralism in the New Testament, although some think I overstate it.

THE CONSTRUCT OF A SYMBOL

The central reason for the appeal to symbol as a christological category lies in the dialectical structure of a symbol: a symbol holds together in a tensive union two perceived or experienced realities that are not the same; a symbol mediates and makes present something other than itself. Moreover, given the apologetic intent and structure of the argument, the fact that this category is common in ordinary life and pervasive across numerous academic disciplines recommends it. In the sphere of the sacred or religious, symbol takes on a meaning synonymous with "sacrament"; description of a symbol and its dynamics thus provides a plausibility structure for, but not an explanation of, an understanding of the unity of the humanity and divinity of Jesus.

Criticism

This is a "mediating" christology that does not succeed because it does not appeal sufficiently to Word of God theologians (Buckley). More strongly, in the end the position that "Jesus is symbol of God" negates the normative claim that "Jesus is God" (Cavadini 4, Moloney 151). At the very least construing Jesus as symbol of God does not explain or reduces the difference between Jesus and others to whom God is present and active (Buggert). Kohler proposes an alternative theory of symbol from the Jungian tradition: symbols are not real or concrete but psychic phenomena which, working "inside-out," allow us to grasp latencies in external reality that we could not appreciate otherwise.

Responses

I do not understand the criticism of Buckley which seems to assign a negative value to a mediating christology used to understand the one whom Christians have traditionally called the Mediator while recognizing that at other times some mediating christologies succeed. His review is a study in compactness, and I simply do not understand his point. The criticisms of Cavadini and Moloney and Buggert move along the same trajectory and are correct in saying that I am wary of saying "Jesus is God" in a nondialectical way. The choice of symbol as a christological category seems called for in the measure that one appreciates Chalcedon's doctrine of one person and two natures as precisely dialectical. One cannot break the dialectical tension between Jesus' being at the same time human and divine with a nondialectical construal such as "Jesus is God" or "Jesus is merely a human being." In contrast to their views, then, I would assert that the doctrine of Chalcedon is strictly dialectical; that the statement "Jesus is God" by itself and without a great deal of explanation is deeply problematic; and that one of the points of Chalcedon was to affirm what the New Testament also teaches, namely, that Jesus is precisely just like us, excepting sin, and like Adam is the new first born of all and the paradigmatic human being. Therefore I do not accept the implicit charge that symbol stands between the divinity of Jesus and its being made present in the world, or that Jesus' divinity lies "behind" his human existence. Symbol precisely "makes present," as does my body and bodily gesture make present my "self" who constitutes the gesture. The only alternative that I see to such dialectical thinking leads to something unimaginable, that is, an unmediated presence of God in Jesus which reduces to some form of docetism.

Shifting now to the relations between Jesus and us, if God is not related to us as God is related to Jesus, he would not be the earnest of our salvation: the very point of incarnation is that Jesus is just like us, and the deeply experienced impulse of an *imitatio Christi* or following of Jesus requires the nonqualitative difference between Jesus and other human beings. But to put it that way sounds reductionist. It is better to think of us, with the help of God's grace, being like Jesus.

Relative to a Jungian theory of symbol, I accept this conception as significant and operative, as in my distinction of "conscious symbols," but the exclusion of the idea of a concrete symbol applicable to Jesus could possibly, but not necessarily, undercut the significance of the historical reality of Jesus and open up the charge of mere projection. In any case, the idea of a concrete symbol, extending beyond Jungian usage, works in religion generally and in theology, for example, in sacramental theology and christology.

INTERPRETATION OF
NICAEA AND CHALCEDON

It is important to recognize the degree to which historical consciousness tends to undermine the relevance of these doctrines of the past: one cannot presuppose today that Christians in our Western culture consider them relevant, or that Christians in non-Western cultures have any idea what they mean without extensive study. But the supposition of JSG is that these are classical doctrines, and although the language of these doctrines no longer works in a postmodern culture, hermeneutical theory allows an interpretation that preserves their point, that is, their historical intention or rationale, but in a different key or language. An interpretive language comprehensible in today's world preserves the meaning of the past analogously, that is, retaining on a deep religious level a common substantive dimension of corporate Christian experience amid significant differences. Indeed, a variety of such theological interpretations may be found consistent with the common Christian experience that is contained in and grounds the doctrines.

Criticism

Favoring a modified Cyrillian Logos christology, Baxter believes that one cannot accept the interpretation of Chalcedon that I have provided (404). From the perspective of a Logos christology, Buggert thinks that my interpretations of Nicaea and Chalcedon appear reductionistic. Moreover, my Antiochene bias endangers the compromise accomplished by Chalcedon (Lane). Moloney finds the definitive criticism of JSG in the complex position (1) that Jesus "is simply and solely 'a human person'" (152), which (2) contradicts the councils; and to explain this error he interprets JSG as (3) confusing between "Christ's [sic] conscious life" and "the ontological centre of the person" (152). Lefebure reminds me that consulting recent agreements between the Roman Catholic Church and Eastern churches can help clear away misunderstandings of these councils and provide further grounds for the reinterpretation of christology proper that I seek.

Responses

I will not attempt to defend my historical reconstruction of various patristic christologies and will yield to experts here. But one cannot hold that a reconstruction of the historical meaning and intent of the Fathers of the church suffices for christology today. And it is equally problematic to think that one form of words can be the criterion of admissibility of another christology in a situation that requires pluralism. I take it that the criterion for the adequacy of any christology today transcends the alternatives of "Alexandria" and "Antioch," and I posit that criterion in a christology's intrinsic capability to coherently explain the experience of salvation mediated through Jesus. It appears to me that these criticisms for the most part stem from another system of theology and language. But even though the imaginative framework set up by a christology from below really differs from that of the councils, my argument does not set out to exclude what is in place or to replace a christology from above. Rather, on the basis of pluralism, I seek to show that this christology constitutes an inculturation for a particular audience, vaguely described as a postmodern culture, which is possible and acceptable.

Moloney's view that I hold that Jesus is simply and solely a human being is false because asserted in too narrow a framework, that is, in the framework of a Logos christology developed from above. I responded positively to the critique with my reflections in the last point on the dialectical character of christological doctrine. Also, I believe that his opinion concerning my confusion between the psychology and ontology of Jesus is projection on his part: I do not explicitly entertain that problematic or use those categories. Both the problem and the significance of the distinction have their origin in a christology from above, and a christology from below, as it were, bypasses them. This objection provides a good example of taking ideas from one imaginative framework and interpreting them within another.

THE MEANING OF SALVATION

The religious question that human existence is to itself provides the anthropological ground of christology. And the experience of salvation through Jesus provides the basis upon which christology is constructed. The New Testament and subsequent tradition offer many views of exactly how Jesus saves, or what he did for human salvation. But the objective metahistorical transaction theories have to be interpreted as expressions of the existential human experience of a salvation from God mediated through Jesus. The essence of the experience of salvation in the Christian framework consists in an encounter with a personal, saving God whom one meets in the person of Jesus, in his ministry and in his resurrection. But salvation cannot be reduced to an individual relationship to God because it includes as a constitutive social dimension an impulse of love of neighbor translated into political-social terms. In the late modern and postmodern period the notions of social salvation and liberation mediated through discipleship of Jesus have taken on a peculiar urgency, not least for the very credibility of Christianity itself.

Criticism

Two critiques of JSG hover around the problem of evil: one author retrieves some positive value to some forms of suffering (Albright), and another feels that the discussion of the God of love mediated by Jesus in the book remains too facile. It does not enter deeply enough into the question of evil and the conflicting responsibilities of God relative to the human situation (Kohler, 60–62).

Response

It is simply true that JSG does not explore the "dark side" of human existence and of God in the Jewish-Christian tradition, and for it to be comprehensive these issues would need further development. I attend to the issue of theodicy only implicitly in the chapters on salvation where Christian faith is interpreted as antithetical to escapism and entailing an absolute mandate to resist evil in all its forms. While the death of God provides no answer to the problem of evil, human resistance, empowered by God's revelation in Jesus and God's cooperative Spirit or grace, addresses the issue concretely. Finally, resurrection surrounds the whole question with hope.

JESUS CHRIST VIS-À-VIS OTHER RELIGIONS

The question of the evaluation of Jesus within the context of other world religions dominates our postmodern situation and consciousness. It is most important to recognize that a method of correlation entails a recognition that this situation and our prevailing attitudinal response to it serves as an intrinsic dimension of the interpretation of Jesus Christ for our times. To put it negatively, one should not construct one's christology as it were independently of our situation, which could only mean relative to another situation, and then apply it from the outside to our own. In other words, probing human and Christian sensibility to this issue is prior to and a condition of the response to the more properly christological question.

But it is a growing phenomenon that many Christians who live within a postmodern culture and those who live in a religious culture where other world religions predominate respond to this question in a way that implicitly assigns other religions a status roughly on a par with Christianity. The chapter on Jesus Christ and other religions in JSG, therefore, explores possible sensibilities and attitudes prior to an examination of the christological question properly speaking. In it I set out a dialectical or tensive position: first, the Christian can recognize that God is at work in other religions so that they provide autonomous mediations of God's saving presence and grace; second, Jesus Christ, insofar as he truly mediates God's salvation, is normative not only for Christians but for all human beings, because truth in such matters is universally relevant; but, third, this also entails recognition that, insofar as other religions mediate truth about God and God's salvation or, more generally, about ultimate reality, they too are universally normative. This position is not based on comparative theology but on the revelation of Jesus Christ: according to the principle that God truly is the way Jesus reveals God to be, God engages all people for their salvation through the cultural and religious media at hand. This position preserves the distinctiveness of Christianity and guarantees the autonomy of other religions, and, as chapter 7 of this book shows, one can formulate an orthodox christology that builds upon and includes this Christian conviction.

Criticism

Those who hold that Jesus is constitutive of or causes the salvation of all human beings, including those who existed before Jesus of Nazareth was born, are critical of the pluralistic and mutually normative position that I have adopted in JSG. The book's dealing with Christ vis-à-vis other religions must be disputed as "an undermining of our traditional doctrine on the uniqueness of Jesus" (Moloney, 150). It is also criticized from the left, because the language of salvation from a

personal God overrides Buddhist language and thus belies the possibility of having a mutual normativity from different religious traditions
(Lefebure).

Response

At the outset one should recognize that these issues cannot be summarized in shorthand; in itself this topic is too complicated, and the
literature and options extend too far. But something has to be said.

Let me begin with this generalization: the universal role of Jesus
Christ has become the subject of open debate today within christology
itself. Chapter 5 of this work, I think, demonstrates this. In this discussion it appears to me that the alternative of whether or not Jesus is the
cause of the salvation of all draws a line that cleanly divides Christian
theologians. The issue in mainline christology is not whether God's salvation is or is not available to all human beings, but whether this saving
grace is *"gratia Christi"* in the sense of attributing to Jesus an actual universal saving agency. It is not clear at all to me that the position of JSG
must be disputed for this is still an open question and Christian theologians hold a variety of positions, and many more agree with the position
I have argued than may be apparent.

In fact I do not abandon Jesus' uniqueness, but it may be equally
important to recognize with Moloney that I understand this uniqueness
in a different sense than formerly, that is, in a sense forced upon us
by a historically conscious framework. The uniqueness I propose does
not set Jesus Christ above other actions of God in history in principle,
even though comparative religion or comparative theology may make
such determinations; rather I suggest that Jesus Christ and the Christian
community that flowed from him are historically unique in the sense of
their individual and irreplaceable self-identity.

In speaking of salvation from a Christian standpoint I did not have
Buddhist experience in mind, and I am sure I made some statements that
sound imperialist when the contexts are fused. But as long as the object
of "religious" attention is transcendent, so that no belief is adequate to
the reality intended, and as long as one supposes that other religions
contain truth, which as such is normative, and as long as one recognizes
that the application of religious norms is complex and must occur in

dialogue, I do not see how a pluralism of norms for religious truth is incoherent.[8]

CHRISTOLOGY PROPER

In the light of our current religiously pluralistic situation, and recognizing a pluralism of christologies within the Christian community and among its theologians, and appealing to the pluralism of New Testament christologies, chapter 15 proposes (but not exclusively) two distinct languages for christology and shows how each can be held to the norms for christology. These two christologies are based on the key scriptural symbols, "Logos" and "Spirit." The christological norms that are invoked are these: christology must respond to and be intelligible in our current situation, be faithful to the tradition of Christian witness, and motivate and empower the Christian life of the community.

Criticism

Criticism of the category of symbol and of the interpretation of the christological councils reviewed earlier come to bear on the proposals for constructive christology. Reviewers divide over the possibility of a Spirit christology: those schooled in a Logos christology from above reject it (Baxter et al); others appear more open to it. Those who imagine or relate to Jesus as God who has taken on a human nature are critical of those who relate to Jesus as a human being who makes the reality of God present in a distinctive and preeminent way.

Response

In many important ways the questions revolving around an adequate christology for our time are decided at earlier stages of the discussion. The formal christology proposed in JSG is the result of a sustained argument involving all of the previous eight steps that I have just reviewed. One cannot see this narrow christological discussion as an isolated unit standing alone, so to speak. Moreover, in the end, reason and argument

---

8. I say more about how and when the principle of noncontradiction may be invoked in the text of *Jesus Symbol of God.*

will not decide this debate; it lies too close to each one's Christian identity for it to be moved around by words. Christological issues are decided
in a place deep in religious sensibility and imagination.

This partly accounts for my casting the debate within the context of
christological pluralism along with a proposal for general norms. In a situation of theological pluralism, the goal is not to offer a christology that
will replace all the others; one christological position does not necessarily
rule out another; and the two christologies that I propose together are
not meant to control the field. In fact, I consistently reiterate the specific
context for this essay, the audience that it addresses, and the method employed in it. None of these are exclusive. The contention regarding the
formal christologies that I propose is that they are viable or "lawful," or
orthodox, or coherent with Christian faith as this is measured by certain
criteria of the discipline. I have not found that any of the critiques of it
thus far warrant any substantial adjustments. Many simply propose other
christologies which, insofar as they meet the criteria of christology, will
by definition prove to be viable.

GOD AS TRINITY

Given the compartmentalization of systematic theology it sometimes
happens that christology is developed with no formal consideration of
the doctrine of the trinity. And one might add that much trinitarian
theology unfolds apart from a consideration of the genesis of the doctrine through christology. Thus one may find that behind christology
from above there lies a tacit or implicit doctrine of the trinity with high
tritheistic tendencies, as the very number "3" indicates. It follows that
the doctrines of Jesus Christ and the trinity are so closely interwoven
together into a single piece that one must consider their connection in
a formal way. In the final chapter I develop the doctrine of the trinity
from below and emphasize its "economic" source and import.

Criticism

Criticism at this point predictably divides on the basis of appreciation
of method in christology and what understanding of the doctrine of
the trinity operates as a premise. A good example is the criticism, which

is difficult to determine as positive or negative, that JSG leads in the direction of modalism (Kilby).

Response

The final chapter of the book presents the reader with some fundamental options. One of these is the classical contrast between the trinitarian theology of Karl Barth and that of Friedrich Schleiermacher, the one appearing at the head of his dogmatics, the other appearing as a summary of his systematics. A christology from below spontaneously gravitates toward the option of Schleiermacher; one might even say that charting the development of the doctrines concerning Jesus Christ and God define christology from below. Christology from below demonstrates that the doctrine of the trinity is derivative. Its content and value depend historically and logically from christology, so that by itself a doctrine of the immanent trinity cannot logically support a christology from above. This does not rule out christology from above in some sense as a possible method in christology, but it shows that such a method rests on the supposition of the development of the doctrine of the trinity in the first place.

It is important to realize that the heresies of the past were historically conditioned so that they may appear differently within the framework of different contexts and presuppositions. I operate on the principle that the language of a given doctrine of the past will not make sense today if all the perception and reasoning that supported it in the past has been undercut. Current theology of the trinity seems to be moving in the direction of reawakening concern for the economy of God dealing with human beings in history. I think of trinity as a narrative doctrine: it compactly summarizes the story of the emergence of Christianity and defines the language of Christian faith and soteriology. This at least de-emphasizes the relevance of the distinctions within the Godhead, but I do not hold that it eliminates them.

CONCLUSION

This schematic review of position, criticism, and response relative to *Jesus Symbol of God* cannot meet the demands of the situation in christology today. Only a broad conversation of many voices can help the church in its churches address the questions that challenge ordinary Christian people. Educated Christians are asking questions. And insofar as the churches do not answer them in terms that meet the questions themselves and appear satisfying, the faithful are cast back on their own resources to make do. Purely dogmatic answers simply do not meet the challenge. Neither does polemic and debate which are increasingly labeled "theological" for their narrow, esoteric, and sectarian mystification. What is needed is broad, sympathetic, mutually enriching and implicitly self-critical conversation. Often realism in theological discussion can be measured by the degree to which construction merely puts in words what the community is already experiencing if not thinking. Christian theologians are more and more called upon to address the world beyond Christianity on the premise that they will address the thinking members of their own church only in the measure in which they succeed in addressing those outside it.

REVIEWS OF
JESUS SYMBOL OF GOD

᥈

Albright, Matthew. "Pluralism Hurts," *Regeneration* 7, no. 3 (2000).

Amaladoss, Michael. *Vidyajyoti* 63 (1999): 870–72.

Astorga, Christina. *Budhi* 4 (2000): 187–219.

———. *Landas* 15 (2001): 114–51.

Baxter, Anthony. *Journal of Theological Studies* 51 (2000): 400–405.

Berkey, R. F. *Choice* 37, no. 2 (1999): 345–46.

Bernad, Miguel A. *Kinaadman* 23 (2000): 269–77.

Buckley, James J. *Modern Theology* 16 (2000): 555–56.

Buggert, Donald. *New Theology Review* 13 (2000): 87–88.

Cavadini, John. *Commonweal,* October 8, 1999, 22–24; November 19, 1999, 60; January 14, 2000, 4.

Cote, Paul E. *The Church World,* December 16, 1999, 8.

Dalzell, Thomas G. *Heythrop Journal* 41 (2000): 222–23.

Gonzalez, Rene. *Mayeutica Revista Filosofico-Teologica* 60 (1999): 650.

Hamilton, Andrew. *Eureka Street* 10, no. 8 (2000): 35.

Hodgson, Peter C. *Religious Studies Review* 27 (2001): 152.

Johnson, Elizabeth. *America,* November 6, 1999, 25–26.

Kilby, Karen. *Reviews in Religion and Theology* 7 (2000): 281–82.

Kohler, Rainer M. *The San Francisco Jung Institute Library Journal* 19 (2000): 51–63.

Lane, Dermot A. *Theological Studies* 61 (2000): 379–81.

Lefebure, Leo D. *Christian Century* 116 (1999): 1139–40.

MacEoin, Gary. *The American Catholic* (November 2000).

Macquarrie, John. *The Expository Times* 111 (1999): 103–4.

Mallon, Colleen Mary. *Dialog* 40 (2001): 238–40.

McFarland, Ian A. *Scottish Journal of Theology* 55 (2002): 250–52.

Miller, Edward J. *Horizons* 27 (2000): 164–78.

Moloney, Raymond. *Milltown Studies* 47 (2001): 147–53.

Nicholson, Paul. *The Way* 40 (2000): 88–89.

Oakes, Edward T. *Journal of Religion* 81 (2001): 303–6.

———. *Leaven* (February–March 2001): 6–7.

Peña, Braulio. *Landas* 15 (2001): 152–66.

Pramuk, Christopher. *Leaven* (December 2000–January 2001): 11–14.

———. *Chicago Studies* 41 (2002): 80–91.

Smith, Susan E. *Mission Studies* 17 (2000): 281–82.

Sykes, Stephen. *Theology* (September–October 2001): 374–76.

Weinandy, Thomas. *The Thomist* 65 (2001): 121–36.

INDEX

ᘓᕽ

abstraction, mental, 17
Adam, Jesus as second, 99–101, 138, 162, 205
Albright, Matthew, 208
Alexandrian christology, 178–79, 206–7
analogy, principle of, 21, 42, 49, 173
angels, 170
"anonymous Christianity," 187
Anselm of Canterbury, 55, 58, 80
anthropology
  cultural, 34–37
  of Rahner, 35, 46, 64, 88–89, 100, 107–8, 111–15
  of Schillebeeckx, 65, 109, 111–15
  theological, 16–19, 151
"anti-kingdom," 143, 146
Antiochene christology, 178–79, 206–7
apologetics, in postmodern context, 39
Aquinas, Thomas
  epistemology of, 16–18, 20, 22, 35, 46, 105
  on nature and grace, 56–57
  on the object of sacred doctrine, 60
Aristotle
  epistemology of, 16–18, 35, 46
  philosophy of nature, 56–57
Arius, 154, 177
Athanasius of Alexandria, 58
atonement theories. See *under* salvation
Augustine of Hippo, 55, 56, 58, 183
  and the human desire to be, 151
  on sin and human freedom, 66–67, 69–70

Barth, Karl, 110, 213
Baxter, Anthony, 199, 202, 206, 211
Berkey, R. F., 198
Blondel, Maurice, 105n3
Buckley, James J., 197, 204

Buddhism, 210
Buggert, Donald, 197, 204, 205, 206

Cavadini, John, 204, 205
Chalcedon, Council of
  dialectical doctrine of, 47, 155, 176, 177, 205
  and imagination, 19–21
  interpretation of, 206–7
  and non-Christian religions, 121, 148
  as response to specific historical problems, 18
Christianity
  as historically grounded, 18–19
  and world religions
    christology, 10–11, 50–51, 148–64, 186–90, 193–94, 208–11
    mission, 10, 123–47
    Rahner and Schillebeeckx on, 9–10, 103–22, 131–32
"Christ kerygma," 25
christocentrism, 116, 118, 119–20, 161n3, 187–88
christology
  "from above," 152, 165–66, 179
  Alexandrian and Antiochene, 178–79, 206–7
  "from below"
    characteristics of, 8, 32–54, 82, 120, 152, 165–66, 197–99, 201, 213
    and divinity of Jesus, 51–53, 153
    loci in, 47–54
  classical, 48–49, 154–55
  criteria for orthodox, 42–43, 159–60
  genesis of, 43–45
  genetic method, 40, 43–45, 82–83, 197–99, 201
  "high," 33, 121, 152, 161, 165
  historically conscious, 130–31

217